BUSINESS
A N D
MANAGEMENT
EDUCATION IN CHINA

BUSINESS AND MANAGEMENT EDUCATION IN CHINA

Transition, Pedagogy and Training

editors

Ilan Alon
Rollins College, USA

John R McIntyre
Georgia Institute of Technology, USA

World Scientific

NEW JERSEY · LONDON · SINGAPORE · BEIJING · SHANGHAI · HONG KONG · TAIPEI · CHENNAI

Published by

World Scientific Publishing Co. Pte. Ltd.

5 Toh Tuck Link, Singapore 596224

USA office: 27 Warren Street, Suite 401-402, Hackensack, NJ 07601

UK office: 57 Shelton Street, Covent Garden, London WC2H 9HE

Library of Congress Cataloging-in-Publication Data
Business and management education in China / edited by Ilan Alon & John R. McIntyre.
    p. cm.
  Includes bibliographical references and index.
  ISBN 981-256-322-9 (alk. paper)
    1. Business education--China. 2. Management--Study and teaching--China.
  I. Alon, Ilan. II. McIntyre, John R. III. Title.

  HF1171.C5B87 2005
  658'.0071'151--dc22

                                                              2005050598

British Library Cataloguing-in-Publication Data
A catalogue record for this book is available from the British Library.

Printed in Singapore by Mainland Press

From Ilan:
To Anna and Kareen

From John:
To my friend, Martine Andriot, China hand, who keeps
rediscovering China through French and American eyes.

Preface

Management Education in the
Twenty First Century: A China-based Perspective

Business and Management Education in China is a collection of masterpieces presented by a group of leading domestic and international scholars. My sincere thanks should to go the editors, Dr. Ilan Alon and Dr. John R. McIntyre, who have been so kind as to invite me to write the foreword. From the unique standpoint of the office of the President of China Europe International Business School (CEIBS)—a "state of-the-art" educational joint venture between the People's Republic of China and the European Union—these prefatory remarks are offered as ground-setting parameters within which to conceptualize the evolution and mutual influence of the long Chinese tradition of educating professionals and the Western management training techniques and philosophy. The mission of CEIBS is to develop entrepreneurs and business leaders skilled in the tools of international competitiveness and endowed with the global mindset that increasingly typifies management in the twenty first century.

I

Entrepreneurs differ from capitalists in that they are not necessarily owners of capital. Some public companies with diverse stock ownership have emerged as multinationals or global companies through technological, management, and system innovation in fierce global competition. The board chairmen and CEOs of these businesses undoubtedly deserve the honorable title of "entrepreneurs". However, not all business leaders can claim themselves as entrepreneurs in the same way that not all school masters or university presidents are educators, or that not all people working in laboratories are scientists. Indeed, only those who have made huge contributions to education and science are respected as educationists and scientists. If this argument holds water, then the title of entrepreneur only belongs to those who have led their businesses to go from good to great through continuous innovations in management.

But are these people trained or born? The answer to me is somewhat obvious: if they are born, then what's the use of human education? It's true that talents are critical to entrepreneurs, educationists and scientists, but talents will come to nothing if they are not developed effectively. The development of talents can be realized through various channels, but without doubt, education is among the most important. The fundamental purpose of education is to provide understanding and tap human potential. It can make a huge difference in an individual. Admittedly, some generals have learned military arts through battles, but more are trained by military institutions like West Point.

In a word, management education offered by business schools has undeniable value in developing entrepreneurs. This is not a question; it has been proven by the practice of management education over a century.

If we all agree that the pivotal role of management education is to tap and maximize the potential of future entrepreneurs, then the next question will be what qualities a successful entrepreneur should possess?

The first quality is a high IQ (intelligence quotient). Without a high IQ, nobody can become an entrepreneur. To make an extreme example, a school can never turn an idiot or a retarded person into an entrepreneur, no matter how smart the training might be.

The second quality is a high EQ (emotional quotient). A high IQ itself is not enough for an entrepreneur. Chen Jingrun was a well-known Chinese mathematician who must have had a high IQ as evidenced by his contribution in proving "Goldbach's Conjecture". However, his EQ was so low that he could not even take care of himself. In this case, any effort to train him as an entrepreneur would have been in vain. A high EQ can help an entrepreneur not only become a charismatic leader and unite the individuals as a cohesive team, but to also establish a harmonious relationship with the external environment and win the market competition.

The last quality is a high SQ (spiritual quotient). This notion is often overlooked but it has proved its staying power and Chinese culture repeatedly identifies it as a critical ingredient for success. Starting a new venture or winning the fiercest of competitions requires courage and daring; seizing rare business opportunities requires courage and daring; managing crisis requires courage and daring. Lacking a high SQ, becoming an entrepreneur is all but impossible.

Therefore, the candidates' potentials in IQ, EQ and SQ should be measured as   important criteria in the selection process of any business school, and it is wise to give the same emphasis to the development of the three Qs as essential foundations for the mastery of management concepts and tools.

II

To develop entrepreneurs and business leaders with international competitiveness skills in the twenty first century, we need first of all to understand what the future social and competitive landscape will look like and what challenges it will pose for management education in the twenty first century.

Based on my understanding, the twenty first century will experience three major historical changes:

1. Scientific-Industrial Revolution

The mid-twentieth century witnessed a new scientific and technological revolution represented by micro-electronics technology, marking the end of the industrial society begun in 1776. Defined by such catch phrases as "post-industrial society", "the third wave", "information society", and "knowledge-based economy", this new technological revolution is opening a new age and kindling a new industrial revolution, just as the steam engine did three centuries ago. Its basic feature is that scientific research has developed into an industry and gradually become the cutting edge sector in society. The key product of science-based industries is knowledge and information which are quickly becoming the most strategic resources of our own century. In a word, humanity is experiencing a vigorous scientific-industrial revolution, ushering a new scientific-industrial society whose contours are emerging. Just like an agricultural-rural economy was replaced by the industrial-urban economy, the industrial economy will be replaced by a scientific-industrial society. This is another epoch-making watershed in human history.

This emerging scientific-industrial society poses a series of revolutionary challenges to business management:

- The organizational form of businesses must be changed. Integration of medium and small-sized technology companies, venture capital and second board will be the common practice, and virtual businesses will emerge as a result of the ever growing use of electronic networks.
- The main object of business and management education is knowledge workers whose creative labor calls for a rethinking of management approaches.
- The extensive use of information, intelligence and technology in business management has not only transformed the internal structure of businesses but also presents sharply distinct and new requirements for the management of quality and the quality of management.

2. Economic Globalization

The most important sign of economic globalization is the emergence of global companies who build their strengths not on size, but on the effective allocation of capital, technology, production, management and other elements on a worldwide basis. As the most advanced mode of production, it will invariably yield maximum economic benefits. Economic globalization is thus an irresistible trend in the twenty first century.

It will also pose new challenges to global business management in the twenty first century:

- Global competition will intensify, and global companies will become more powerful. Consequently, infusing a global perspective in business strategy formulation and execution has become the paramount issue in management.

- The national characteristics of businesses are fading while their global characteristics are asserting themselves, making many popular and traditional management philosophies obsolete.
- As autonomous economic actors with their influence extending to every corner of the world, the vitality of large-scale global companies depends on their choice of internal structures to create appropriate synergy.
- A global company's management philosophy and team should be multi-culturally relevant and competent, as the successful resolution of conflicts generated by the blending of cultures often determines optimal outcomes.

3. China is the Locomotive of the World Economy

With its annual income per capita exceeding one thousand U.S. dollars, China has reached the turning point on a rapid growth curve, well known to experts in development economics; with its population of 1.3 billion, China now boasts the largest consumer market in the world; endowed with cheap and high-quality human resources, it has become "the world's factory"; finally, with World Trade Organization accession, companies from all countries are flooding to China as Chinese companies step onto the world's commercial stage. All these are patent confirmation of recent historical trends that China is fast becoming the world's locomotive, as predicted by numerous entrepreneurs and economists.

Given such a shifting competitive landscape, any business must adapt rapidly to the emerging tendencies, and more importantly, develop the ability to manage multi- and cross-culturally, if it wishes to succeed. History has amply proven that Western and Chinese cultures are each the depositor of large reservoirs of vitality. Hence, it is not unreasonable to expect Chinese businesses to acquire the "global perspective" manifest in the Western cultural mold and Western businesses to acquire a deep appreciation for the unique "Chinese martial arts" in engaging the complex process of economic globalization. The creative integration of a "global perspective" and of "Chinese martial arts" perspective is keystone in reaching leading ranks in the global competition race.

III

Who was recognized as the best business school in the twentieth century? British-based *Financial Times* rankings show that the list has often been topped by a few American schools. Indeed, people always think about Wharton, Harvard or Sloan whenever they talk about the best business schools. A few years ago, however, I was surprised to find, in an influential US magazine, that the answer should be "West Point". Why a military institution? According to my own survey, West Point has produced more than 1,500 board chairpersons and CEOs for Top 500 and 5,000 business leaders at the board director level – an achievement hardly matched by any business school in the world. What is the most critical factor behind this resounding success? In my exclusive interviews with numerous business gurus, I have been given various reasons, among which one impresses me most - "business schools teach us leadership, but West Point teaches the lifestyles of leaders." This might be the source of the leadership gap between the education provided by a business school and that of a West Point-type institution, which calls for a reconsideration of business education in the twenty first century.

In my opinion, business schools can learn from West Point. They should not only continue to invite good faculty for classroom instruction, but also develop a new learning style for business leadership. This can be understood as the revival of seminal ideas advocated in traditional Chinese culture in the new century - "Education should enlighten people along with knowledge dissemination", and "students should learn how to be a worthy human being before they learn how to do things." A good faculty member should not only teach knowledge, but also teach how to be a "man," and in the case of a business school, how to become a great entrepreneur. In the selection chain from recruitment to placement, business schools ought to stress the exercise of leadership and train accordingly--a prerequisite for visionary, innovative leadership. The former requires sustained efforts by the faculty while the latter requires innovative reforms of curriculum. China is uniquely positioned to respond to this professional educational challenge.

However, we would be remiss to copy the educational philosophy of a West Point blindly or turn a school into a military camp. It is the spirit and philosophy underpinning the success of a West Point that matters most, and better results can be achieved in the twenty first century within the canons of current business education.

Liu Ji
President, China Europe International Business School

Contents

List of Contributors

Herman Aguinis

Herman Aguinis (Herman.Aguinis@cudenver.edu) is Associate Professor of Management in the Business School at the University of Colorado at Denver. He has been a visiting scholar at universities in several countries focusing his teaching, research, and consulting activities are in the areas of human resources management, organizational behavior, and research methodology. He is the author of *Applied Psychology in Human Resource Management* (with Wayne F. Cascio, 6th ed., 2005, Prentice-Hall), the author of *Regression Analysis for Categorical Moderators* (2004, Guilford), and the editor of *Test-Score Banding in Human Resource Selection* (2004, Praeger). In addition, he has written over 40 refereed journal articles in well recognized and prestigious publications. Aguinis served as Division Chair for the Research Methods Division of the Academy of Management (2003-2004) and currently serves as Editor-in-Chief for the journal *Organizational Research Methods* (2005-2007).

Ilan Alon

Ilan Alon (ialon@rollins.edu) is Associate Professor of International Business and Co-Director of the Global Practicum Program at Crummer Graduate School of Business, Rollins College. He is the author, editor, and co-editor of 9 books and over 60 published articles, chapters, and conference papers. His two recent books *Chinese Culture, Organizational Behavior and International Business Management* (Greenwood, 2003) and *Chinese Economic Transition and International Marketing Strategy* (Greenwood, 2003) are widely distributed among US research and university libraries. Alon is a recent recipient of the Chinese Marketing Award, a dual award from the Tripod Marketing Association (China) and the Society for Marketing Advances (USA). He is also an international business education consultant and a featured speaker in many professional associations.

Peter H. Antoniou

Peter H. Antoniou, MIBA, DBA, (DrPHA@aol.com) is president of Pomegranate International, a firm involved in *International Venturing, Educational* Programs and *Consulting* activities with a particular focus on matching US and Asian companies, and principal of Ansoff Associates, a firm specializing in *Strategic Transformations.* He has authored and co-authored 15 books and numerous articles published internationally, including a bimonthly column on U.S. - China trade issues published in the Development News of Tianjin, China from 1992 to 1995. In addition to teaching courses in International Business and Strategic Management, he frequently travels to Europe, Mexico and China delivering seminars and consulting in the areas of International Marketing and Strategic Management, and has worked with companies including IBM, Johnson Wax, Infotec and the Pearl River Investment Company. Antoniou has been a principle in the founding of trade and strategic management firms with extensive reach. He serves on several boards and is the recipient of many awards and honors.

Xue Bai

Xue Bai recently completed a Master of Management Studies (MMS) degree at the University of Waikato, Hamilton, New Zealand. She is now working for her family business in Anshan, China.

Paul W. Beamish

Paul Beamish (pbeamish@ivey.uwo.ca) is Professor of International Business at the Richard Ivey School of Business, University of Western Ontario, London, Canada. He is the author or co-author of 40 books, and over 100 articles or contributed chapters. At Ivey, he has responsibility for Ivey Publishing, the distributor of Ivey's collection of over 2000 cases. Beamish has authored nearly 100 case studies, primarily in the international management area. These have appeared in *Asian Case Research Journal, Case Research Journal,* and in 60 books. As Director of Ivey's Asian Management Institute, he is overseeing a process which generates applied research useful to managers doing business in Asia, and which has resulted in over 200 new Asian cases being prepared.

Fabienne Bressot

Fabienne Bressot (fbressot@yahoo.com) has worked on management development in intercultural contexts in Europe and Asia since 1995. Currently with Metizo, she specializes in personal and career development strategy and training in education and in the corporate world. She conducts organizational diagnoses resulting in recommendations to plan and facilitate definition of key roles and functions in the organization and designs assessment tools and strategies to align the right people with company objectives. She is a Ph.D. candidate in Organizational Management at the Institute of Business Administration of Nice with a specialty in Intercultural Management in China and teaches personal development at Marseille Euromed School of Management (France). She frequently speaks at professional conferences and publishes on the topics of intercultural and management development.

Peter Enderwick

Peter Enderwick (peter.enderwick@aut.ac.nz) is Professor of International Business at Auckland University of Technology, Auckland, New Zealand. His research interests include international human resource management, international service firms, and Asian business. He has written or edited several books and numerous papers on these topics. He has taught in a number of European and Asian countries. He serves on the editorial board of *International Business Review* and is currently an adjunct professor at the University of South Australia, Adelaide, Australia. The work described in this chapter was completed while he was Professor of International Management at the University of Waikato, Hamilton, New Zealand.

Wei He

Wei He, (mfhe@isugw.indstate.edu) is Assistant Professor of Management at College of Business, Indiana State University. He has been a faculty member at School of Management, Dalian University of Technology, Dalian, China between 1989-1996 and received his Ph.D. in organization studies from Boston College in 2004. His current research interests include the reform of Chinese state-owned enterprises, the transformation of management education in China, and the corporate philanthropy of multinational corporations. He has published in both English and Chinese in journals such as *Organization Science, Journal of International Management, Journal of Social Psychology,* etc.

Jonatan Jelen

Jonatan Jelen (JJelen@mercy.edu) is currently assistant professor of Business at Mercy College, Dobbs Ferry New York. Additionally, he holds responsibilities as Coordinator of Online Learning and is Director of the MS in MIS that he is currently creating for the College. Additionally, he is an avid instructor at several other colleges in the US and internationally and is completing his thesis for his PhD in Business-Computer Information Systems at Baruch College. His research interests focus on Leadership at large, Distance Education and Pedagogy, Information and Network Economics, Cyberlaw, and the Management of Techonology. Jelen holds a doctorate in law from Universite de Pau, France, as well as MBAs from Ecole Superieure de Commerce de Paris, Edinburgh Business School of Heriot-Watt University, and Baruch College, as well as a JD form Ludwig-Maximilians-University, Munich.Germany, and LLMs from Universite de Pau, Universite de Paris II-Pantheon-Assas, and Fordham University School of Law.

Liu Ji

Liu Ji (Faye Zhang: zfaye@ceibs.edu) is the Executive President, China Europe International Business School and has successively held posts of Deputy Chairman, Research Fellow and Member of the Academic Board, the Chinese Academy of Social Science during the past ten years. He has also been chiefly involved in leadership of the Association of Science and Technology of the Shanghai Municipality, the Commission of Economic Restructuring of the Shanghai Municipality and the Research Institute of Combustion Engine under the Ministry of Electromechanics, Shanghai.

Howard Kleinmann

Howard H. Kleinmann (hwrqc@cunyvm.cuny.edu) is the Director of the Academic Support Center, College English as a Second Language (ESL) Program, and China Program at Queens College, city University of New York. He holds a B.A. in Linguistics from Queens College, M.A. in Teaching English as a Second Language from UCLA and Ph.D in Linguistics from the University of Pittsburgh. He has written on a wide rang of subjects including second language acquisition, ESL reading and writing, consumer English, and Indochinese refugee education. Since 1985, he has been involved in developing cooperative programs in English and business education with higher education institutions in China.

Kern Kwong

Kern Kwong (kkwong2@calstatela.edu) is the Full Professor and Chairman of the Department of Management, California State University, Los Angeles. He is also the Director of Asian Pacific Business Institute (APBI), a President chartered institute at California State University, Los Angeles. He consults extensively with companies such as Saudi Aramco, Southern California Edison, Goldlion Holdings (U.S.A) and other international firms. He has also conducted extensive executive management training programs for national, provincial and municipal governments as well as enterprises of the People's Republic of China.

Catherine Levitt

Catherine Levitt (clevitt@ggu.edu) holds multiple degrees including Southeast Asian Studies, Vietnamese Language and a Doctorate in Business Administration in Strategic Management from United States International University. Levitt has more than 15 years of private industry experience at an executive level, several years with Department of Defense and is a certified Commercial Contracts Negotiator. She has lived, worked and taught in several Asian and European countries with a particular area of interest and expertise in the privatization process that accompanies the transition from a command economy to free-market practice. Currently, Director of the Center for East-West Entrepreneurial

Studies in Southern California she also consults on privatizing industries in transitional economies. Levitt is the Representative for the Americas to the Executive Council of the International Association for Chinese Management Research. She was Provost of Golden Gate University's Southern California Region from 1998-2000. Levitt was a nominee for the PriceWaterhouseCoopers' Ansoff Prize in Strategic Management, 2000.

Mingfang Li

Mingfang Li (mli@csun.edu) is Professor of Management at California State University, Northridge. He joined the Northridge management faculty in 1990 after completing his doctorial degree from the Department of Management, Virginia Tech in 1990. Mingfang Li's teaching area focuses on strategic management, technology and innovation and global management. In addition to his regular appointment he has offered executive seminars and guest lectures. Mingfang Li's research focuses on corporate governance, technology and innovation, and emerging economies. He has published in outlets such as *Strategic Management Journal, Advances in Competitive Research, Information & Management,* and *Asia Pacific Journal of Management.*

Shaomin Li

Shaomin Li (sli@odu.edu) teaches international business at Old Dominion University. He obtained his Ph.D. from Princeton University and was a post-doctoral fellow at Harvard University. He has extensive academic and business experiences in China, Hong Kong, and the United States, including being a founding CEO of a high-tech firm in Hong Kong. His research interest is in business environment in societies undergoing rapid political and economic transitions.

Romie F. Littrell

Romie Littrell (romie.littrell@aut.ac.nz) is Associate Professor of International Business at Auckland University of Technology in New Zealand since 2002. Prior academic experience includes stints teaching business and management at university in Germany, Switzerland, China, and the USA. His business background includes several decades in marketing and information technology with UNISYS, Xerox, IBM, and managing his own international IT trading company. Experience in China includes teaching at Sheng Da University, Xinzheng, and four years as a training manager and human resources manager in a multi-hotel complex in Zhengzhou, both cities in Henan Province.

Le Lu

Le Lu (lllule@online.sh.cnis) Professor and Dean of the Shanghai-New York International Language Institute, University of Shanghai for Science and Technology. Her research covers lexicology, semantics, and cross-cultural communications. She has written numerous academic papers which were published in prestigious Chinese journals, books and Western journals. Her books include a translation of Tradition by Edward Shils, an American sociologist, two co-edited dictionaries, and a number of textbooks used widely throughout China. She delivered 15 TV lectures broadcasted nationwide by China Central Television. She and her research partner successfully finished a project, funded by Ford Foundation, concerning Social Changes in China and Vocabulary Changes in the Chinese Language. She has recently participated in research funded by US universities, aimed at exploring China's market and have co-authored a few reports and articles published in business oriented journals resulting from this research.

Nandani Lynton

Nandani Lynton (lyntonn@t-bird.edu) is Vice-President for Executive Education, Greater China of THUNDERBIRD. Lynton has been based in China since 1993 and has extensive international consulting experience in both the private and the public sectors, with expertise in organizational development, human resource systems, process facilitation and intercultural management. In Europe, the Americas and Asia, Lynton has consulted for Fortune 500 multinationals and for joint venture corporations. Internationally her work focuses on assisting companies and their managers to meet the challenges of globalization. She has also taught and done research at several prestigious universities in the US and abroad. Since 1995, Lynton has co-founded and chaired the Beijing Trainers' Network, organized the Beijing Human Resource Forum for HR executives, and served on the Board and on committees for the American and the Australian Chambers of Commerce and the Rotary Club (Provisional) of Beijing. Her team received the 1998 China Staff / Euromoney award: Best China HR Consultancy, and she herself received the special award: Outstanding contribution to HR in China from the same organization in 1999.

Steven D. Maurer

Steven D. Maurer (smaurer@odu.edu) is a Professor of Management with a Ph.D. in Human Resources Management from the University of Oregon. He has over 20 years of research, teaching, and consulting experience in areas such as employment/labor law, conflict resolution, compensation management, and the recruitment, selection, and retention of technical/professional workers. He has served as a visiting scholar at the Hong Kong University of Science and Technology and an invited lecturer at the Romania Polytechnic University of Bucharest. Maurer's research has been published in scholarly reviews, conference publications such as those by the Academy of Management, the American Society for Engineering Management, the Society of Industrial and Organizational Psychology, and in several top management journals such as the *Academy of Management Review,The Journal of Applied Psychology, Personnel Psychology*, and *The Journal of High Technology Management Research.* He is a three-term member of the editorial review board for *The Academy of Management Journal* and has nearly ten years of experience as a project engineer and engineering employment manager with an AT&T operating company.

John McIntyre

John R. McIntyre (ciber@mgt.gatech.edu) is the director of the federally funded Georgia Tech CIBER and a professor of international management and international relations, with joint appointments in Georgia Tech's College of Management and Sam Nunn School of International Affairs. He is also a senior fellow of the East-West Trade Policy Center of the University of Georgia in Athens, Georgia. He has had work experience with multinational firms in the U.K. and Italy. He has published articles in many journals, published numerous book chapters and is author and co-editor of six books on international business government relations, political economies and international trade. His non-academic activities include international business strategy consulting with Southeastern U.S., Japanese and European firms. He has served as a member of the Delegation of the European Communities Commission "European Union Task Force of Experts", in the U.S., since 1988. He was editor of the annual Japanese Investment Yearbook in the Southeast of The Japan-America Society Inc. from 1990 to 1997.

J. Mark Munoz

J. Mark Munoz (jmunoz@mail.milikin.edu) is an Asst. Professor for International Business at the Millikin University in Illinois, USA. He is also a member of the Board of Directors for two companies operating in Asia-Pacific. Munoz is a graduate of MBA and PhD in Management, and has worked in senior level posts in the international arena including International Sales and Marketing Director for a retail group, Country Manager (Asia) for a European technology company, and Account Director (US & Asia-Pacific) for a leading market research firm specializing in the travel and tourism industry. He has been awarded two Best Research Awards in international conferences, and has publications in academic and business journals. His research pertaining to globalization and the travel industry has been cited at eHotelier.com and the Travel Daily News. Munoz is listed in the 58th edition of *Who's Who in America*.

Glenn Pearce

Glenn Pearce (g.pearce@uws.edu.au) is a senior lecturer in Marketing at the University of Western Sydney, Australia. He recently completed the

EdD degree at the University of Technology, Sydney and his thesis investigated the use of educational drama by university students in learning about marketing. He has authored articles published in the *Journal of Organizational Change, Assessment and Evaluation in Higher Education, Research in Drama Education, Drama Australia Journal, The International Journal of Management Education, Acta Horticulturae, the Australasian Marketing Journal and the Australian Journal of Experiential Learning.* Glenn has won numerous prizes for teaching excellence and been recognized at the national level by being a finalist in the Australian Awards for University Teaching on two occasions -1998 and 2002.

Heidi A. Roth

Heidi A. Roth (Heidi.Roth@cudenver.edu) received her master's degree from the University of Chicago and her Ph.D. in psychology and religion from the University of Denver and Iliff School of Theology. She has held teaching positions at the University of Denver and the University of Colorado at Denver-International College in Beijing. Her research, teaching, and consulting interests include the relationship between psychology and culture, and the effects of religion on morality. Currently, she a psychotherapist in private practice in Denver, Colorado.

Joanne Shoveller

Joanne Shoveller, (jshovell@uoguelph.ca) Vice-President, Alumni Affairs and Development, of the University of Guelph in Canada, joined the University of Guelph following a 17-year career at The University of Western Ontario that included work in marketing, communications and development as well as alumni and corporate development and graduate program management. During her tenure at UWO, Joanne initiated the University's outreach to Asian alumni, took a central leadership role in the planning and implementation of the successful $75 million Ivey Campaign, and was instrumental in establishing Ivey's Hong Kong campus. In 2001, Joanne was appointed as the Director of Ivey's MBA Program Office, managing the marketing, recruiting, admissions, program services, and administration of the Ivey Business School's core academic program. Joanne has a B.A. in English Language and Literature from Wilfrid Laurier University and a Masters in Business Administration from UWO's Ivey Business School. She has made presentations and written articles on global student recruiting, alumni and fundraising to several organizations including the National Association of Asian American Professionals, Council for the Advancement and Support of Education, and the Canadian Association for University Continuing Education.

Y. James Song

James Song (watervillesz@yahoo.com.cn) graduated from Peking University, and received his Ph.D. from University of California Berkeley, and an MBA from Cornell. He has taught at Shanghai Jiaotong University (SJTU) School of Management, Nanjing University Business School, and the Sydney Graduate School of Management. His most popular courses include *Communication and Negotiation, Competitive Intelligence,* and *Cross-Culture Management.* A Chinese native and US citizen living in Shanghai, Song is currently managing director of Waterville International Management Information Inc., adjunct professor in SJTU's IMBA program, and senior consultant with Negotiation Resource International. He has advised and served as senior executive in many leading global organizations in America and China, in finance, marketing, information technology, and international business education.

Catherine Sutton-Brady

Catherine Sutton-Brady (c.sutton-brady@econ.usyd.edu.au) is a Lecturer in the Discipline of Marketing, School of Business at The University of Sydney. She has considerable industry experience, having worked in multinational marketing companies in Europe. Sutton-Brady is also an experienced educator who has more than ten years experience in undergraduate and postgraduate teaching. She has been invited as a visiting professor, to both Hong Kong and mainland China, on numerous occasions. She values innovation in teaching and constantly strives to improve her teaching and maintain student interest and enthusiasm for learning. Testament to this is her receipt of the Faculty of Management Annual Teaching award 2000 for her teaching innovation in International Marketing and in 2001 she was highly commended, by the College of Law and Business, UWS, for team teaching in Guangzhou. In 2003 she was a nominee for the Australian and New Zealand Marketing Academy (ANZMAC) Marketing Educator of the Year Award. Sutton-Brady has published in the area of international and business marketing and in marketing education.

Mary Vielhaber

Mary Vielhaber, Professor of Management at Eastern Michigan University, received her M.A. and PhD from the University of Michigan. She teaches managerial communication, human resource development, organizational behavior, organization development, and leadership. Vielhaber served two years as an Acting Associate Graduate Dean, and three years on a special assignment in the President's Office at Eastern Michigan University. She has served as the co-director (with Dr. Fraya Wagner-Marsh) of our Master's program in Human Resources and Organizational Development. Her research focuses on team interviewing and executive coaching strategies. Vielhaber co-authored with Dr. Rick Camp a book, *Strategic Interviewing: How to Hire and Keep Good People*, published by Jossey-Bass. For over eighteen years, Vielhaber has been on the faculty of The Executive Education Program at the University of Michigan where she teaches in the Strategic Interviewing Program with Dr. Rick Camp.

Fraya Wagner-Marsh

Fraya Wagner-Marsh has a doctorate in Management from the University of Memphis and is the Department Head of the Management Department of the College of Business at Eastern Michigan University. She teaches graduate and undergraduate courses in Human Resources Management, is the co-director of the Master of Science in HR/OD program and is the chapter advisor for the national award winning student chapter of SHRM (Society for Human Resources Management). Fraya is a member of the Greater Ann Arbor Society for Human Resource Management, is the Past-President of the HRAGD (Human Resources Association of Greater Detroit), is the former HRCI (Human Resources Certification Institute) State Coordinator for Michigan, and is the past Treasurer and current State Director-Elect for the Michigan Council of SHRM. Fraya is the program coordinator and facilitator for the SHRM University Learning System. She does management and HR consulting and training for various corporations including General Motors, City of Detroit, and Masco Corporation. Her current research interests include strategic human resources, team interviewing, compensation, business ethics and spirituality in the workplace. She has had numerous research articles published in various conference proceedings and articles published in the Journal of Organizational Change Management, Journal of Management Systems, Journal of Teaching in International Business, Mobility, and the Journal of Business and Economic Perspectives.

Qun Wang

Qun Wang, Ph.D. in Technology Economics and Management of Hohai University, is Associate Professor of Management. Her teaching area focuses on strategic management, human resources management, and organizational behavior. Qun Wang's research focuses on corporate strategy and human resources management. She is serving as consultant, advisor to the private sectors such as Shenzhen An-yuan Company, and is the author of many scholarly and industry publications as well as an experienced trainer in the public and private sectors.

Xiaoyun Wang

Xiaoyun Wang (xiaoyun_wang@umanitoba.ca) is Assistant Professor of Asper School of Business, University of Manitoba. She has joined the University of Manitoba as an Assistant Professor since 2001 and received her Ph.D. (Organizational Behavior) from McGill University in year 2001. She received her M.Ed and B.Ed in Psychology from Northeast Normal University, Changchun, China. Wang's research interest is in cross-cultural adjustment, social networking, value creation and international human resource management. She has published in both English and Chinese in journals such as *International Journal of Human Resource Management, International Journal of Cross-Cultural Management*, etc.

Gigi Wong

Gigi Wong (gwong@ivey.uwo.ca) is the Assistant Director of the Asian Management Institute at the Richard Ivey School of Business, University of Western Ontario, London, Canada. Born and raised in Hong Kong, Wong is fluent in English, Mandarin, Cantonese, and several other Chinese dialects. After graduating from the University of Western Ontario, she worked in the educational sector in Hong Kong for a number of years before rejoining Western. Wong joined the Ivey Business School at the inception of the Asian Management Institute in 1997, which has a mandate to develop and disseminate management education intellectual capital with Asian relevance. She played a major role in the development of more than 300 new Asian business cases, and more than 70 Asian publications edited by Ivey faculty. She visits China regularly to promote and make arrangements for case method workshops across China.

Yim-Yu Wong

Yim-Yu Wong (yywong@sfsu.edu) is a Professor and former Department Chair of International Business at San Francisco State University. Her research covers strategic management, global strategic issues in emerging and transitional economies, international diversification, cultural values at workplace, and knowledge transfer. Her works have been published in 28 articles in academic journals, 8 contributions to books, and 56 papers presented at academic conferences. She has taught at business programs in the United States, France, and China. She received her Honor Diploma at the Hong Kong Baptist

College (now Hong Kong Baptist University), B.B. in and M.B.A. at Western Illinois University and a Ph.D. at University of Nebraska-Lincoln.

Diana J. Wong-MingJi

Diana J. Wong-MingJi, (Diana.wong@emich.edu) is Assistant Professor of Management at Eastern Michigan University, completed her PhD in strategic management at the University of Massachusetts, Amherst. She teaches graduate and undergraduate strategic management, organization development and change, entrepreneurship, and teams and teamwork. She also has experience teaching leadership, international management, research methods and data collection, and organizational behavior to undergraduate, graduates, and executive graduate students. Wong's areas of research interests include strategic alliances, merger and acquisition integration, learning and technological innovations, and international management of global strategies. She chaired the planning committee for developing and implementing the International Cultural Competence Institute for faculty and staff at Eastern Michigan University. In addition, she consults with executive managers who focus on strategic change for leading organizations. Her publications can be found in the journals *Organization, Organization Development Journal,* and *Personnel Review.* Wong's professional involvement includes the Academy of Management, Academy of International Business, Strategic Management Society, North American Case Research Association, Eastern Academy of Management, Southern Academy of Management, and the Caribbean Studies Association.

Kaicheng Yu

Kaicheng (K.C.) Yu (kcyu@dlut.edu.cn) is Professor of Management (retired) at School of Management, Dalian University of Technology, Dalian, China. He was one of the first generation professors in promoting the development of management education, organizational behavior, and teaching with cases in China in 1980s-1990s. His major research interests included organizational commitment, distributive justice, and motivation to manage. He has published extensively in both English and Chinese in journals such as *the Journal of Applied Psychology*, *Journal of International Management*, *Indigenous Psychological Research in Chinese Societies,* etc.

Wenxian Zhang

Wenxian Zhang (wzhang@rollins.edu) is an Associate Professor at Rollins College in Winter Park, Florida, USA. He holds a BA from Peking University, Beijing, China, a MS in business and economics and a MLS from Southern Connecticut State University in New Haven, Connecticut. His research interests include international business, Chinese history and cultures, and comparative librarianship.

Yenming Zhang

Yenming Zhang (yzhang555@yahoo.com.cn) is the CEO of the Beijing Taiji Times Educational Management Consultants, Inc., and a Senior Research Follow at the Chinese Management Academy. He received his BA in English from Henan Normal University in Xinxiang, China, MA in educational management from Southern Connecticut State University in New Haven, Connecticut, and Ph.D. in educational leadership from Harvard University in Cambridge, Massachusetts.

Introduction

Ilan Alon

Rollins College

In recent years, China's rise to prominence was noted by most writers and business analysts. The country is now a member of the WTO, host to the world's largest flows of foreign direct investment, and the second largest economy when measured by purchasing power parity GDP. With these notable achievements, there is a growing need for a more educated, more flexible, and more highly trained management cadre.

The chapters of this book are divided into three sections:

Part I: Economic Transition and International Cooperation

Part II: Pedagogical Issues

Part III: Professional Business Training in China

This book is the first of its kind to combine such diverse content from world experts on the topic of business and management education in China.

Part I: Economic Transition and International Cooperation

The first chapter by Li and Wong defines the study area of the Greater China economy as the totality of the economic activities of Chinese communities across the globe, and considers the management education challenges in this greater context.

Companies in the Greater China economy may exhibit different degrees of global integration (e.g., expansions into global arenas, and increased interactions with multinationals). Furthermore, they may utilize skilled human resources available through increased brain circulation. Different degrees of global integration and different degrees of brain circulation utilization will lead to managerial challenges that can be described from relatively simple to very significant. Furthermore, different areas of the world may exhibit different cultural characteristics (such as values and assumptions), and different institutional characteristics (such as different markets, and different degrees of available laws and enforcements).

The authors develop a regional typology which compares and contrasts the cultural and institutional characteristics of the Greater China economy. The demands placed on managerial knowledge and managerial education can be relatively simple and straightforward if the company management challenges are simple, and the contextual gap is limited; while complex and multifaceted if the managerial challenges are significant, and the contextual gap major. Managerial educational responses will then need to consider the content (including teaching materials), process (different teaching activities and pedagogies), and the trainee types (such as MBA students, executives and onsite training).

Chapter 2 by Bai and Enderwick considers the transition that has occurred in the Chinese market leading to higher demand for management personnel, particularly those with a strong appreciation of managing in a market-based economy. Traditional Chinese management approaches have been primarily shaped by experience under a centrally planned economy. This has led to a lack of understanding of market-oriented management approaches. As the Chinese economy has evolved and developed, the shortage of management personnel able to understand and master Western management skills in marketing, financial management, inventory control, human resources, and international business rules has become increasingly evident.

The chapter presents an audit of likely skill deficiencies within four key sectors: the SOE sector; the private sector; foreign-owned and joint venture firms; and the emerging 'high technology' sector. The audit identifies the most deficient skills as effective HRM, financial management, intellectual property management, marketing and strategic planning. Potential sources of the supply of management skills are discussed. The chapter concludes with some implications of the analysis for international business educators.

While Bai and Enderwick discuss deficiencies in Chinese management and business education, in chapter 3, Li and Maurer discuss deficiencies in Western business and management education as it relates to emerging markets. Li and Maurer discuss evidence that the majority of expatriate managers from the United States of America and other Western countries often fail in their job assignments in developing countries and that such failures commonly inflict enormous financial and opportunity costs on the expatriate's employer. Still, international business educators have yet to go beyond attributing such failures to "cultural differences" when teaching how to manage in developing countries.

Their chapter addresses this deficiency in management education processes by adopting extant research on working relationships and a recently developed framework of rule-based verses relation-based economies, to consider performance of expatriate managers in terms of their ability to form and manage effective working relationships in relation-based societies. First, the authors introduce a theoretical framework based on potential gaps in the working relationship expectations of expatriates from rule-based countries and employees in relation-based societies. Second, they propose a teaching agenda for training expatriates, in particular, and business students, in general, on how to effectively manage in a relation-based environment.

In chapter 4, Song discusses an emerging global need to better educate businesspeople on ethical issues. As China's preoccupation with economic growth deepens, ethics has become a focus of persisting public concern and incessant rhetoric by policy makers and opinion leaders. Yet as a curricular subject, business ethics remains virtually absent from the country's management education programs, even though some business schools are beginning to consider including the subject as either a required or an elective course.

Shortage in qualified faculty is a leading cause for the slowness in building up a critical mass. In the mean time, the subject's propinquity to cultural values, ideological doctrines, nationalistic sentiments and political taboos seems to interfere with potential focused effort to foster broader interest among academics, students, and executives. This chapter discusses the prospect of business ethics education in China by probing current understanding among MBA students at several universities and trainees in managerial development programs.

Reported in the chapter are results from a survey based on 180 respondents, which reveals complex patterns in views on and attitudes towards such issues as ethical criteria, moral development, and cross-cultural considerations. Three quarters of respondents agree that "Chinese organizations are less ethical than those in western countries." Two thirds believe that "lack of ethics is a price poor countries pay to get rich." Slightly less than half do not doubt that "everybody cheats if there is no danger of getting caught," whereas more people see honesty as a hindrance to wealth. A stark contrast exists between the dismissal, by a clear majority, of the "lower" or "pre-conventional" moral development stages and the unequivocal embracing, by nearly all, of the "higher" or "principled" level stages in Kohlberg's cognitive developmental model.

The investigation provides a basis for exploring the factors that may have helped shape current beliefs and attitudes. The findings shed new light on the discussion and program development of business ethics in contemporary China. A new model of culture, expanded from Trompenaars' three-spheres to accommodate analysis of formative processes, is introduced as a general framework for discussion.

Jelen and Alon discuss in chapter 5 the intersection of globalization and technology as the two most powerful forces that have shaped trade, investment, industrial development and people in the 20th and 21st centuries. Faced with these forces, Universities, on the one hand, internationalized their curriculums, students and faculty and, on the other hand, enhanced their technological base, such as the use of computers, internet infrastructure, and technology-based instructional capabilities. These two efforts have largely been mutually exclusive with little intersection between the two. This chapter analyzes the crossover between a university's potential to internationalize with respect to China, and to use its technological capabilities to extend its educational outreach.

Indirect presence in the Chinese market through Internet-mediated distance-learning education is thus proposed because of its attractiveness from effectiveness and efficiency perspectives, and because China has experienced an increase in its technological and infrastructural environments that enable this mode of entry. Distance learning education via e-commerce in China can be economically viable, consistently scalable, politically feasible, and expediently realizable.

Part II: Pedagogical Issues

Chapter 6, chapter 7 and chapter 8, taken together, significantly add to our general knowledge on pedagogy and educational transformation China and can help professors wishing to teach or administrators designing programs for the Chinese market. Chapter 6 starts the second part of this book with Littrell discussing in general the unique characteristics of culture, education, learning styles and cultural values specific to Confucian cultures, with an emphasis on China. Prescriptions that can facilitate success for non-Chinese lecturers in the tertiary classroom in China are provided.

Related to Littrell's chapter, in chapter 7 Aguinis and Roth discuss the cultural elements that are different between China and the West and their impact on educational efforts. China hosts dozens of United States based higher education institutions offering management and business programs and this number is increasing at a rapid pace. However, cultural differences between the U.S. and China make teaching particularly challenging for U.S. instructors in China. The authors review general cultural differences between the U.S. and China, as well as some unique features of Chinese culture, and link these differences to specific instructional challenges. Based on theoretical considerations, they offer nine testable propositions to guide future empirical research on education in China. Finally, they suggest pedagogical approaches and techniques that may prove useful for non-Chinese instructors teaching in China.

Chapter 8 written by Wang, He and Yu add to the pedagogical knowledge of chapter 6 and chapter 7 by acknowledging the growth in management education in China over the last couple of decades, examining the transformation of China's management education, and identifying the pedagogical problems in China's management education. The future orientation of China's management education and the roles of western educational institutions are also discussed.

Building on the more generalized information in chapter 6 through chapter 8, in chapter 9, Sutton-Brady and Pearce document a case study of successful team teaching of a business course - International Marketing Management - in an international MBA program held in China. Their chapter highlights how two lecturers using their individual areas of expertise work effectively together to enrich the learning experience of MBA students in Southern China. The chapter begins with a description of the setting for this team teaching experience. This description is followed by a discussion of use of the team teaching approach in education, which includes the advantages and disadvantages of the method. The logistics of team teaching are then presented. The student evaluations of the unit are discussed in support of the effectiveness of the method. Finally, lessons learned from the team teaching case study are presented.

Another specific case is discussed in chapter 10, where Beamish, Wong and Shoveller share the experiences of the Richard Ivey School of Business at The University of Western Ontario, London, Canada, in its endeavours to assist in modernization of the MBA programs in China by the introduction of a large body of teaching materials – mostly in the form of case studies – and faculty training programs. While they have found success in their involvement in China as an institution, there remains a long road ahead for educators and material providers to ensure the efforts are sustainable and the benefits transferable.

The case method has been hailed as an efficient and effective way of teaching business, a belief shared by most at top business schools such as Harvard, Ivey and Darden. Recognizing this, China's National MBA Education Supervisory Committee mandated that 25 per cent of China's MBA curriculum be delivered using the case method. The committee's endorsement of the case method created an immediate need for teaching materials and qualified instructors. Ivey saw that as an opportunity to assist in the development of China's institutional capacity for management education.

In Chapter 11, Antoniou, Kwong, and Levitt depart from the approach taken by the other chapter in this section, and examine education from a corporate and knowledge transfer perspective over a six year timeframe. During a 3 month period in 1997, they conducted a study to examine the agency factors that contribute to successful transfer of soft technology of management skills to Chinese firms. In the original study, 93 Chinese firms selected by the Ministry of Light Industry were surveyed in a small group interview process designed to capture both qualitative and quantitative data. These firms were re-contacted and interviewed again in 2003. Changes in the structures of firms and the relationships of firms had changed. The type of skills sought had modified. The expectations for the transfer agents had also changed. These changes, taken together, offer significant insight into curriculum development and the pedagogy of teaching management and business subjects to Chinese students, government officials and business practitioners.

Part III: Professional Business Training in China

Part III covers professional and business training specific to management practice, human resource management, organization development, management consultants, and travel executives.

In chapter 12 Lynton and Bressot discuss the ironic situation that while corporations in China are in great need of good managers (as acknowledged in previous chapters), the press is rampant with stories of students with MBAs from Chinese and overseas institutions who cannot find jobs. This apparent contradiction reflects both demographic and historical factors in China. The generation that should represent the senior managers of today was denied a formal education during the Cultural Revolution. While there are some CEOs and numerous entrepreneurs from this group, the bulk are not trained managers and few speak foreign languages. On the other hand, the young MBAs of today tend to lack lengthy work experience but have high position and salary expectations. This divergence leaves a gap that must be filled if corporations are to grow and function well in today's global economy.

Chapter 13, written by Wong-MingJi, Vielhaber, and Wagner-Marsh, discusses innovations in human resource management and organizational development education in China. According to the authors, the first graduate human resource management program in China provides illustrations of three innovative pedagogical practices that enable future Chinese managers to deal with major organizational transformations. The three pedagogies are the 3-D ASIMCO case study, a photo-change research project, and a Masters of Science in Human Resources and Organization Development e-portfolio. An important purpose underlying the three pedagogies is to bridge western oriented management knowledge with the dynamic Chinese cultural and economic context. The approached aimed for not only cognitive, but also affective and behavioral level learning to develop the managerial competencies. Given the rapid pace of economic restructuring in China, the three pedagogical practices address critical needs and major change processes at the human and organizational level. Future graduate business education must continue developing innovative pedagogy and more supply sources in order to keep up with demands for professional managerial competencies in China.

In chapter 14 Zhang and Zhang discuss the training of management consultants in China. Management consultation is defined generally as a contract advisory service provided to organizations in order to identify management problems, analyze them, recommend solutions to these problems and, when requested, help implement the solutions. The chapter discusses the development of market and management consulting services in China, professional development and certification of management consultants in China, the development of the profession and consulting companies in various regions, and the training such consultants have to undertake. Such training is not radically different for the training that management consultants in the United States of America receive, with perhaps the exception of the modules relating to the Art of War in business operations.

Munoz in chapter 15 discusses the education of Chinese travel executives by analyzing travel executives' perceptions on business, governance, technology, cross-border communication and knowledge flows resulting from an increasingly global market environment. His study provides strategies by which Chinese travel executives can manage the emerging challenges and opportunities brought about by the global spread of knowledge. Business organizations today are no longer as restricted and compartmentalized as in the past. Where companies in the past kept knowledge and information within an internal vacuum, business models in the New Economy have demonstrated aggressive approaches towards information gathering and dissemination across borders. National boundaries no longer curtail the spread of knowledge and information. The world has been transformed into a virtual information paradise and implications are evident to China's travel industry.

Kleinmann and Lu in chapter 16 write about the need of business education in language students in China. What these students need to be apt in the marketplace is cultural flexibility, communicative competence in both general and business English, and familiarity with business standards and practices. To achieve this purpose, the local educational system must deal with a spectrum of difficulties, including textbook availability, business education concepts and Chinese tradition. The chapter describes how an experimental business educational program, co-sponsored by two universities, one Chinese and one American, addresses these difficulties. The chapter further discusses how an integration of business knowledge, language and culture within the curriculum distinguishes the program but also creates other pedagogical and program administration problems.

I. Economic Transition and International Cooperation

Chapter 1

Management Education in the Greater China Economy: Challenges and Tasks

Mingfang Li
California State University, Northridge

Yim-Yu Wong
San Francisco State University

Qun Wang
Hohai University

1. Introduction

Management education is an important institution that transfers theoretical knowledge, nurtures managerial talents for enterprises big and small, and influences successful business practices and public policies. Management has played a significant role in the development of various countries and regions (Drucker, 1974). Business and commercial activities no doubt will constitute an integral part of the Greater China economy, as business enterprise operations clearly become competitive and critical for the continued economic development of the Greater China economy.

The authors suggest, however, that effective operations of business enterprises in the Greater China economy will depend on how well these businesses meet their managerial challenges, and these managerial challenges are amplified by contextual differences among the regions involved in the Greater China economy. Furthermore, the authors believe that the existing management education entities fall short of meeting these challenges as there exist significant gaps in theoretical knowledge, teaching materials, and educators, and furthermore there exist gaps in management education practices including teaching methodologies, and teaching interactions. In this paper the authors first develop an understanding of the management education challenges by

3

examining the managerial challenges the businesses in the Greater China economy confront, and contextual differences that these businesses must contend with, and then describes the combinations of management education contents, processes and trainee types that may help fill in the void identified.

First of all, in this paper we define the Greater China region as the geographical cluster that includes Mainland, Taiwan, Hong Kong and Macau, and the Greater China economy as the totality of economic activities of Chinese communities in the world (Kao, 1993). While the definition of the Greater China region relates clearly to certain geographical areas, the definition of the Greater China economy relates mainly to cultural commonalities of the business communities involved even though they may be scattered around in different parts of the world (Kao, 1993).

The Greater China economy thus defined distinguishes itself from other economic entities in several ways. All other major economic entities, namely, the Triad that includes US, Europe, and Japan (Rugman & Hodgetts, 2001), are geographically bound. The Greater China economy represents a significant part of world economic activities but defies easy descriptions because of the dispersion of economic activities across various regions and the diversity of business activities and management challenges. Regional cultural differences and institutional arrangements further increase complexities in business management.

Another notable feature relates to the emerging and transitional nature of the economic entities in the Greater China region. While the significant cultural bond may enable businesses in the Greater China region to collaborate with those Chinese based firms in other regions more easily than if they are to collaborate with other multinationals, institutional differences may complicate business undertakings. Furthermore, Western advancement in management theories has had a pervasive influence on business practices in modern multinational enterprises, while firms in the Greater China region must pursue their internationalization steps combining unique local management practices and modern advances. Systematic management research in emerging economies remains an underemphasized area. Existing management education practices may either emphasize Westernized contents or local contents but meaningful combinations of theories and case materials remain exceptions.

To identify effective responses to these managerial education challenges we first present a theoretical framework that depicts how managerial challenges and contextual differences demand more systematic management education solutions.

2. Business Management Challenges

Two important dimensions capture the business management challenges firms in the Greater China region may face. The first is the extent to which these domestic firms engage in international business flows of capital, currency and commerce (*global integration*) or utilizing global activities as a strategic part of their operations. The second is the extent to which these businesses utilization human resources made available through brain circulation or labor market mobility (*utilization of "brain circulation"*). We first describe the need for global integration, and speculate on the existence of varying degrees of global integration among firms in the Greater China region.

Scholars concur that two powerful forces have been at play in the global environment (Bartlett & Ghoshal, 1998). The first force is the pressure to globalize. Scale economies and scope economies, ever-expanding R&D costs, and increasingly shortened product life cycles all point at the need for companies to seek global power and efficiency in their business activities. Global integration from political and cultural perspectives, and advances in transportation and communication technologies reinforce this thrust as well. It must also be noted that many companies have succeeded remarkably by pursuing global or world product strategy – Japanese home electronics companies are but some of the examples. To many the world is becoming one, and meeting the global challenges quintessential recipe for corporate success. At the same time, the second force, the pressure to localize is asserting itself anew. Local cultural traditions persist in spite of global economic integration. Regional political forces are actively influencing various social processes. Violent demonstrations in cities where global economic conferences are being held serve to reinforce people's concern about globalization. Technological forces responsible for globalization are also accommodating and possibly reinforcing localization trends. For example, utilizing advanced manufacturing technologies enables firms to produce highly customized products to meet unique customer needs and tastes without sacrificing scale economies.

Clearly the opposing forces have put conflicting demands on businesses, big and small, multinationals as well as domestic. Multinationals that pursued either pure global strategy (world product orientation) or multi-domestic strategy (multi-local product orientation) are now facing both pressures (Bartlett & Ghoshal, 1998; Devinney, Midgley, & Venaik, 2000). Furthermore, the need to create global power and efficiency and local differentiation and responsiveness simultaneously leads companies to seek another important advantage, that of worldwide innovation and diffusion. Innovations along various aspects of businesses are critical for responding to localization pressures. Diffusing those innovations when appropriate on a greater scale is also critical for gaining, and enhancing global power and efficiency. Product innovation popularized in one market may help enhance a firm's competitiveness in another market. Effective marketing strategies uncovered in one region exhibit their prowess in another. Fuji-Xerox produced miniature copying machines to meet Japanese market's demand, but helped Xerox to fend off potential competitive onslaught in US as well. Acer's desktop computer designed in US served the world market. These are but some examples of the competitive implications of worldwide innovation and diffusion. Global power and efficiency, local sensitivity and responsiveness, and worldwide innovation and diffusion become the tripod on which a successful multinational enterprise builds its success. They can also be a source of insights for domestic firms in emerging economies and point out the related management challenges.

As noted earlier, the Greater China region as defined is home to many domestic businesses that are seeking to gain competitive advantage alongside powerful multinationals actively competing in the same arena. Many of these firms may find it advantageous to limit the extent of global activities by focusing on unique niche markets or regional customer bases. Other firms may find it essential to develop truly global oriented strategies to compete head to head against the multinationals.

Still others may find it beneficial to collaborate with multinationals for mutual gains. In many sectors, firms in the Greater China region are expanding internationally and multinationals are collaborating with domestic firms actively. Examples might include Acer (Bartlett & Ghoshal, 1998), Haier (Liu & Li, 2002; Yi & Ye, 2002; Zeng & Williamson, 2003) and numerous other companies. To the extent that greater global integration brings greater managerial complexity and risk, we suggest that effective global integration requires more focused and polished managerial skills and "state of the art" knowledge.

Closely related to but significantly different from the global scope of business activities identified above is the nature of human resource management practice or more specifically the utilization of talented managerial and technical resource skills in business processes. Two phenomena are relevant. First, contrary to the brain drain or the flow of human talents from developing to developed countries, and to the "reverse" brain drain or the flow of human talents from developed to developing countries, scholars have noted another important phenomenon, that of "brain circulation" (conceptualized alternatively as the movement of managerial elites and the creation of knowledge networks) (Saxenian, 2002a, 2002b) or the mobility of human talents from location to location and the formation of geographical clusters and even networks composed of highly skilled labors from different locations. For example, the Hsinchu-Shanghai-Silicon Valley semiconductor industry network benefits significantly from "brain circulation." A variety of competitive companies established their home base first in the Silicon Valley, then, in Hsinchu, and now in mainland China. These transplants combine interesting characteristics unique to each particular geographical area. Apparently various local governments recognize the importance of this human resource mobility and are developing attractive measures to recruit these individuals as well. The emphasis by businesses and governmental agencies on attracting high quality employees and managerial materials is especially appropriate given that competitive advantage is believed to be linked to geographical clusters (Porter, 1998). Indeed, in those "transplant" companies, employees stay and work at different regions part of the time.

Another equally important move by firms in the Greater China region relates to recruitment of senior level executives from multinationals to work for their local and overseas subsidiaries. Acer for example hired former IBM executives to head its North American operation. Various technology firms from the Mainland also have relied on the assistance from overseas Chinese executives, managers, business experts and professors, among others, who have garnered significant managerial and technique experience in multinationals.

In both cases of the utilization of brain circulation, we must recognize that the management team and key functional teams may be composed of people from diverse backgrounds and therefore will represent a unique challenge to management.

Considering the two dimensions of business activities, the degree of global integration, and the degree of utilization of "brain circulation," we may envision the managerial challenges to vary from relatively simple and homogeneous to significantly complex and heterogeneous. Figure 1 captures the varying degrees of business management challenges.

Conceptually several possibilities arise. If a firm engages in limited global integration and limited utilization of brain circulation, we would assume that the management challenge would be relatively homogeneous, and simple. On the other hand, with extensive global integration and extensive utilization of brain circulation, we would assume that managerial challenges become multi-faceted and heterogeneous.

Utilization of Brain Circulation	Extensive	Greater challenges	Significant challenges
	Limited	Simple challenge	Increased challenges
		Limited	Extensive
		Global Integration	

Figure 1. Business Management Challenges

In addition to considering firm level issues we must also look at differences among different regions in terms of institutional arrangements, and dominant cultural values of each society. This perspective is relevant since we now also need to consider the Greater China economy as an entity when considering management education challenges.

3. Contextual Gap

As Khanna and Palepu (1997; 1999) point out, several major aspects of the institutional environment in emerging economies, such as the product market, capital market, and labor market, are substantially different from those in developed economies. We may characterize these differences as the institutional arrangement difference or deficiency. These differences pose unique challenges to competing companies (Li & Wong, 2003; Li, Li, & Tan, 1998). Furthermore, availability of laws and regulations, and enforcement of contracts may present additional challenges. We may characterize this as institutional behavior uncertainty (Li & Wong, 2003). To effectively deal with institutional arrangement differences and institutional behavior uncertainty, companies may develop different strategic behaviors (Li, Li, & Tan, 1998; Whitley, 1999). In fact, it is possible that these firms may combine paradoxical strategic elements such as public and private ownership; practical goals and pluralistical goals; and innovation and imitation effectively. These behavior differences may become barriers to effective interaction and collaborations among the business enterprises within the Greater China economy. For example, businesses in emerging economies may work actively with governments to secure institutional supports while those in developed economies may emphasize predominantly market competitiveness and firm resource and core competence development. Different strategic orientations and motivations present significant challenges to inter-firm collaborations (Parkhe, 1993). These challenges are amplified if firms in the Greater China region exploit *ad hoc* and multiple strategic combinations.

In a theoretical discourse on competence transfer across multinational enterprises, Kostova (1999) uses the three dimensions in institutional theory, viz., regulative, normative, and cognitive (Scott,

1995), to describe the institutional environment. She suggests there are systematic quality variations in these three dimensions across different institutional environments. By combining these three institutional dimensions (Scott, 1995) with major institutional aspects relevant to company strategic behavior (Khanna & Palepu, 1997), we come to a realization that institutional arrangements and characteristics will affect business behavior in long-lasting fashion. In fact, the differences in institutional arrangements, or more specifically, the capital market, labor market and product market functions as well as laws and regulations may become normalizing forces to define the way economic actors perceive external factors, form preferences and value judgments, and develop behavior patterns. When we look at two businesses respectively in two different institutional environments, company behavior and activities may reflect closely their institutional environment. This embeddedness or fit is important for the survival and success of these businesses (Granovetter, 1985). Firm behavior differences, because of institutional differences, will also present challenges for effective inter-firm collaboration across the regions. Management education--if it is to be effective as an important means to bridge differences and serve as an enabler for interregional firm collaboration and interaction—must pay heed to this set of issues.

We also need to consider the underlying cultural values, attitudes, and belief systems of different societies constituting the firm's regional environment. It is worth underlining the notion that the Greater China economy does not have a specific geographical boundedness. Businesses in this economy in flux may have their home bases in different countries and regions. The dominant cultural value orientation of the society where these firms reside will no doubt also have a bearing on their strategic behavior and firm management practices.

Several schemes exist to highlight the key cultural value differences (Hofstede, 2001; Mead, 1998; Trompenaars & Hampden-Turner, 1998). Two important conclusions can be drawn from these research streams. First of all, there exists stable and commonly shared cultural values in different societies, and there are inter-society differences. Secondly, cultural values affect both strategic behavior at the firm level and human resource management practices at the intra-firm level. These two observations underscore the importance of integrating cultural differences when considering interregional firm collaborations (more specifically collaborations and interactions among firms within the Greater China economy).

We find the research work of Inglehart and Baker (2000) to be particularly effective for our purpose, as we develop a broad brush treatment of the management education challenges. Inglehart and Baker (2000), in an important project on modernization, studied two salient dimensions of cultural values. One dimension is related to the basic decision making orientation, and has two respective end points on a continuum: traditional value vs. rationality. The second dimension is related to the overarching goal of a society. The two respective ends on a continuum are survival and self expression. On a cultural map using these two dimensions, tested countries and regions can be found array in a broad range of positions. The authors concluded that *cultural values are relatively stable*. Economic developments and other societal changes do not alter the basic orientations readily. Other researchers clearly reached similar conclusions (Hofstede, 2001). Secondly, and more interestingly, the authors discover that immigrant communities share the same broad cultural values as society which they join.

This latter conclusion is especially relevant to our pursuit of a broad model of management education in the China context. We hypothesize that firms in the Greater China economy call different parts of the world their home bases, and the home base cultural values, shared by the employees and management of these firms, has significant bearing on these firms' strategic behavior and management practices. These firms will engage in interregional collaboration and interaction with their counterparts in the Greater China economy for mutual gain and with ease. We would assume that the differences in the strategic and management practices due to culture could form an intangible barrier to successful collaboration and interactions.

After identifying two significant contextual differences – institutional environments, and cultural values, and explaining how they relate to barriers for successful interregional firm collaboration in the Greater China economy, we are in a position to formalize the contextual difference aspect as described in Figure 2.

Cultural Value Differences	Large	Greater gap	Significant gap
	Minimal	Little gap	Increased
		Minimal	Large
		Institutional Environment Differences	

Figure 2. Contextual Gap

As illustrated in Figure 2, if two firms collaborating are from two regions that share similar cultural values and institutional environments, we would assume the contextual gap to be rather small, and therefore few barriers would be found. On the other hand, if the two firms are from two regions with marked cultural differences as well as institutional environment differences, we would assume a significant contextual gap, and subsequently the existence of real barriers to successful collaboration and interaction. Management education must then assume the task of bridging the gaps to facilitate task-driven collaboration through better understanding of inter-firm behavior differences.

Combining the contextual gaps thus conceived, and managerial challenges identified earlier, we can formulate another framework for a management education demand curve. Figure 3 presents this framework.

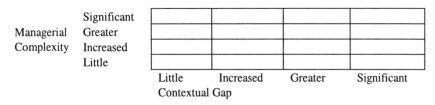

Managerial Complexity: Significant / Greater / Increased / Little

Little — Increased — Greater — Significant
Contextual Gap

Figure 3. Need for Managerial Knowledge and Education

4. Management Education Challenges

It is clear that firms in the Greater China economy will engage in various competitive moves, from purely domestic to truly global integration, and utilize 'brain circulation" differently. It is also clear that firms in the Greater China economy will engage in collaborative and interactive moves with firms from regions that exhibit little contextual differences to firms from regions that represent significant contextual differences. We may then be able to locate firms on the managerial knowledge and education map (Figure 3). Some firms may need a relatively straightforward and simple set of managerial knowledge and skills (if they face lower managerial complexity and limited contextual gap), while others may require a complex repertoire of managerial tools for their undertaking. Still others may fall in between. What is clear from this "map" is that management education as an enabling institution in the Greater China economy must perform several important tasks.

First, there is a patent need for a region-specific theory of management development and applications. Much of the existing body of business and management knowledge has been developed with Western and developed countries in mind. Its applicability to other environments must wait for further testing and verification. Furthermore, closely associated with the region-specific theory and knowledge is region-specific business cases and simulations. Business cases for specific regions require some analytical and theoretical pegs which are also conscious of regional specificities.

Secondly, there is a need for continued training and development of business and other educators to insure they are responsive to the Great China economic area issues and approaches. Business schools, corporate universities, and business research institutes have been a main vehicle of business knowledge generation, transfer and application in and for developed countries. Their future in the Greater China region, while promising, but they have not yet risen to the managerial challenges faced by this region's business actors.

Third, there is a dire need to elaborate effective pedagogies for future management leaders of the Greater China economy. It appears that most business and management education in the Greater China region simply borrow pedagogies and methodologies from the Western countries. While these may be useful approaches, cultural, work, and societal and economic system differences are often given short shrift.

Fourth, there is also an evident need to think through and offer optimal mixes of theory, applied material, cases, courses with educators schooled in methodologies and culture.

The need for tailor-made content (theories and cases), appropriate selection of educators, pedagogies sensitive to culture and language, as well as an optimal combination of contents and pedagogies is a formidable task for management education. Management education institutions in the Greater China economy must offer a diverse range of knowledge and skills utilizing effective educational processes suited to a different type of trainee. We now look at the basic offerings of management education institutions.

5. Business Management Education – Content, Process, and Trainees

Management education institutions are charged with the task of transferring relevant skills and knowledge to nurture the abilities of those who will become future business leaders. Accomplishing this task requires the involvement of educational content that can be broadly conceived to include theoretical materials, ideas, business cases as well as simulations. Furthermore, it requires the utilization of various teaching methodologies that range from lectures, classroom interactions, case discussions, simulations, experiential methods, team projects and report writings (Vance, 1993). A causal survey of the business schools and other training facilities may reveal that we utilize a variety of contents and a variety of processes. Finally, it is important to recognize that business management education involves different types of trainee with different needs and capabilities. We may quickly identify, for example, undergraduate students, MBA students, training programs for mid-level executives, distance learning, onsite training, and training programs for senior executives. Figure 4 may be a useful framework to identify the possible combinations that could be advantageously utilized by management education institutes to accomplish their tasks. (Note that we only captured two dimensions--the content of business education and the process of business education. Overlaying onto this Figure should be the third dimension – trainee types).

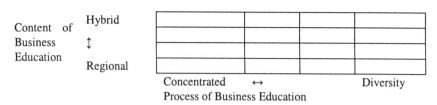

Figure 4. Varieties of Business Education Modes

Just as Figure 3 identified a variety of management educational needs, Figure 4 identifies a variety of educational modes to meet those diverse needs. It is interesting to note from the comparison of Figure 3 and Figure 4 that there is demand for a variety of management educational institutes. Some institutes may focus on regions and build core competences in a specific delivery methodology. Others may explore hybrid content and delivery methods. Still others may find an optimal mix of content mix and process mix for one given experience. A diversity of management education institutes (including business schools, training centers, corporate universities as well as consulting arms) may well be a requisite condition for the success of the management education in the Greater China economy, given the complexities of the tasks identified.

6. Responding to Management Education Challenges

Judging from the managerial challenges and educational needs presented above, management education must emphasize a number of important aspects. They range from concentrated educational methodology utilizing region-based teaching materials to diversity in teaching processes and combined teaching contents.

Significant efforts must be made to develop teaching materials relevant to specific regions. These materials cover both business theories and models, and cases as well as teaching exercises. Western publishers have recognized the market potential of emerging economies and developed textbooks focusing on those areas (e.g., Chow, Holbert, Kelley, & Yu, 1997). In general, however, these textbooks tend to mix localized cases with Western management and business theories. This approach, while beneficial, does not go far enough in truly transferring management theories developed and tested within the specific local environments and may fail to provide a relevant skills set and knowledge base to future generations of business leaders.

There is also a need for educators who are also active researchers with more regionalized topics. Theory development in business and management in developed countries has essentially assumed a given context and researched relationships among various business behavior aspects. Many advances have been made in business management knowledge. The significant economic successes in the Western developed countries would often invite borrowing and imitation. This is useful. We must, however, never forget theoretical understandings developed in one setting may not work in another as the key assumptions may be quite different. The coverage of institutional environment differences (Khanna & Palepu, 1997), and cultural value differences (Inglehart & Baker, 2000) are but some more notable examples. Sociologists have long recognized the powerful forces of the external institutions (DiMaggio & Powell, 1983; Granovetter, 1985). We believe that regional focus would be important to enrich theoretical understanding and to provide relevant theoretical lenses for educational materials.

Cross-regional collaborations and teaching activities would be another viable direction to pursue. Bringing educators from multiple regions to teach students would open up the possibility that students will benefit from different ways of thinking, and appreciate different perspectives more. Such training and education are important for future business leaders if they are to engage successfully in interregional collaborations and interactions. Stressing the influences of cultural values differences and institutional differences will help future business leaders to recognize the additional task of working with colleagues from different parts of the world even though they might share the native culture together.

Educators themselves are and should be lifetime learners. As of now, many management educators in the Greater China economy were born and raised in the Greater China but trained the West. Although they have cultural understanding and management expertise, the limited contacts they have makes the transfer of management knowledge often problematic. Hence, there is a need to provide "live-in" opportunities to these educators to strengthen their ties between Western management theories and their practice in the Chinese communities. This is also true of educators who were born, raised, and trained in the Chinese communities abroad but teach Western management. The need for these educators to be in Western countries to experience how theories are applied will enhance the value of the education they provide to Chinese managers.

Cross-region researchers fill a very important void in management theory development. By identifying broader contextual conditions and predicting how businesses will behave not only validate theory but also add boundary conditions to those theories and expand them in new contexts. Whitley (1999), as a noted theoretician of comparative management systems, researched capitalist systems in different regional settings and extended our understanding of business behavior across the regions.

Regional focused research and cross region research, however, must need to be integrated into the teaching offerings to become effective. Course material development must go beyond moving extant research from the dynamics of triadic and developed areas to regional differences. The example of corporate diversification comes to mind. The Western theory of management has emphasized the importance of strategic focus, business scope, and core competences development. Researchers should question the applicability of accepted wisdom and thinking and consider the market deficiency and institutional behavior uncertainty of emerging markets and economies.

This leads us to consider a sophisticated blend of teaching materials to address the range of business behaviors so students can appreciate the region-specific obstacles they will encounter. Theories are important and relevant not only for their explanatory power but also for sharpening critical thinking. Alternative theories may lead open minds to creative ways to perform the challenging tasks they are facing. If teaching material preparation emphasizes an eclectic approach to problem solving, skill development, and ability enhancement, future business leaders will reap evident benefits and ultimately their societies too.

Moving beyond the teaching contents, it is useful to recognize the role that mixed participants play in management education. We already discussed the utilization of cross-regional collaboration in teaching; we also need to emphasize the role of collaborative learning through a diverse student population, as well as a diverse learning community.

The discussion of cross-region research, collaborative teaching, collaborative learning and diverse learning communities leads us to another promising avenue, the mix of technology-based distance education and learning, and in-person immersion experiences. The advancement of information technology enables us to pursue more innovative and impactful educational experiences. Online communication, web-based learning communities, simulations across different regions represent telling examples.

We have reviewed some of the tasks management education institutions need to address for the Greater China economy to maintain its ascent on the development growth curve. Such tasks range from material development, programs with a regional-specific and cross-regional foci, new methods sensitive cultural specificities, and the teaching process optimization. Obviously we only scratched the surface of the existing challenges. We raised more questions than answered. Some preliminary answers have been suggested for consideration and action.

Acknowledgements

The first author's work is supported in part by the Wang Faculty Fellow Grant, California State University.

References

Bartlett, C. A. & Ghoshal, S. 1998. *Managing across borders: The transnational solution* (2 ed.). London: Random House Business Books.
Chow, I., Holbert, N., Kelley, L., & Yu, J. 1997. *Business strategy: An Asia-Pacific focus.* Singapore: Prentice Hall.
Devinney, T. M., Midgley, D. F., & Venaik, S. 2000. The optimal performance of the global firm: Formalizing and extending the integration-responsiveness framework. *Organization Science*, 11: 674-695.

DiMaggio, P. J. & Powell, W. W. 1983. The iron cage revisited: Institutional isomorphism and collective rationality in organizational fields. *American Sociological Review*, 48: 147-160.

Drucker, P. F. 1974. *Management: Tasks, responsibilities, practices.* New York: Harper & Row.

Granovetter, M. 1985. Economic action and social structure: The problem of embeddedness. *American Journal of Sociology*, 91: 481-510.

Hofstede, G. H. 2001. *Culture's consequences: Comparing values, behaviors, institutions, and organizations across nations* (2 ed.). Thousand Oaks, CA: Sage Publications.

Inglehart, R. & Baker, W. E. 2000. Modernization, cultural change, and the persistence of traditional values. *American Sociological Review*, 65: 19-51.

Kao, J. 1993. The worldwide web of Chinese business. *Harvard Business Review*, 71(2): 24-36.

Khanna, T. & Palepu, K. 1997. Why focused strategies may be wrong for emerging markets. *Harvard Business Review*, 75(4): 41-51.

Khanna, T. & Palepu, K. 1999. The right way to restructure conglomerates in emerging markets. *Harvard Business Review*, 77(4): 125-134.

Kostova, T. 1999. Transnational transfer of strategic organizational practices: A contextual perspective. *Academy of Management Review*, 24: 308-324.

Li, M. & Wong, Y. Y. 2003. Diversification and economic performance: An empirical assessment of Chinese firms. *Asia Pacific Journal of Management*, 20: 243-265.

Li, S., Li, M., & Tan, J. J. 1998. Understanding diversification in a transition economy: A theoretical exploration. *Journal of Applied Management Studies*, 7: 77-94.

Liu, H. & Li, K. 2002. Strategic implications of emerging Chinese multinationals: The Haier case study. *European Management Journal*, 20: 699-706.

Mead, R. 1998. *International management: Cross-cultural dimensions* (2nd ed.). Malden, MA: Blackwell Business.

Parkhe, A. 1993. "Messy" research, methodological predispositions, and theory development in international joint ventures. *Academy of Management Review*, 18: 227-268.

Porter, M. E. 1998. Clusters and the new economics of competition. *Harvard Business Review*, 76(6): 77-90.

Rugman, A. & Hodgetts, R. 2001. The end of global strategy. *European Management Journal*, 19: 333-343.

Saxenian, A. 2002a. Brian circulation. *The Brookings Review*, 20(1): 28-31.

Saxenian, A. 2002b. Transnational communities and the evolution of global production networks: The cases of Taiwan, China and India. *Industry and Innovation*, 9: 183-203.

Scott, W. R. 1995. *Institutions and organizations.* Thousand Oaks: Sage Publications.

Trompenaars, A. & Hampden-Turner, C. 1998. *Riding the waves of culture: Understanding cultural diversity in global business* (2 ed.). New York: McGraw Hill.

Vance, C. M. 1993. *Mastering management education: Innovations in teaching effectiveness.* Newbury Park, CA: Sage.

Whitley, R. D. 1999. *Divergent capitalisms: The social structuring and change of business systems.* Oxford: Oxford University Press.

Yi, J. J. & Ye, S. X. 2002. *The Haier way: The making of a Chinese business leader and a global brand.* Dumont, NJ: Homa & Sekey Books.

Zeng, M. & Williamson, P. J. 2003. The hidden dragons. *Harvard Business Review*, 81(10): 92-99.

Chapter 2

Economic Transition and Management Skills: The Case of China

Xue Bai
University of Waikato

Peter Enderwick
University of Waikato

1. Introduction

For any economy to grow and develop, key resources and capabilities are essential. Research over many years has highlighted the importance of land, labor, capital and entrepreneurship. A modern complex economy places increasing demand on the key factors of information and skilled labor. Since such economies depend critically on market processes, current development emphasizes the creation of appropriate market institutions (including legal, financial, and regulatory) and high levels of organizational ability. Indeed, there is growing recognition of the importance of so-called 'soft' technologies, organizational and management skills, over traditional hard technologies such as scientific and engineering know-how. A high level of technological know-how is of very little value if it cannot be translated into commercial value.

Globalization has become a more pervasive factor in the world economy. International competition has forced transition for many economies while others are trying to catch up in the process of structural adjustment to open-type market policies. China chose a "pragmatic" transition approach to economic reform from its centrally planned economy to a market economy, nevertheless an accelerated one compared with economic evolution in the West. China's specific "socialist market economy" is a capitalist economic system and an autocratic, communist political system.

Since the start of economic reform in 1978, the Chinese economy has enjoyed dramatic growth. In 1993, China's economy was the world's third largest and if recent growth rates are sustained, China is expected to surpass the USA and Japan to become the world's largest economy within this decade (Child & Lu 1996). An important by-product of economic reform is the growing demand for management personnel to manage an increasingly diverse, sophisticated and complex economy.

As the Chinese economy has evolved and developed as a market system, the shortage of management personnel able to understand and master Western management skills in marketing, financial management, inventory control, human resources, and international business rules has become increasingly evident. Furthermore, this shortage is intensified with China's accession to the World Trade Organization (WTO) at the end of 2001.

For anyone involved in the study and teaching of international business, meeting the management needs of China is both a significant conceptual and practical issue. The aim of this paper is to explore these issues and develop implications for the field of international business. We begin by providing a comparison of management skills likely to exist in a former planned economy such as China and those necessary in a modern (Western) market economy. Section III surveys the evolution of the Chinese economy and the implications of this for changing management needs.

An important contribution of the discussion is the recognition of differences in likely existing management skills and emerging needs in four distinct sectors: the state-owned enterprise (SOE) sector; private firms; foreign-owned and joint-venture businesses; and the emerging high-technology and 'new economy' sector. This section also provides a skill audit by sector. Given the gaps in management skills, section IV outlines the main ways in which skill deficiencies can be overcome and the relative contribution of these to the Chinese transition. The final section develops some important implications of the preceding discussion for international business practitioners as well as offering concluding thoughts.

2. Chinese and Western Management Systems and Skills

This section describes the main characteristics of a centrally planned economy like China and identifies the main differences between a centrally planned economy and a market economy.

2.1 *Management in a centrally planned Chinese economy*

In 1953 China introduced its First Five-Year Plan and created a centrally planned economy in that the State Planning Commission allotted productive resources (including the human resource) and controlled the production, distribution, and consumption of all goods. In the Chinese centrally planned economy, the planning authority (a group of economic planners) controlled all physical productive resources, including land, machinery, and other capital goods (Chan 1996). It controlled all sources of supply of inputs and assigned production targets for each factory and farm (Chow 1985). So, directly and indirectly, the planning authority controlled all factories, farms, and firms. The supplies of all consumer goods were under the control of the planning authority.

On the human resource side, the worker's job was assigned by a government labor bureau and a farmer could be assigned to work in a different farm. It is obvious that the need for market-oriented management personnel was virtually non-existent in China's centrally planned economy because the planning authority controlled nearly all flows and decisions.

By contrast, in a market economy all flows go through markets. In a market economy, consumers decide what to buy. Enterprises in different fields compete to satisfy consumers' demands. The government does not directly participate in the majority of economic activities (Chow 1985). Child and Lu (1996) demonstrate the key differences between the Chinese management approaches under a centrally planned economy and typical Western management approaches under a market economy (Table 1). In their description, Chinese management is mainly shaped by the pre-reform centrally planned economy, even though Chinese cultural values do influence management approaches.

It is apparent from Table 1 that there are marked differences between the two systems. This is clear from areas such as managerial autonomy, procedural formalization, information flows and reward policies. It is also clear that as the Chinese business environment has changed, existing practices have become increasingly less appropriate. In a turbulent and changing environment, managers must be given greater autonomy, it is not clear that they can be expected to simultaneously meet economic, political and social obligations. Similarly, vertical information flows and the absence of performance-related incentives may be acceptable in a stable or incrementally evolving environment, but this is no longer the case in China.

Table 1 also highlights the interrelationships between these practices. If one wishes to emphasize improved performance then organizational performance goals need to be carefully formulated, procedures need to reflect this new reality and appropriate management

Table 1. A Comparison of Chinese and Western Approaches to Management
(Source: Child and Lu (1996), p. 3)

Concepts and practices	Chinese management under a centrally planned economy	Western management under a market economy
Decision-making authority	Industrial bureaus or ministries	Boards of directors and CEOs
Managerial autonomy	Little before the reform, much improved now	CEO enjoys autonomy under the board
Organizational performance criteria	Multiple rationality-economic, political and social obligations	Economic rationality, tempered by social responsibility
Degree of procedural formalization	Low formalization but highly personalized process	Highly formalized and relatively impersonal
Information communication	Mainly vertical; little horizontal flow	Multi-directional
Management training and development	Not emphasized before mid-1980s	Highly emphasized
Reward policies and incentives systems	Rewards dependent on age and long service; incentives not closely related to performance	Performance-related

incentives be devised. Partial change involving one or two concepts is unlikely to bring success.

Chinese management approaches have been primarily shaped by experience under a centrally planned economy. This has led to a lack of understanding of market-oriented management approaches. However, Chinese cultural values also influence traditional Chinese management skills. Cultural values such as high power distance, high uncertainty avoidance, and low individualism, that are dramatically different to Western values such as low power distance, low uncertainty avoidance, low masculinity, and medium individualism, are consistent with a hierarchical planned economic system. As a result, traditional Chinese management displays a number of distinct traits:

- Top-down decision-making: Workers simply follow orders from the upper levels. Workers lack creative thinking on feedback, because the reward system in a centrally planned economy depends on age and service time, not performance. This results in a considerable separation of manual and intellectual labor.
- Vertical communication: There is lack of flexible communication between different layers. In addition, the feed back from the bottom takes a long time as the vertical organizational structure has many layers. Vertical communication is not only present in SOEs; it is firmly entrenched in the whole Chinese economic system.
- Focus on production: In order to achieve production targets allocated by the planning authority, managers focus on production. Achieving production targets is a primary criterion for evaluation of managers' performance in the Chinese centrally planned economy. As a result, managers focus on production and have limited understanding of many aspects of 'soft' knowledge (management skills) such as advertising, HRM, inventory control, accounting, and financing.

The traditional management skills required within a largely administratively planned economy means that Chinese managers are unlikely to have much experience in:

- The appreciation and management of risk. The nature of a planned economy is to encourage risk averse attitudes since it is unlikely that risk takers will participate in rewards. In contrast, risk taking attitudes and experience are of critical importance in the development of private sector firms;

- The linking of pay and performance. In most Chinese enterprises, managers are political appointees, they are not selected for their potential performance, nor does their employment security depend on performance. For these reasons there are few incentives to link pay and performance. Such arrangements are far more common in the private sector and, in particular, in new high technology ventures;

- Financial management skills. Most Chinese managers operate along budgeting lines; there are few incentives to adhere to such budgets ('soft budget constraints') or to innovate in financial management. Chinese enterprise managers are likely to have little experience with sophisticated financial tools such as derivatives or concepts such as financial gearing. Similar weaknesses exist in related areas including dividend policy, foreign exchange management and hedging.

- Marketing activities. The underlying rationale of a planned economy is production or a supply focus. The disposal of output is an issue for planners not the individual enterprise. For this reason, managers invest little in the way of marketing resources such as marketing research, branding, and distribution networks or after sales servicing. In a competitive market economy, particularly one that permits overseas competition, marketing becomes a fundamental locus of competition.

- Investment in the creation and maintenance of competitive advantage. Again, where the company focus is on supply not demand and competition is deliberately restricted, there are few incentives to understand and create competitive advantage. However, in a competitive market economy, differentiation may become an essential means of survival and successful managers will be those that have experience with the wide range of advantages that can be developed;

- Corporate governance and leadership skills. In a planned economy, plans replace governance and political acumen substitutes for corporate leadership. If Chinese managers are to build and lead internationally competitive businesses, they will need to develop the appropriate higher level skills;
- Cross-functional integrative skills. SOEs tend to operate with high levels of functional fragmentation and separation, often with a 'silo' mentality. Levels of cross-functional or holistic skills are likely to be low.

As a result of these differences generated by a centrally planned economy we would expect to see Chinese managers as both less well qualified and less focused than their western counterparts. Available evidence, while limited, seems to support these expectations.

First, a survey of 3,000 Chinese executives nationwide showed that only 23.9 percent of the respondents had a university degree. One-third of the executives came from production workers (Sun 2000). Lack of managerial competence in a market-oriented competitive environment may be one of the major reasons that cause many Chinese managers to avoid taking personal responsibility.

Second, "Chinese managers were generally political appointees." (Child & Lu 1996, p.2). They have to maintain close relationships with the higher governmental officials upon whom they depend. As a result, "the effort they put into the different areas of management is: 27.6 percent into the coordination of the relationship with local or central government, 17.3 percent into sales, 14.2 percent into production." (Sun 2000, p.385). Typically, Chinese managers have to take account of multiple criteria that include social, political, and economic considerations in their decision-making.

3. Evolution of the Chinese Economy and Changing Skill Needs

Like any successful growing economy, China has experienced structural economic change. The pace and precise form of such change depends on a range of influences, the most significant of which are likely to be external factors and domestic policy choices. Externally, China's reintegration into the world economy and increasing participation within international institutions such as the WTO suggest that changes in the world economy will be rapidly transmitted to the Chinese economy.

Furthermore, such involvement is likely to accelerate the rate of structural change that might have been expected to occur anyway. This suggests that China's transition from a planned, predominantly agriculturally-based economy will be rapid from a comparative or historical perspective. This expectation is supported by domestic policy that has emphasised the dynamic and diverse nature of change in China. A willingness to focus limited resources into a small number of high growth clusters (EPZs, the coastal cities and more recently, science parks) coupled with a propensity to experiment (to 'let a hundred flowers bloom'), means that economic change and upgrading is recognised as a legitimate developmental goal by Chinese policy-makers.

The broad parameters of economic change are similar for most developing economies, including China. As modernisation occurs, resources are shifted from predominantly low productivity agricultural activities into higher value manufacturing production. This transition involves the movement of labour and a commitment to high levels of productive investment. Both of these features are apparent in China today. The human exodus from the Chinese countryside to the factories of the cities is one of the largest human movements ever recorded. At the same time, a high rate of domestic savings coupled with the ability to attract more than half of the all-foreign direct investment destined for Asia means that a very high rate of capital formation has been possible.

Growth of the manufacturing sector brings change not just to the broad sectoral composition of an economy (between the primary, secondary and tertiary sectors), but also within sectors. For example, within manufacturing a gradual process of upgrading may be expected to occur. This manifests itself in three key ways.

First, firms acquire and develop their production capability through an increase in scale, experience and quality. Increased engineering and production know-how are the drivers of this stage. As scale and experience increase, it is expected that cost will fall and quality improve. The second stage involves the development of improved marketing capability to ensure that increased production is moved into markets and sold. During this stage, firms invest heavily in market research, distribution and brand building. The third stage sees a geographical diversification of manufacturing activity out of increasingly costly high growth centres and in the pursuit of lower costs. This process has begun in China, with industry spreading out of the coastal cities into related regions but is attenuated by the plentiful supply of cheap transient labour. Chinese firms are heavily concentrated within the first stage of upgrading and often produce under contract or for overseas markets. Thus, at this time there are relatively few widely known Chinese consumer brands, the best known of which include Legend and Haier.

As the market economy of China has grown it has become both more complex and specialized. As the market has deepened there has occurred a growth in specialist organizations and services. Examples include the provision of market research or management consultancy services, specialist financial instruments and merger and acquisition advisory services. As with any market-based economy, markets do not operate in isolation. They must be supported by a range of non-economic institutions that support economic processes. Rodrik (2000) identifies five key institutions. These relate to property rights and regulation, as well as institutions encompassing macroeconomic stability, social insurance, and conflict management. The development of these institutional mechanisms has important implications for management know-how in China.

First, policy makers must have an understanding of the operation of a market economy if they are to design and create appropriate institutions. Second, these institutions must be staffed by bureaucrats with commensurate knowledge and experience to ensure that they play an effective role in facilitating the development of a productive economy. Third, for enterprise managers the growth of institutional regulation suggests that they must develop an understanding of the implications of this for the development of corporate strategy. Furthermore, such institutions may be expected to substitute for the pervasive personal relationships (guanxi) characteristic of the Chinese economy. Over time, we might expect to see an increase in rules based as opposed to relationship based constraints impacting on managerial decision-making although Child and Tse (2001) recognize the inherently political nature of institutional development in China and the likelihood that institutions may substitute political for efficiency goals.

At the same time that the Chinese economy is becoming more complex and extensive, a fragmentation of ownership and operating forms is also occurring. The state's effective monopoly of the means of production has given way to a variety of new ownership structures. According to Child and Tse, pre-reform China was dominated by state-owned enterprises (SOEs) that produced three-quarters of industrial value. Reform has brought a much more diverse productive structure. In 1998, state-owned enterprises accounted for only 28 percent of industrial output with urban and collective enterprises accounting for approximately 38 percent, foreign investors 15 percent and private firms 17 percent.

The future importance of state-owned enterprises depends in part on their ability to restructure and respond to changing conditions. Reform, while slow, is already underway. More than 12,500 SOEs had been converted into joint stock companies by 1997. Collective enterprises, the Town and Village Enterprises, have benefited from the decentralization of industrial development and now constitute a significant sector. Because they suffer from problems such as uncertainty over property rights and poor levels of managerial capability, they are found in lower technology activities. Foreign-owned firms have brought a range of important resources to the Chinese economy and now enjoy greater freedom in their ownership forms as wholly owned subsidiaries (WOS) were permitted in 1986 and now exceed joint ventures.

The most dynamic sector has been private enterprise that now employs more than 13 million (Child and Tse 2001). In the future we might expect to see strong growth of high technology firms forming part of the so-called 'New Economy'. While at the present time the number and importance of such firms is limited, and their operations are largely confined to industrial or scientific parks, they are likely to become more important in the future as China seeks to upgrade into specialist high-value activities.

With the fundamental changes of economic structure, human resources face new demands in providing the quality workforce needed for development of a new knowledge-driven and technology-intensive economy. Moreover, a by-product of economic reform is the growing demand for management personnel to manage in a series of positions that have emerged with the process of economic restructuring such as the new phenomenon of privatization, the bankruptcy and merger of SOEs, the increasing number of joint ventures with foreign companies, and the expansion on foreign trade and international business.

All these have created a huge need for a new generation of managers who can understand the principles of marketing, advertising, finance, accounting, inventory control, human resource, and international business rules, in order to compete in the global economy.

A series of market-oriented reforms in China, for example, the introduction of stock markets and bankruptcy laws, the establishment of social security systems and free labor markets, have already put pressure on traditional management skills. Table 2 shows the main changes in China's economy and the relevant implications for management skills.

According to Table 2 as the result of reform, growing international integration and increased competition, Chinese management will need to change radically. However, the implications for management skills vary with different sectors. We focus on four different sectors: SOEs; the private sector; foreign and Chinese joint-venture firms; and the new economy.

3.1 *SOEs*

The more than 305,000 SOEs are the backbone of China's industrial sector; they now face more intense competition and the challenges that result from SOE reform. Organizational theory and managerial wisdom suggest that organizations must be compatible with their environments in order to flourish. The operating environment of SOEs has changed dramatically in recent years and as a result the implications for management in the SOEs sector are broader and deeper than for other sectors, because the SOEs management inherited all the traditional Chinese management characteristics from the centrally planned economy.

Table 2. Changes in the Chinese Economy and Implications for Management Skills

Changes in China's Economy	Implications for Management Skills
Greater reliance on market forces	Market positioning; quality, reputation, and advertising of products; determinants of supply, demand, pricing.
Greater international influences	Intensive competition; new competitors; new technologies and ideas; international rulers and regulations; Organizational structure; and international communication (language).
Workforce / HRM	Performance reward system, recruit system, training and staff development.
Financial Sector	Financial budget; corporate governance. Management of risk. Familiarity with sophisticated financial instruments.
Welfare and social safety net	Lay-offs and corporate restructuring (breaking of 'iron rice bowl' policy). Need to maintain social stability, labor mobility and opportunities for re-training
Creativity and innovation	R & D, patent protection and knowledge management. Shortening of the PLC. Growth of the new economy has increased the demand for knowledgeable skilled labor with creativity and innovation characteristics.
Consumer laws and protection	Customer services such as post-purchase service; and public relations. Role and value of branding.
Competition levels necessitate competitive advantage	Need to identify, create, maintain and utilize distinctive forms of competitive advantage. Need to understand and effectively manage the underlying sources of such advantage e.g. skilled labor
Shift from a production to a marketing orientation	Need to recognize the growing importance of the marketing function. Investments in the stages of marketing and appreciation of the elements of the marketing mix. Appreciation of the integration between marketing and other functions e.g. production, R&D.
Development of market supporting institutions	Recognition of the operating constraints provided by such institutions. Shift from relationship-based to rules-based management.

Official statistics show that in 1996 and the first half-year of 1997, Chinese SOEs laid-off nearly 2 million workers (Sun 2000). The 'lay offs' are not an occasional phenomenon, because market competition is forcing firms to adopt a more flexible employment and wage system. In a labor surplus economy, with an estimated one-fifth to one-third redundant workforce (World Bank 1999), the system of lifetime employment cannot be sustained. With China's bankruptcy law and company law taking effect, "a total of 6,232 firms declared bankruptcy in 1996" (Sun 2000, p 380). Since the mid 1990s, the slow transformation of the operating system of the state-owned economy has become more evident. The state-owned economy has experienced a considerable drop in growth. According to the World Bank, about half of all industrial SOEs made a loss in 1996, up from one-third just two years earlier. Official Chinese estimates are even more pessimistic, that 43 percent of SOEs make losses, and another 30 percent only make a profit by false accounting (Sun 2000). Compared with the non-state sectors, the most significant problems that the SOEs face include:

- The SOEs have fixed production and prices, the non-state sector is capable of responding to high demand with higher prices
- The SOEs have employment and social welfare function, the non-state sector could take advantage of the unlimited labor supply from rural areas at lower wages
- The SOEs are guided in their investment towards strategic and comprehensive production; the non-state sector can selectively invest in the most profitable market sectors.
- The SOEs tend towards traditional management and old technologies; the non-state sector is more responsive to modern management and new technologies.
- The long-term protection from the government means that SOEs lack experience of the competitive environment.
- The managers of SOEs are still assigned by government officials.
- The increasing turnover of skilled personnel from the SOE sector seeking higher salaries and more attractive conditions.

SOEs are the sector most urgently requiring a change of management approaches if they are to survive in the competitive market-oriented environment. However, SOEs are also the most difficult sector to reform. The recruitment system for SOE managers is an example of the continuing problems. Government still plays a critical role in assigning managers and determining the fate of business leaders.

3.2 *The private sector*

China's market-oriented reforms have resulted in a rapid growth of privately owned enterprises as well as township and village enterprises (Sun 2000). The private economy has overtaken the state-owned economy to become the most active, the fastest developing and the largest contributor to economic growth. The growth of private businesses has been significant, from almost none in the mid-1970s to 1.04 million registered private firms in 1999 (Lawrence 1999).

Private firms should have a better understanding of the market position, pricing system, recruitment system, and a more flexible organizational structure than SOEs. However, the private sector still faces several problems. The major form of private firms in China is family business. As a result, the limitations of Chinese family business inevitably appear within these firms. Chinese family firms are likely to be characterized by:

- Highly centralized decision-making processes
- Reducing transactions costs by doing business within Chinese networks
- Arranging financing within Chinese networks (capital is raised through accumulated profits from operations and from successful business deals)
- Low margin and high volume in order to penetrate markets
- A rigorous control of inventory in order to maintain a low capital investment and high rate of stock turnover
- Simple organizational structures which may be inappropriate when firm size increases.

3.3 *Foreign owned and joint venture businesses*

The demand for educated management skilled labor increased as a result of foreign investors' localization and domestic firms' internationalization. "A total of 19 out of 20 of the largest industrial firms in the USA; 19 out of 20 of the largest industrial firms of Japan; and nine out of ten of the largest industrial firms in Germany have already invested in China"(Sun 2000, p. 380). "General Motors (GM) had invested $2 billion by the end of 1998 and has four joint ventures. More than 120,000 foreign-funded enterprises with 18 million employees were already in operation across China." (Sun 2000, p.380). Foreign investors are normally associated with the importation of management skills. Indeed, such skills are identified as one of the principal benefits of inward investment.

The impact of such investors on the skill base depends, in large part, on the nature of the operations and ownership structure of the foreign venture. Where an affiliate performs a highly specialized task, is closely integrated into a regional or global production system, depends on proprietary technology and expatriate managers, the spill over effect is likely to be low. A wholly owned subsidiary is less likely than a joint venture, to encourage the diffusion of skills. Similarly, where foreign investors enjoy a strong bargaining advantage, they are less likely to make provision for the transfer of management knowledge.

At the same time it must be acknowledged that foreign investors are also major users of skilled labour. Where they localize their management, this can result in fewer skills being available to local firms or even the loss of such skills if outstanding management talent is shifted overseas within the corporate network. Because of cultural differences, Western investors are most likely to seek those with strong cross-cultural abilities and experience of living and working overseas. These are just the types of employees most in demand by domestic firms.

On the other hand, Chinese domestic companies such as Legend and Haier are beginning the process of internationalization. By expanding economic cooperation with other countries, China faces the need for a generation of management personnel who understand management principles, management styles and management practice in the West.

3.4 High technology and the new economy sector

The 'New Economy' is built on the wealth created from know-how by selling it, exchanging it for something else of value or leveraging it to create added value. By comparison, the traditional economy relies on raw resources and primary processing to generate income and wealth. As a result, competitive advantages from the old sources are becoming less important. In the knowledge economy, individuals and firms must focus on maintaining and enhancing their biggest asset: their knowledge capital. The knowledge economy places great importance on the diffusion and use of information and knowledge as well as its creation. The determinants of success of enterprises, and of national economies as a whole, is ever more reliant on their effectiveness in gathering and utilizing knowledge. It is clear that the demand for education and training will increase in the knowledge economy, particularly management training and education.

Economic and social changes are creating new market standards (productivity, quality, variety, customization, convenience, timeliness). Meeting these standards requires great changes in organizational structures, and skill needs. The new competitive framework requires a broader set of skills, both 'hard' skills (technical know-how) and 'soft' skills (managerial skills). It is suggested "to compete and prosper in this new environment, China has to move away from factor-intensive growth toward knowledge-based growth, become more open, and harness the forces shaping the global economy" (World Bank 2001). Now, 22 university-based scientific parks and six university-based centers for commercializing technological findings have sprung up in China. These parks and centers will be further developed to help reinforce technological innovation and fuel the development of information technology and other high-technology industries (Cui 2002).

4. Skill Audit

Examination of the problems of a centrally planning economy highlights that planning from the top (planning authority) is not an efficient way of managing the economy. With the process of institutional structure reform in China, the decentralization of decision-making not only transferred authority from central government to local governments, but also transferred authority from ministries to firms (Chan 1996). This empowerment of decision-making has increased the demand for management personnel with market-oriented management skills, because firms are responsible for buying and sourcing input materials as well as selling the products to the market and to their customers.

So, management personnel must be responsible for strategic planning, production and marketing for a firm to maintain efficient operations and profitability. However, existing skills are not in adequate supply. Different economic sectors have particular skill needs. Table 3 provides a comparison between likely existing skills and deficiencies by principal sector.

Overall, the state-owned sector reveals the most serious shortage of management skills for a market-oriented economy. SOEs are likely to possess skills in production, technical and engineering, and relationships, but skills in marketing, creativity, innovation, effective HRM, financial management, strategic planning, and international markets are likely to be deficient. Two factors probably explain this shortage; one is the composition of management personnel, the other is the low emphasis on management education and training.

However, a problem of skills shortages is also apparent in the other three sectors of Table 3. Overall, the most deficient skills (occurring twice or more in different sectors) are effective HRM, financial management, intellectual property management, marketing and strategic planning. Those skills are hard to master without training during a transition period that has no blueprint to follow.

4.1 *Meeting future skill needs*

The shortfall between the available supply of skilled managers and China's likely future needs is very significant.

In 1998, the Chinese Vice-Minister for Education, Lu Fuyuan, noted that China has about 400,000 state-owned enterprises, 300,000 joint ventures and 200,000 township enterprises. If each of these enterprises needed three trained managers then the total requirement would be 2.7 million. The demand for trained managers accelerated with China's access to WTO. However, management education was not emphasized before 1978, which led to a critical shortage of management resources in the whole country (Sun 2000). We can identify three main processes by which the supply of management skills can be increased.

Directly, it could be done through increased investment in management training within China, by domestic universities, the entry of foreign business schools or through exchange programs. Indirectly, the number of suitable managers could be enhanced through spillover effects from foreign firms that have entered the Chinese market. Thirdly, there may be a 'demonstration' effect as Western consultants increasingly influence management practice through their business in China.

Two points are worth noticing here. First, these different sources of skills are complements not substitutes. At the same time that additional resources are provided within the formal education system, skill diffusion from consultants or overseas investors can also occur. Second, China is likely to benefit from a diversity of sources. This is because the different sources provide different types of skills from the theoretical and conceptual tools emphasized by tertiary management training to the more applied training offered by consultants.

4.2 *Chinese university education*

Management courses were reduced or cancelled and smaller colleges offering management education were closed or merged with bigger universities as the need for management personnel was nearly non-existent in the centrally planned economy. The education system was even further retarded during the ten-year period of the Cultural Revolution (1966-76), resulting in many universities and colleges closing.

The first year that students registered for management studies in tertiary education in China was 1976 when 2,453 students enrolled (Chan 1996). Since 1980 over 150,000 students have been enrolled in under-graduate programs in management education (Chan 1996). For undergraduate management education, "there are over 270 universities and colleges offering undergraduate degree programs" (Chan 1996, p. 244). At the master's level, there were 78 universities offering master's degrees in management in 1992 (Chan 1996). Around 1996, only 20 universities and colleges offered doctoral degrees in management, due to the lack of qualified supervisors.

Table 3. Skill Audit by Sector in the Chinese Economy

Economic Sector	Likely Existing Skills	Likely Deficient Skills
State-owned sector	Production Technical, Engineering Administrative Budgeting Supply chain Multi-plant management Large scale operations Social welfare provision Political and personal relationships	Research, innovation Marketing distribution Quality management Effective cost management Effective HRM Competitor intelligence Market intelligence Competitive advantage Financial management Strategic planning Flexibility Change management Leadership and governance skills Rules based competition International markets Risk management Holistic management Competing for resources
Private sector	Product or service idea Holistic management Project management Flexibility/small scale Niche or limited markets Family and personal relationships Competitive advantage Risk management Market intelligence	Effective HRM Financial management Strategic planning Stakeholder interests Large scale operations Political skills Market development International markets IP management
Foreign-owned and JV	Range of functional skills Access to world class capabilities Financial management Brands, Experience, Scale	Market knowledge Competitor intelligence Cultural understanding Risk assessment Communication Political relationships
High technology, New Economy	Small scale, limited experience Working with limited resources Partnerships with universities, government institutions Highly skilled employees Technical risk management	Market making Commercialisation skills IP management Commercial risk management Effective HRM Knowledge management

Chinese universities have offered a Western style MBA from the autumn of 1990. By the end of 2000, 66 universities and colleges were offering MBA programs with a total recruitment of about 35,000 students (Song 2001). Since the beginning of 1992, there has been a tremendous push to introduce management education to senior managers in SOEs. In 1996, a nationwide three-month MBA-type of short training program was launched for managers from SOEs. By the end of 1998, 288,000 managers had participated in this program. Since then, about 5,000 managers each year have passed national MBA entrance examinations and entered into on-the-job MBA programs with a target of 200,000 managers to go through MBA training. This will greatly enhance the quality of management personnel in China's SOEs.

4.3 *Joint venture business schools*

By 1998, it was estimated that there were 50 indigenous management schools in China. However, some of them fall short of international standards (Southworth 1999) in terms of faculty, textbook use and facilities. The most obvious solution was to establish links with foreign business schools forming educational "joint ventures" (Southworth 1999). About 30 Chinese universities have joint ventures with top foreign institutions, such as the MIT Sloan School of Management, mostly offering MBA courses (McGregor 2001).

China's enormous population and immense potential market attracts educational investment from overseas. Joint ventures business school can profit both sides. China obtains the management skills and develops a management skills labor pool to meet increasing demand. Universities and institutions from overseas get the profits and valuable experience of the Chinese market (Anderson 2002).

4.4 *Spillovers from FDI*

The attraction of FDI to any developing economy is the bundle of resources that it brings. In addition to capital inflows, foreign investors often undertake technology transfer and management development as well as providing access to overseas markets. In such a case Chinese managers can gain access to valuable technical, marketing and more general managerial skills. The likelihood of such spillover is higher in joint ventures where the provision of such resources may form an explicit part of the agreement.

With the process of FDI, both 'hard' technologies and 'soft' technologies have passed to China. In the spillover process China has learned the management skills and foreign investors get the experience of Chinese culture and build up cross-cultural management skills.

4.5 Chinese students overseas

The overseas placement of Chinese students has grown very rapidly in recent years. Able technical and management students are now studying at a range of universities and research centers around the world. Many of these students will return to China upon completion of their studies. They will have gained access to leading edge scholarship and research as well as becoming increasingly familiar with other cultures. They represent a considerable source of future management talent for China.

4.6 Consultancy firms

Consultancy firms, like other multinational corporations, are attracted to the opportunities offered by China, particularly since China joined the World Trade Organization. Following in the footsteps of the Boston Consulting Group in 1992, Bain & Co., McKinsey & Co. (1993), and Ronald Berger (1994) have moved into the Chinese market. Several of the world's leading consultancy firms have greatly increased their presence in China, because they see huge opportunities for their business in the future.

According to Saywell, "China's vast market means that consultants, even when they aren't making money, feel they must be there now to position themselves for the long term" (Saywell 2002, p. 29). McKinsey & Co. has 80 consultants based in mainland China (Dolven 2002). Germany's Roland Berger, Europe's largest consultant company, has put together a new financial group and set up in Shanghai in the past six months (Dolven 2002). Boston Consulting Group, with 70 consultants based in Shanghai and Hong Kong, recently set up a Beijing office (Dolven 2002). Other American companies, such as PWC

Consulting, Deloitte Consulting, KPMG Consulting and Bain & Co., are in the country too (Dolven 2002).

At first, the consultancy firms mostly focused on helping multinational firms trying to enter Chinese markets. But now, most are dealing primarily with Chinese companies trying to restructure or cope with the competitive pressures of deregulation (breaking up monopolies), privatization (ownership diversification), liberalization, and China's WTO membership. (Dolven 2002).

As China integrates further into the international economy and companies operating there face more sophisticated problems, company managers will increasingly need to consider using consulting services. Consultancy firms' involvement ranges from technical assistance at the level of the individual firm to high-level regulatory reform and institutional development at the national policy level. Such firms often combine a range of related competencies including accounting, auditing and general consultancy. Some of the largest firms already have experience of the Chinese market through their work with large MNEs investing in China. They are now keen to move into the lucrative business of privatization and SOE reform where they have experience from working in other transitional economies. While their rates mean that they are only likely to be engaged by the largest organizations, their principal impact may be in the design and implementation of institutional infrastructure that underpins any successful market-based economy.

5. Implications and Conclusions

The discussion presented here has important implications for all those involved in teaching international business.

First, our discussion has highlighted the considerable management needs that China faces. This is true in both quantitative and qualitative terms. Like any transitional economy, China carries a huge burden in the form of the legacy of central planning. The skill set of managers who operated under the centrally planned model is totally inadequate for the emerging market oriented economy. The need to expand and upgrade market oriented management skills is pressing. We would not expect to see this process occurring through the widespread provision of in-company training. This is because of a lack of resources within many Chinese organizations, and in particular, the absence of a sufficient critical mass in the necessary skills upon which training programs could be based. This suggests that an external stimulus or intervention will be required. While a competitive stimulus is provided by China's transition to an open market-driven economy and, more recently, its accession to the WTO, the supply of suitable managerial talent is still deficient. Government intervention in the form of increased provision for management education, whether through the expansion of Chinese based programs or the increased utilization of foreign training courses, will be necessary. The contribution of foreign investors, consultants or visiting scholars is likely to complement this process.

Second, it is likely that many international business teachers have been, or will be, involved in helping to try to overcome these skill deficiencies. Many Western universities now teach in China, through satellite campuses, articulation agreements or visiting positions. Many others experience Chinese management students on exchange or overseas placement programs. China's decision to require leading universities to teach in the medium of English within seven years will create huge opportunities for visiting scholars.

For foreign universities and scholars, involvement in the Chinese education market will require resolution of important strategic decisions. While the focus of the present discussion has been on the likely quantitative deficiency of desirable skills, there is an equally important qualitative dimension. It is not just curriculum content that must be considered, but also the ways in which the material is presented. Traditional Chinese learning styles, which focus on rote learning and the attainment of minimum standards, are of limited value in a dynamic, transitional economy which provides little in the way of a development blueprint. What becomes critical is a desire for ongoing learning and the ability to foster creativity and the management of ambiguity. These are traits which are rarely encountered in Chinese organizations, particularly SOEs. A weakness of traditional Chinese teaching methods is that they are quite passive, with one-way delivery of lectures and test-paper examinations. The majority of instructors lack business and practical experience. Their lectures are based on information from textbooks with limited practical value (Newell 1999).

Third, our discussion enables management teachers to more carefully focus on the critical areas of deficiency. As identified in Table 3 the most widespread weaknesses are in effective HRM, financial management, intellectual property management, marketing and strategic planning. Furthermore, the discussion highlights the variation in needs across the principal sectors of China's industrial economy. While we have identified a number of functional areas of management where further training is desirable, it does not follow that these subjects should be taught in isolation. Rather, there is a strong case for integrative approaches which highlight the many interdependencies between, for example, marketing and finance or strategic planning and human resource management. This would suggest the value of case-based approaches. Such cases would be of benefit to not just Chinese participants, but also to Western students who are increasingly likely to find themselves involved with the Chinese market in years to come.

China's reintegration into the world economy and increasing participation within international institutions such as the WTO suggest that changes in the world economy will be rapidly transmitted to the Chinese economy. The transformation from a centrally planned system to a market system and the opening of the economy (so called Open Door Policy) are two main components of China's economic reform policy that have resulted in dramatic economic growth. Chinese management approaches have been primarily shaped by the centrally planned economy. This led to a lack of understanding of market oriented management approaches. In the Chinese centrally planned economy, the main management goal is to meet management targets that are assigned by the upper level ministries or planning authority. With the development of a socialist market economy traditional Chinese approaches to management face a number of challenges.

References

Anderson, L. (2002). Paris trains Chinese faculty. *Financial Times,* 11.
Chan, M., & Porter, R. (1996). Management education in the People's Republic of China. In D. Brown (Ed.), *Management Issues in China Volume I* (Vol. 1, pp. 237-257). London: Routledge.

Child, J., & Lu, Y. (1996). *Management Issues in China: International Enterprises Volume II* (Vol. 2, pp. 1-10). London: Routledge.

Child, J., & Tse, D. (2001). China's transition and its implications for international business. *Journal of International Business Studies.*

Chow, G. (1985). *The Chinese Economy.* New York: Harper & Row.

Cui, N. (2002, January 22). Chinese education goes global. *China Daily, New York*, p. 1.

Dolven, B. (2002). The great consulting pile-up. *Far Eastern Economic Review*, pp. 26-29.

Lawrence, S. (1999). Answer to a prayer. *Far Eastern Economic Review*, pp. 50-51.

McGregor, R. (2001, Oct 8) Western educators want profits, while the Chinese want full credit for course. A compromise is needed on both sides. *Financial Times*, p. 4.

Newell, S. (1999) The Transfer of Management Knowledge to China: Building Learning Communities Rather than Translating Western Textbooks? *Education and Training*, 41(6/7), 286-293.

Rodrik, D. (2000, February). *Institutions for high quality growth: what they are and how to acquire them.* Boston, Mass: National Bureau of Economic Research. (7540)

Saywell, T. (2002). Despite the China allure, consulting elsewhere isn't a losing game: business may be down, but it's far from out. *Far Eastern Economic Review*, 16.

Song, W. (2001, March 12). Seeking qualified business managers. *China Daily*, p. 3.

Southworth, D. (1999). Building a business school in China. *Education and Training*, 41(6/7), 325-330.

Sun, J. (2000). Organization development and change in Chinese state-owned enterprises: a human resource perspective. *Leadership & Organization Development Journal*, 21(8), 379-389.

World Bank. (1999). *The China Human Development Report.* Oxford: Oxford University Press.

World Bank. (2001). *Making the Most of the Knowledge Revolution for China's Development.* Washington: Author.

Chapter 3

Managing in a Relation-based Environment: A Teaching Agenda for International Business

Shaomin Li
Old Dominion University

Steven Maurer
Old Dominion University

1. Introduction: The Issue

One of the most common and costly problems facing Western firms doing business in developing countries is the poor record of effectiveness among expatriate managers. For instance, the inability to simply survive their assignments is shown by evidence that about 70% of all American employees assigned abroad return to the US before their appointment period is concluded (Shay and Bruce, 1997; Black and Gregersen, 1999). Perhaps even more disturbingly, studies show that about a third of American managers perform below expectations (Black and Gregersen, 1999) and that 30 – 50 % of all American managers and other highly paid workers who are able to remain in their assignments are regarded by their firms to be only marginally effective, at best (Black, Mendenhall, and Oddou, 1991).

The cost of such failure is very high. For instance, costs per failure have been estimated to be about three times the expatriate's domestic salary plus relocation costs (Harvey, 1983) or about $250,000 to $1 million (Caudron, 1991) a decade ago. In terms of total costs, evidence that multi-national companies (MNCs) have grown to the point where they now account for more than one-tenth of the world's total GDP and one-third of the world's total exports (UNCTAD, 2002) suggests that annual costs of turnover among American expatriate managers have almost certainly risen above the $2 – $2.5 billion per year estimate offered about ten years ago (Lublin, 1992).

Persistent reports of poor performance and the fact that the developing countries are attracting a substantial and increasing amount of foreign direct investment ($190 billion in 2000 with an average growth rate of 12% (United Nations, 2001) present an obvious need for employers to better understand and manage the effectiveness of expatriate managers, especially upper-level managers, in developing economies. Unfortunately, international business (IB) educators have yet to provide any theory-based guidance or explanation of expatriate success in emerging economies. Most simply attribute the failure to the expatriate's inability to adopt the local culture.

While this attribution of expatriate failure to "cultural" differences is intuitively appealing, it is not particularly useful for at least two reasons. First, ever since IB became a valid teaching subject, the emphasis on culture has been prominent. There is no single IB textbook or IB introductory course that does not feature culture as one of the most important topics. In addition, most companies provide cross-cultural training courses to their employees, in general, and international assignees, in particular. Thus attributing the failure to a general lack of cultural awareness adds little to an acute awareness of such differences that has served as a basis for decades of culture sensitivity education and promotion. Second, aside from attributing the failure to cultural difference, IB educators have been unable to develop a general framework to explain such failure across cultural settings. Hence, prescriptions are ad hoc at best: in order to reduce the chance of failure, an expatriate must learn the particular culture of the country he/she is going to. If he/she is reassigned to another country, then he/she must learn the culture of his/her new destination. If this is the advice we as IB educators can give, we do not add much value, as there are hundreds of countries and thousands of cultures to learn.

While recognizing the difference in culture and its importance, we argue that culture is not the only exogenous variable that ultimately determines the success in an expatriate assignment. Culture is endogenous and is shaped by the political, economic, and legal systems of a society. The culture that exists in a society is greatly influenced by the political system and the level of economic development, and therefore is a result of rational choice collectively made by the people (Li, forthcoming). The common features among the developing countries are not culture, but the political, economic and legal systems. Because most developing countries tend to lack rule of law, officials are more prone to corruption, and business activities are governed by personal connections rather than public rules. Thus, we believe that Western managers operating in developing economies are ill-served by education efforts that focus on general characteristics of culture. Instead, we assert that expatriate managers should be educated to understand that their success lies in their ability to create an effective working relationship in a prevailing governance environment created by the social, legal, and economic institutions that affect the means by which individuals and firms govern their property rights in social and economic exchanges (Li, *et al.*, 2003; Li and Filer, 2004).

In this article, we will substantiate our argument by examining the working relationships between expatriates and host country employees. We will use a newly developed framework of "relation-based" and rule-based" governance developed in recent economic and business research (Li, 1999; Li and Li, 2000; Li, 2002; Li, *et al.*, 2003) to consider the managerial effects of basic differences in work relationships in Westernized (rule-based) and developing (relation-based) economies. From this, we will propose a more theory-based approach to examine expatriate failure and present a teaching agenda for improving the ability of Western expatriates to manage in developing countries. The teaching ideas presented here can be used to develop a component of an IB survey/introductory course for degree programs in business schools, or to design stand alone seminars for corporate training.

2. A Framework Explaining Expatriate Failure

Our framework combines two streams of research: the research on expatriate failure and the research on governance environment. In the following three subsections, we develop our framework based on a review of the literature of both of these streams.

2.1 Expatriate failure

There is a rich literature on expatriate failure (e.g., Tong, 1979; Black, Mendenhall, and Oddou, 1991; Shay and Bruce, 1997; Black and Gregersen, 1999). Some focus on the selection criteria for international assignments. Their basic premise is that a well-designed, effective selection process will reduce the failure rate. They find that most MNCs' selection criteria are culturally based (Hoecklin, 1994). Most scholars in this stream emphasize that the "ability to adopt", or the "adaptability to cultural change" is the most important factor determining expatriate success (e.g., Stone, 1991; Hodgetts and Luthans, 2000; Hill, 2003). This emphasis on cultural adaptation is founded on research characterize by Hill (2003) who notes that the failure of expatriates is primarily owing to an "inability to adjust" that "seems to be caused by a *lack of cultural skills* (emphasis added) on the part of the manager being transferred." (p. 613).

To reduce expatriate failure, international human resource management scholars have proposed methods of screening, interviewing, testing, and training expatriate candidates (Hodgetts and Luthans, 2000). Most of the training activities focus on culture, language, and adaptability. Some have attempted to develop models that help explain the factors involved in effectively adjusting to overseas assignments. Black *et al.*, (1991) propose a model that consists of two major types of adjustments: anticipatory adjustment and in-country adjustment. To improve anticipatory adjustment, they suggest that the candidate take pre-departure training such as cross-cultural seminars. They identify a number of major factors that affect in-country adjustment. One of the most important factors is the ability to correctly evaluate the host country's culture, values and norms.

While recognizing that the effort to emphasize the role of culture in expatriate management is helpful, we contend that this approach overlooks the development of working relationships with host country nationals (HCNs) as an important factor to the expatriate manager's success. In order to examine the particular importance of working relationships to expatriate managers in developing economies, we must consider the macro environment in which social and economic activities are governed. Recent studies on governance systems may provide us a new and useful perspective from which to better understand working relationships between expatriate and host country employees.

2.2 *Governance environment*

Li (1999) and Li *et al.*, (2003) propose a framework that distinguishes two mode governance systems. One is called rule-based governance system and the other relation-based governance system. A *rule-based governance* system exists in societies where most transactions are based on impersonal and explicit agreements that can be impartially enforced by the state. On the other hand, *relation-based governance* exists in societies where the legal system is not fair and the state is generally unable to impartially enforce contracts.

These basic differences reveal several significant distinctions in rule-based and relation-based systems summarized in Table 1. First and foremost is the distinction in rule of law. In order for rule-based governance to become the dominant mode of governance in a society, the majority of people and firms must voluntarily follow the formal and public rules.

This requires that the rules be fair, universally and equitably applied, and efficiently enforced. Thus, rule-based societies require a well-established legal infrastructure with effective checks and balances among the legislative, judiciary, and executive branches, to provide efficient and fair mechanisms of drafting, interpreting, and implementing contract and corporate laws.

In contrast, relation-based societies tend to lack checks and balances in their political and legal systems. The legal infrastructure tends to be nonexistent or poorly developed. Laws are opaque, and courts and judges are not independent (usually controlled by the ruling political party). People depend on their private connections with the authorities for protection. Since social exchange relies on private protection, the need for "law and order" is minimal. As long as there is no rampant larceny or complete anarchy, people and firms can actively pursue and profit from business.

Table 1. Differences between Relation-based and Rule-based Governance
(based on Li *et al.*, 2003, and Li, in press).

Relation-based Governance	Rule-based Governance
Relying on private and local information	Relying on public information
Implicit and non-verifiable agreements	Explicit and third-party verifiable agreements
Person-specific and non-transferable contracts	Public and transferable contracts
Costly to develop business relations and thus requiring mutual commitments, implying high entry and exit barriers	Low entry and exit barriers
Requiring minimum social order	Requiring well-developed legal infrastructure
Low fixed costs to set up the system	High fixed costs to set up the system
High and increasing marginal costs to govern relations and transactions	Low and decreasing marginal costs to develop and govern transactions
Effective in small and emerging economies	Effective in large and advanced economies

The second distinction is in public information infrastructure. In order for the rule-based system to function efficiently, it requires that public information, such as auditing reports, financial data, and credit ratings, be highly accurate. This requires a high level of public trust and a well-establish information infrastructure (independence of accountants, auditors, and rating agencies and free flow of information).

In contrast, public information in relation-based societies tends to be unreliable. The state often monopolizes the right to disseminate information. Media are controlled by the state. Many types of information that would be free and publicly available in a rule-based society are classified as state secrets and restricted. Business information providers, such as accountants, auditors, and rating agencies, tend to be dependent on dominant business groups and/or the ruling political party. As a result, public financial information, such as auditing and accounting reports, are less accurate. Fraudulent information is commonplace (Li and Filer, 2004).

As a result of the above two features (well-established legal infrastructure and efficient public information system) in rule-based governance, the fixed costs of establishing these infrastructures are high. And the marginal costs of enforcing an additional contract between an additional transaction pairs are negligible because the exchange contract is explicit, impersonal, and standardized, and the legal enforcement system is available to all.

In contrast, a relation-based governance system involves few fixed costs, but significant marginal costs, since business transactions are governed by private relationships. There is little economy of scale in developing relationships. Each relationship requires time, resources, and personal attention and effort to cultivate and nurture. In fact, as one's relationship development effort expands from siblings and friends to strangers, the cost of relationship building increases (Li, 1999; Li and Li, 2000; Li et al., 2003).

When a market is small, a relation-based governance system has a cost advantage since it avoids significant costs in legal and information infrastructures. When a market expands from local to national and to international, relation-based governance will become more costly. For markets with large scale and scopes, rule-based governance is more efficient and competitive. Thus, as the markets of developing countries grow, these countries face the pressure to transform their governance system toward rule-based (Li, 1999; Li and Li, 2000; Li et al., 2003).

2.3 Our propositions

The governance environment of a society, to a great extent, defines the employee-management working relationship in a firm. We argue that the main reason that causes expatriates from rule-based countries to fail in managing employees in a relation-based country is the expectation gap in working relationship between them. Specifically, the perception of working relationships between rule-based expatriates and relation-based local employees differs as discussed earlier by Maurer and Li, (2004) in the following ways:

2.31. Scope of working relationship. For rule-based managers, working relationships tend to be narrowly defined based on laws, codes of conduct, and job descriptions. Their perception of working relationships tends to be task-oriented and narrowly defined (e.g., the employer cannot interfere or inquire about an employee's personal life).

However, relation-based workers may view the working relationship more broadly to include personal affairs (because getting personal is an effective way to build good relationships). They may emphasize the need to forge individual understandings on matters that will enhance their relationship with an expatriate executive or senior manager.

For relation-based workers, anything is negotiable and the line between personal life and work life is fuzzy. They expect their supervisor to advise and help in their personal affairs. Such differences in perception often cause confusion and misunderstanding. For example, a Western manager may want to project a "professional" style by avoiding "personal" questions in his/her dealings with local employees." However, local employees may interpret this practice as the Western manager's lack of concern or interest in establishing a personal relationship.

2.3.2 Precision of the terms of working relationships. Following our argument on the scope of working relationships, rule-based managers and relation-based workers differ in precision of the terms of working relationships. Rule-based managers tend to make precise terms, whereas relation-based workers tend to favor a fuzzy relationship, which provides more room to gain favorable treatment from the manager and to develop closer relationships.

2.3.3. Investments in working relationships. In a relation-based system, managers are expected to invest personal time and resources to cement harmonious working relationships with key managers and other personnel. Such investments may include elaborate gifts, private dinner parties, and other hosted social events that afford opportunities for mutual obligation and understandings. Although rule-based expatriates may also host social events for employees and co-workers, the purpose of such events tends to be more superficial (e.g., have a "good time") and less inclined to serve as a venue for establishing interpersonal working agreements.

Moreover, because many Western companies have "no-gift" policies that prohibit managers from giving co-workers or superiors any personal items of value, Western managers may studiously avoid such investments in co-worker relationships and react badly to these overtures from subordinates or peers. In short, rule-based managers are less likely to invest time and resources in developing personal relationships in the work place because they assume that such understandings ought to be based more on formal rules and tangible agreements than by ingratiation efforts.

2.3.4. Differences in process priorities. In a relation-based society, the common practice is that business dealings can only come after the creation of effective personal relationships. In contrast, Westerners focus on creating successful transactions that will eventually lead to effective working relationships. The implication of these differences is that there is an inherent conflict in assumptions about the priority and timing of events for developing an effective working relationship. Specifically, Westerners tend to rely on rules to govern a relationship and therefore, begin by assuming that new employees are "trustworthy unless proven otherwise".

However, in a relation-based society, ineffective public enforcement leads to business dealings restricted to a private network of tested partners. There is a lesser need to deal with strangers and strangers tend to cheat. As a result, the level of public trust is very low and the prevalent view is that potential partners are "presumably untrustworthy unless proven otherwise."

Thus, relation-based employees may not trust the expatriate manager at the beginning. They expect that effective working relationships will take a long time to develop, and their first priority is on forging such relationships as a mandatory basis for their cooperation and commitment. Clearly, these differences in priorities at the early stages of the expatriate's experience with host country workers may pose a significant and irreversible impediment to the ability to create truly functional working relationship.

From the basic differences in working relationship perceptions just presented, Table 2 identifies six specific differences in the operating expectations of rule-based expatriates and relation-based HCN employees. Based on these six dimensions, we present in Table 3, four potential types of working environments defined according to the level of fit (or disparity) in working relationship expectations of expatriates and local employees.

In the first environment, Quadrant I of Table 3, both parties view the working relationship as relational. In this scenario, the working relations between the foreign executive and local employees tend to be harmonious. Both expect the relationship building to take some time and both tend to make a long-term investment in doing so.

Since the development of relations is time consuming and costly, the expatriate executive cannot develop a relation-based working relationship with every local employee if the number of employees is large. He/she must spend a long time to observe, test, and select a small number of local employees to develop such close, personal relations.

Table 2. Expectations of Working Relationship Formation between Rule-based and Relation-based workers/managers (based on Maurer and Li, 2004)

Dimensions of expectations	Relation-based workers/managers	Rule-based workers/managers
Terms	Vague	Clear
Scope	Wide and deep (it may include all sorts of activities and relationship between an employer and a worker)	Narrow and specific, task-oriented.
Duration	Long	Short
Time needed to develop the working relationship	Long	Short
Costs of developing the relationship	High	Low
Learning curve	Flat, slow learning process, since relations are secretive and particularistic	Steep, fast learning process, since rules are by their nature transparent, public, and general

Table 3. Expectations of Expatriate Executive and Local Employee in Forming Working Relationships (based on Maurer and Li, 2004)

Expatriate Executives	Rule-based	II Expatriate imposes a rule-based governance system onto local employees who are relation-based. Short run: Confusion and misunderstanding Long run: migrating to III	III Expatriate and local employees converge on rule-based system Working relations can be established quickly Efficient when scale and scope are large and market is global (A rare case in relation-based societies)
	Relation-based	I Expatriate and local employees converge on relation-based system Working relations takes time to build, harmony preserved Efficient when scale and scope are small and market is limited	IV Expatriate imposes a relation-based governance system onto local employees who are more rule-oriented. Short run: confusion and misunderstanding Long run: migrating to I (A rare case in relation-based societies)
		Relation-based	Rule-based
		Local Employees	

The second environment suggests that the expatriate executive views the working relationship as rule-based, while the host country employee views it as relation-based (Quadrant II in Table 3). Differences between such expectations create misunderstanding. For example, the expatriate executive may fully trust the local employee and may expect a quick establishment of a positive working relationship, while local employees may reserve their trust and take time to develop a close relationship before devoting themselves to the work effort. Host country employees may compete to invite the expatriate executive to family dinners and other relation-building activities. The expatriate executive may think that these activities are not necessary and decline them. Such declinations, no matter how politely offered, may be incorrectly interpreted by local employees as the expatriate's refusal to enter into a relation-based working relationship, which may affect the local employees' performance.

Poor performance by local employees may, in turn, be viewed by the expatriate executive as a failure to fulfill rule-based working relationships. Alternatively, the expatriate may accept a local employee's dinner invitation as a chance to have a "good time", while the local employee may misinterpret the acceptance as an endorsement of a special relationship.

In summary, there will be confusion and chaos at the beginning that may, in time, evolve to a convergence in the working relationship expectations. In particular, because the expatriate is formally in charge, it is most likely that the working relationship will gradually converge on a rule-based system (Quadrant III) as local employees become familiar with the expatriate executive's rule-based expectations.

In Quadrant III, both parties view the working relationship as more rule-based. Ideally, in this scenario the expatriate executive and local employees will quickly establish a positive working relationship. The period devoted to adjustment, testing, and learning is short for both parties. The efficiency gain from the convergence on rule-based governance is especially significant for firms with a large and expanding scale and scope.

Quadrant IV represents the opposite of Quadrant II. The local employee has a more rule-based expectation while the expatriate views the working relationship as more relation-based. Although this scenario is symmetrical to the Quadrant II, the outcome is systematically different. The process for the more rule-based local employees to learn how to build relationships with the expatriate executive is more difficult, since personal relationship building is, by its nature, exclusive, secretive, particularistic, and based on few known rules.

2.4 *Instructional lessons*

Based on the framework presented in Table 3, we suggest the following basic propositions for teaching expatriates to successfully manage working relationships in Relation-Based economies. First, as the host country economy and the expatriate's firm grow in scale and scope, Quadrant III (both expatriate and local employees are rule-based) will become increasingly more effective and outperform the other quadrants. Hence, expatriate education should focus on strategies for leading the host country employees toward a rule-based system. Second, Quadrant II is more progressive than Quadrant IV, as the expatriate is leading the local employees to adopt a rule-based system. In order to succeed, the expatriate must be taught methods for maintaining a relationship that is healthy and conducive to the transition from a relation-based to rule-based system. Third, Quadrants I and IV both indicate that the expatriate will eventually fail through attempts to act as a relation-based manager. Hence, expatriates should be taught to recognize and avoid the tendency to engage in relation-based strategies that lead to failure due to the inability to effectively respond to the needs of rule-based HCN's (Quadrant IV), or promote the ability of relation-based employees to emulate rule-based counterparts as the scope and scale of the business increase. (Quadrant I).

3. A Teaching Agenda for Managing in Relation-based Societies

In summary, the discussion to this point reveals what we believe is a compelling need to teach managers and business students from rule-based societies how to effectively conduct business and manage in relation-based societies. To meet this requirement, we propose that management educators are faced with an agenda that includes a need to better understand relation-based systems, develop basic elements of instructional content, and determine effective teaching methods. In this section we explain each of these instructional agenda elements and consider their implications for educating future expatriates.

3.1 *Understanding relation-based relationships*

In order to teach managers to develop effective working relationships in a relation-based system, the first challenge is to understand how such systems work. In approaching this task, two major challenges emerge.

First, because relation-based governance systems rely on private agreements (rather than public rules) and individual patterns of relationship development, it is difficult to separate noises from generalizable patterns of relationship creation. Second, due to its nature (private, secretive, and one-to-one relationship), it is extremely difficult for outsiders to even observe relation-based governance at work.

An extreme case of these difficulties is found, for instance, in the relation-based governance of the mafia organization. Obviously, outsiders to that organization (e.g., a professor) tend to lack the understanding of mafia relationships needed to teach someone how to become an effective leader within the secretive and little known rules of mafia culture   Further, sources of needed information are rare since people who are successful in such relation-based societies tend to carefully guard their secrets of success. The ability to obtain current information is diminished because those who write "insiders' stories" have either quit the game deliberately, or are forced outside the organization after they revealed the secrets (see, e.g., Chang, 2001; Gutman, 2004). For these reasons, there is little publicly available and verifiable information on how a relation-based governance system works.

A possible hint for helping Western-trained IB educators develop and teach relation-based management is suggested in the literature on IB education.   For example, a key conclusion of that literature is that business education based on the Western (especially the American) model has not been very successful, partly because it does not fit the business practice of the adopting countries. This concern is expressed by executives of international business who believe that formal IB education adds little to the preparation of business professionals for international business (Reynolds and Rice, 1988; Beamish and Calof, 1989; Ball and McCulloch, 1993; Voris, 1997; Marion, *et al.*, 1999).

We believe that a main reason for this conclusion is that, because a majority of countries are developing countries that rely on relation-based governance, Western-based IB teachers lack the insights and experience needed to explain how such societies work. To remedy this problem, both business leaders and academics agree that IB educators must acquire first-hand knowledge of international business through active involvement in international business, by teaching and living in foreign countries, or at least traveling abroad (Chuck, *et al.*, 1994; Marion, *et al.*, 1999). We strongly agree with the above observation and propose that IB educators must try to learn firsthand how relation-based governance systems work by participating in IB with relation-based countries, or by teaching and/or traveling in such countries.

3.2 Content development

With regard to the question of what to teach prospective managers in relation-based economies, the ideas presented here suggest two fundamental principles. First, the mode of governance environment should be treated as the main determinant in IB patterns across countries. The framework of relation-based governance system and rule-based governance system can be used to classify countries into two groups based on the degree to which a country relies on relation-based or rule-based governance system (Li and Filer, 2004). This can be done using the Governance Environment Index (GEI), developed by Li and Filer, to determine a country's governance structure according to its level of political rights, rule of law, trust, accounting standards, and freedom of press.

Based on the argument that the governance environment (i.e. the fundamental political, economic, legal, and social infrastructure) is the center force that affects all aspects of business, measures such as the GEI can be used by educators to emphasize the practical importance of the governance environment as a major independent variable in all areas of IB (see Li *et al.*, 2003; Li and Filer, 2004; Maurer and Li, 2004; and Li, forthcoming) for detailed discussion on how governance environment affect management, strategy, investment, and trade).

A second principle to be gleaned from our arguments here is that the study and presentation of governance environment should be both multidisciplinary and interdisciplinary. According to a survey, multinational executives believe that IB education must provide interdisciplinary curricula to prepare better qualified IB graduates (Webb *et al.*, 1999). The teacher should be clearly aware of this feature and prepared to expand our knowledge of governance environments through collaborations with experts in related disciplines such as industrial sociology, legal studies and political economy.

3.3 Teaching method

The methods for teaching managers to function in relation-based societies, is closely related to the nature of the subject and to the content development. As we discussed earlier, a relation-based governance system is characterized by secrecy, private dealings, and lack of clear and transparent rules. These characteristics suggest that conventional lecture mode will not be effective. The best way to teach a relation-based governance system is "learning by doing." Specifically, we suggest the following methods:

3.3.1. Case studies. Because the merits of case studies in business education are well known (see, e.g., Barnes *et al.*, 1994) they are not reiterated here. However, we believe that the nature of relation-based governance makes the case study method particularly useful. Although cases about business activities in relation-based environment are relatively rare, there are at least some well-written cases on relation-based business activities with revealing details (e.g., Hogan, 1998). Such cases, without a theoretical underpinning, are merely stories. Thus the instructor should use the framework of relation-based and rule-based governance presented here to analyze the success/failure of managers in the case.

3.3.2. Guest lectures. Another "learning by doing" method is guest lectures. However, we are not proposing "any" guest lectures; we are proposing that guest lectures should be "insiders" of relation-based business dealings. This is perhaps the best way to learn how relation-based businesses operate. Candidates for such lectures should include managers who have managed in a relation-based environment, business professionals who have conducted business transactions, such as marketing, trade, or finance in relation-based societies. Their "war stories" can give us a rare "insider" glimpse of the workings of relation-based governance.

3.3.3. Exchange programs. An exchange program between schools (or firms) from rule-based and relation-based countries may be extremely effective in teaching different governance systems. For example, one may organize a governance systems seminar that consists of two groups of participants, one group includes experienced MBA students from a rule-based country, and the other group includes experience MBA students from a relation-based country. They can bring their respective views on a topic and learn from each other.

4. Concluding Remarks

In this article we propose a teaching agenda to help managers and business students from rule-based societies effectively manage in a relation-based society. We argue that the "cultural" explanation for expatriate failure/success is too broad and fails to address the fundamental determinants of expatriate performance. Thus, we introduce the framework of governance systems to explain expatriate performance and provide an outline of a teaching agenda designed to improve the ability of rule-based students and managers to better understand how to manage in a relation-based governance system.

In conclusion, we would like to draw the reader's attention to the dynamic nature of governance systems and the role of an IB educator in the dynamics. Relation-based governance is not static. As a relation-based economy grows in scale and scope, the relation-based mode of governance will become inefficient. In order to keep its economy competitive, a relation-based country must embark on a transition toward a rule-based governance system. Currently, some of the relation-based countries are undergoing such a transition, countries like China, Russia, and other former communist countries. Thus the framework of relation-based and rule-based governance is not only descriptive, but also normative. IB educators face a choice for their role in the transition.

As IB educators, we may choose to be passive observers of such a transition, or we may choose to actively promote the transition though research and teaching, such as offering policy advice and consulting. This is a question that IB educators must consider. Furthermore, there is an ethical issue for rule-based business people working in relation-based societies. Cultivating relations with the authorities in a relation-based society (most are not democratically elected and are dictators) may involve gift and favor exchanges. Some may even involve significant briberies. In such an environment, a foreign firm must cultivate good relations with the authorities to be competitive or merely survive, since its rivals will do the same. If a foreign firm does not seek favors from the authorities, it may face a higher tax rate and other extortions.

However, if every foreign firm behaves under the same rationale and tries to outperform others by bribing the authorities, then collectively they will drive up the bribery price and they will all be worse off. Their action will also delay the transition toward a rule-based system. Alternatively, if all foreign firms cooperate and refuse to bribe the authorities, collectively they will be better off and they will accelerate the transition.

Game theorists may quickly point out that under such an environment, cheating, instead of cooperating, is the dominant strategy. However, we argue that the role of IB educators should be to take the ethical stand and show the students the big picture by demonstrating the collective benefit of anti-corruption. Such an approach will not only be in the long-run interest of managers (or future managers) from rule-based societies, but it will also facilitate relation-based countries in their transition towards rule.

References

Ball, D. and McCulloch, W. (1993). The views of American multinational CEOs on international business education for prospective employees. *Journal of International Business Studies*, 24(2), pp. 383-391.

Barnes, L, R. Christensen, and Hansen, A. (1994). *Teaching and the Case Method*. Boston: Harvard Business School Press.

Beamish, P. and Calof, J. (1989). International business education: a corporate view. *Journal of International Business Studies*, 20(3), pp. 553-565.

Black, J.S., and Gregersen, H.B. (1999). The right way to manage expatriates. *Harvard Business Review*, Mar.-Apr., pp. 52-63.

Black, J.S., Mendenhall, M. and Oddou, G. (1991). Towards a comprehensive model of international adjustment. *Academy of Management Review*, 16, pp. 291-317.

Caudron, S. (1991). Training ensures overseas success. *Personnel Journal*, Dec., p. 27.

Chang, G. (2001). *The Coming Collapse of China*. New York: Random House.

Chuck, K., Arpan, J. and Folks, W. (1994). A global survey of international business education in the1990s. *Journal of International Business Studies*, 25(3), pp. 605-623.

Gutman, (2004). *Losing the New China: A Story of American Commerce, Desire and Betrayal*. San Francisco, CA: Encounter Books

Harvey, M.G. (1983). The multinational corporation's expatriate problem: An application of Murphy's law. *Business Horizons*, 26, pp. 71-78.

Hill, C. (2003). *International business: Competing in the Global Marketplace*, 4th Ed. New York: McGraw-Hill.

Hodgetts, R. and Luthans, F. (2000). *International Management: Culture, Strategy, and Behavior*, 4th Ed. New York: Irwin-McGraw-Hill.

Hoecklin, Lisa, (1994). *Managing Cultural Differences*, p.124. Workingham, England: Addison-Wesley.

Hogan, H. (1998). Shanghai real estate ((A) and (B)), *Harvard Business School Cases*, 9-398-088 and 9-398-089.

Li, S. (2002). Does East love *guanxi* more than West? The evolution of relation-based governance: Contemporary and historical evidences. *Global Economic Review*, 31 (1) pp. 1-11.

Li, S. The impact of information and communication technology on relation-based governance system. *To appear in the Journal of Information Technology for Development*.

Li, S. and Filer, L. (2004). Governance environment and mode of investment. *Academy of International Business Annual Meeting*, Stockholm, Sweden, July 10-13.

Li, S., Park, S. H. and Li, Shuhe, (2003). The great leap forward: the transition from relation-based governance to rule-based governance. Paper presented at the Academy of International Business Annual Meeting, Monterey, CA, July 5-8. Reprinted in *Organizational Dynamics*, (2004). 33(1) pp. 63-78.

Li, S. and Li, S. (2000). The economics of guanxi. *China Economic Quarterly*, (Q1) pp. 40-42.

Li, S. (1999). Relation-based versus rule-based governance: an explanation of the East Asian miracle and Asian crisis. Paper presented at the American Economic Association Annual Meeting in New York, January. Listed on the Social Science Research Network (http://papers.ssrn.com/paper.taf?abstract_id=200208), (2000). Reprinted in *Review of International Economics*, (2003). 11(4) pp. 651-73.

Lublin, J.S. (1992). Companies use cross-cultural training to help their employees adjust abroad. *Wall Street Journal*, Aug. 2, B1, B6.

Marion, W., Mayer, K., Pioche, V., and Allen. L. (1999). Internationalization of American business education. *Management International Review*, 39(4) pp. 379-397.

Maurer, S. and Li, S. (2004). Governance issues and psychological contracts as determinants of expatriate manager performance. Academy of Management Annual Meeting, New Orleans, Louisiana, Aug. 6-11.

Reynolds, J. and Rice, G. (1988). American education for international business. *Management*

Shay, J., and Bruce, T.J. (1997). Expatriate managers, *Cornell Hotel & Restaurant Administration Quarterly*, Feb., pp. 30-40.

Stone, Raymond, (1991). Expatriate selection and failure, *Human Resource Planning*, 14(1).

Tong, R. (1979). U.S. multinationals: A study of their selection and training procedures for overseas assignments, *National Academy of Management Proceedings*, Atlanta, pp. 298-299.

UNCTAD, (2002). *World Investment Report, (2002)*. New York and Geneva: United Nations.

United Nations. (2001). Global financial profile. http://www.un.org/reports/financing/profile.htm, June.

Voris, W. (1997). A retrospective of international business education in the United States over the past fifty years. *International Executive*, 29(2) pp. 271-282.

Chapter 4

Business Ethics Education in China: Current Understanding and a Mechanistic Model of Cultural Evolution

Y. James Song
Waterville International Management Information Inc.

1. Introduction: Ethics Education in China–Who Wants It and Why

As China' economy increasingly integrates with those of the more developed nations, ethical practices are becoming a priority on the national agenda. Like the legal system, the subject of ethics is often discussed in the context of national pride, community harmony, social justice, and more recently the very legitimacy of the political system itself (various speeches and publicized CPC documents in the past three years). The ruling political party, which regards itself as heir to the millennia old tradition of autocratic benevolence, finds in moral ethics a new instrument for sustaining and stabilizing the basic foundation of a governing system over a nation that is progressing at a speed unsurpassed by any period in her history (Rohwer, 1996; Schell and Shambaugh, 1999; Smadja, 2001). The highly publicized prosecutions of top-level bureaucrats, some by capital punishments, are intended as stern warnings in an effort to suppress mushrooming corruption (Lewis, 2001; Xiao, 2001).

More recently, renewed national campaigns aimed at rebuilding and uplifting the sense of righteousness amongst teenagers and preteens represent an ongoing struggle to straighten out moral principles deemed to have been severely damaged during the virulent Cultural Revolution in the 1960's-1970's and the go-go economic liberalization in the past quarter century. Such campaigns, spearheaded by the new CPC designated administration, dubbed the "fourth generation leadership" of the party, have apparently been a continuation of the "rule by morality" (*yidezhiguo*) drive initiated by the "third generation leadership."

State media began to feature singular hero whistle-blowers who stood up against mighty corporations while risking their personal well-being. Increasingly, news organizations leverage their newly bestowed power to push for transparency, exposing unflattering environmental disasters, official corruptions, government policy failures, and rights violations by agencies and businesses (Li, 2001). Whether as "megaphones for the party or free-standing independent watchdogs," members of the journalist community realize the critical role of the media in enabling supervision by public opinions, in maintaining a benign political and economical cycle of society, and indeed in moving the country towards political democracy and "modern civilization." Most China observers would agree that the Chinese media today has basically outgrown its former mandate to *xiaoma dabangmang* ("nick picking to save face and aid the grand cause"), driven by market forces that are transforming media organizations from party and government institutions to enterprises.

Outside the bounds of political mandate and governing platform, the business community, consisting of a growing number of multinationals and a rapidly growing private sector, increasingly recognizes the importance of promoting social responsibility and environmental accountability. More and more private enterprises are becoming aware of the benefits of forsaking unethical business conducts. Some of the newly successful and influential even openly advocate a more enlightened ethical orientation, at a time when many have experimented with and exhausted questionable, expedient means to acquire wealth (Chen, 2003).

1.1 Teaching ethics in China: challenges to building up the critical mass

Unlike developed nations such as the United States and Germany, where long held cultural values and a strong, uncensored academic infrastructure allow for timely responses to fulfill new demands by society at large, should they arise, such as calls for enhancing ethics teaching in the aftermath of major corporate scandals, China's decades long relentless demolition of cultural heritage and erstwhile deliberate, systematic destruction of the country's intelligentsia left in place a weak and much improvised management education system, which appears distracted and overstrained in the rapid, record-setting socioeconomic development in this vast country's eventful recent history (De Crespigny, 1992).

Faced with the challenge to provide professional quality education and training in a subject as unconventional as ethics, the system is found inadequately prepared, and shortage of qualified faculty is even more severe than in other disciplinary subject areas. To make matters worse, amateurish indoctrination under the auspices of party propaganda organs in place of instruction by qualified expert academics further deepens the cynicism among a people who have long been conditioned by mendacity, corruption, blatant manipulation, and unashamed exploitation, which have been an institutionalized reality for generations.

The push to rebuild national prominence, in particular the supposed leadership in moral philosophy, and the thrust to strengthen profitability and competitiveness, together, will place business ethics on programs at leading Chinese business schools, slowly but steadily. Given that isolated efforts to teach ethics has achieved less than satisfactory results, the void now begs to be filled with a balanced, focused and culturally localized syllabus. It is therefore opportune to examine some of the basic questions on hand in order to better understand the challenges and tasks ahead.

1.2 *Perceived Chinese attitudes towards ethics*

Western researchers studying ethical attitudes by Chinese citizens report divided views by the subjects. Day (1997) for instance finds a near perfect tripartite split in answering the question of acceptability of increasing profits at the expense of business ethics (Figure 1). Such observations have typically led to the conclusion that the Chinese work on a distinctive set of values, beliefs, and ideas (Ferrell, Fraedrich and

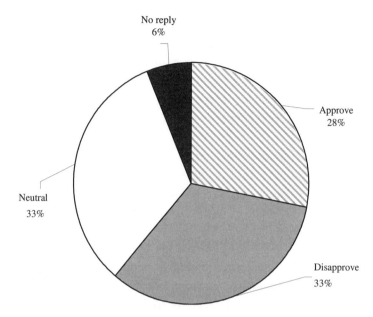

Figure 1. Responses by Chinese managers to the question "Do you find it acceptable to increase profits at the expense of business ethics?" (Based on Day, 1997)

Ferrell, 2000), which sounds to be a truist assertion of little practical use to those seeking to understand the Chinese reality.

Some visiting western academics admit privately that lecturing to Chinese business students on the subject of ethics is greeted by apathy. It appears that, often, the less than enthusiast response could be in reaction to the perceived condescension by western instructors whose seemingly aggressive and imposing approach tends to have an alienating effect. Given the strong still "central kingdom" mentality and mixed feelings among the citizens towards ideas from outside China, cross-cultural considerations must be an integral, indeed essential, component in the development and effective delivery of any ethics program intended to cater to the contemporary Chinese context, no matter where the starting point is along the universalist-relativist spectrum (various authors in Warner and Joynt, 2001).

To understand, on a deeper level, current awareness of and attitudes towards ethics by the Chinese business students, the current study has been conducted with the aim to gain insights into four basic questions: (1) What considerations and priorities are Chinese organizations giving to ethics, both in concept and in practice? (2) What are the general attitudes towards the current level of ethical development in Chinese society? (3) What are the perceptions of the gaps between China and other nations? (4) What stages of moral development do Chinese students feel akin to?

2. Survey and Results

A total of 200 survey questionnaires, distributed to students enrolled in MBA and managerial development programs in Nanjing, Shanghai, and Guangzhou, resulted in 180 validated returns. The surveyees are presented with 40 questions, and four choices are allocated, namely *"strongly-agree," "agree," "disagree"* and *"strongly-disagree."* The reason for not allowing the "no-opinion" choice is to purge, as much as possible, intended or unintended neutrality. On each side of the opinion divide, two levels were afforded to enable the gauging of intensity on various issues.

The absence of a neutral field makes the *strongly-agree* fields more important, when the simple *agree* and *disagree* fields are discounted for including the otherwise neutral answers. Another possible adjustment should apply to the simple *agree* field, which might include a better half of the potential neutrals. In such cases the size of the *disagree* group is of more interest.

Table 1 lists questions presented in the survey. Summarized survey results are discussed below (Tables 2 and 3, Figures 2-5).

2.1 Ethical practices: perception or reality?

The first half of the survey deals with evaluating the importance given to ethical practices by respondents' organizations. Complex patterns emerge from the answers (see rankings in Table 2).

Table 1. Survey Questions

Part 1 Regarding the organization I work for...

1 The organization's founder/top leadership put business ethics on their agenda.
2 The organization has a shared value system and understanding of ethical behavior.
3 There are ethical policies and rules communicated to all employees.
4 There are rewards and penalties regarding ethical behavior.
5 There are open discussions on ethical dilemmas.
6 Employees treat each other with respect, honesty, and fairness.
7 Ethics is an important factor in employee promotions.
8 Ethics is an important reason for employee dissatisfaction/high turnover.
9 Ethics is an important reason for customer dissatisfaction/high turnover.
10 Ethics is an important factor in product/service promotion.
11 The organization believes in serving all customers fairly and honestly.
12 The organization deals with suppliers & subcontractors completely fairly & honestly.
13 The organization treats competitors as enemies that should be wiped out.
14 The organization has clearly identified its stakeholders.
15 The organization puts short-term profits above everything else.
16 The organization gives high priorities to customers, the environment, and society.

Part 2 In my opinion...

17 As a reality, most people choose short-term interests over ethics.
18 In theory, people should put ethics above short-term interests.
19 Lack of ethics is a price poor countries pay to get rich.
20 Everybody cheats if there is no danger of getting caught.
21 It is impossible to become wealthy while being totally honest.
22 People are born to be ethical.
23 Ethics is cultivated.
24 China has a long way to go before giving business ethics serious consideration.
25 Chinese organizations are less ethical than those in western countries.
26 Asian organizations are less ethical than those in western countries.
27 Ethics is a tool for rich, developed nations to control and exploit developing nations.
28 Being ethical is to avoid punishment.
29 Being ethical is to serve individual interests.
30 Being ethical is to serve the interests of others.
31 Being ethical is to fulfill duties/responsibilities, and to maintain social order.
32 Being ethical is to uphold of basic rights, values and legal contracts of society.
33 Being ethical is to advance universal rights, principles and justice.

Table 2. Questions

Part 1 Ranked by "Agree" and "Strongly Agree" Responses...

14 The organization has clearly identified its stakeholders.
1   The organization's founder/top leadership put business ethics on their agenda.
6   Employees treat each other with respect, honesty, and fairness.
9   Ethics is an important reason for customer dissatisfaction/high turnover.
10 Ethics is an important factor in product/service promotion.
2   The organization has a shared value system and understanding of ethical behavior.
11 The organization believes in serving all customers fairly and honestly.
16 The organization gives high priorities to the customers, the environment, and society.
3   There are ethical policies and rules communicated to all employees.
4   There are rewards and penalties regarding ethical behavior.
12 The organization deals with suppliers and subcontractors completely fairly and honestly.
7   Ethics is an important factor in employee promotions.
8   Ethics is an important reason for employee dissatisfaction/high turnover.
5   There are open discussions on ethical dilemmas.
13 The organization treats competitors as enemies that should be wiped out.
15 The organization puts short-term profits above everything else.

Noticeably

(1) *We prioritize ethics, don't we?* On questions regarding the organization's general attitudes towards business ethics, a clear majority of respondents give positive appraisals. Over two thirds report clearly identified stakeholders, business ethics placed on leadership's agenda, ethical promotion of products and services, and mutual respect among employees, and most recognize ethics as an important factor in customer satisfaction and turnover.

(2) *My organization values ethics.* In the mean time, most respondents believe that their organizations compete fairly and are not single-mindedly focused on short-term profits.

(3) *In practice, however...* However, a considerably lesser majority agree on more tangible, operational issues such as shared value system and understanding, priorities given to social responsibilities, ethical policies and rules, and rewards and penalties regarding ethical behavior.

(4) *Who gets promoted? It depends...* Further, nearly half of the respondents rejects the notion that employee promotion takes ethics into account, although a substantial number (14%) strongly agrees, showing a clear separation of opinions.

(5) *Do ethics really matter to all?* Over half of the respondents consider ethics no reason for employee dissatisfaction and turnover, whereas a definite majority reports no open discussion on ethical dilemmas, with few strongly agreeing that discussion happens inside the organization.

(6) *Regarding suppliers and contractors, well let's see...* Very few strongly believe their organizations deal with suppliers and subcontractors fairly and honestly, with nearly half seeing the opposite.

Overall, respondents confirm broad acknowledgement of the importance, and perhaps even value, of ethical leadership and practices. That acknowledgement, however, is largely offset by a lack of specific practical measures (Figure 2). The most outstanding

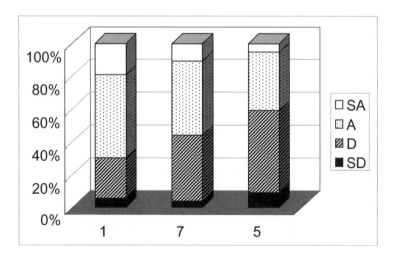

Figure 2. Ethical Practices: Perception or Reality? 1-The organization's founder/top leadership put business ethics on their agenda. 7-Ethics is an important factor in employee promotions. 5-There are open discussions on ethical dilemmas. (A-Agree, SA-Strongly Agree, D-Disagree, SD-Strongly Disagree.)

issues are employee promotion and supplier/contractor relationship. Employee dissatisfaction/turnover is also worth noting: When people admit an indifferent attitude, could that imply a more deeply rooted detachment? Could that be a sign of cynicism?

2.2 Are people born to be ethical?

Part 2 of the survey explores three different areas in people's understanding of business ethics. When asked to assess the basis for ethical behavior, respondents display a tendency of pragmatism and, on one key issue, self-contradiction.

Table 3. Questions

Part 2 Ranked by "Agree" and "Strongly Agree" Responses...
Are People Born To Be Ethical?

23	Ethics is cultivated.
18	In theory, people should put ethics above short-term interests.
17	As a reality, most people choose short-term interests over ethics.
19	Lack of ethics is a price poor countries pay to get rich.
21	It is impossible to become wealthy while being totally honest.
20	Everybody cheats if there is no danger of getting caught.
22	People are born to be ethical.

China and the Rest of the World

24	China has a long way to go before giving business ethics serious consideration.
34	Being ethical is to serve the development of the motherland.
25	Chinese organizations are less ethical than those in western countries.
19	Lack of ethics is a price poor countries pay to get rich.
26	Asian organizations are less ethical than those in western countries.
27	Ethics is a tool for rich, developed nations to control and exploit developing nations.

Kohlberg's Cognitive Developmental Stages

32	Being ethical is to uphold of basic rights, values and legal contracts of society.
31	Being ethical is to fulfill duties/responsibilities, and to maintain social order.
33	Being ethical is to advance universal rights, principles and justice.
30	Being ethical is to serve the interests of others.
29	Being ethical is to serve individual interests.
28	Being ethical is to avoid punishment.

Respondents tend to agree that ethics should precede short-term interests, and, in the mean time, that people rarely carry out that principle. Whereas a clear majority believe that unethical practices are related to a country's underdevelopment, a much smaller majority embraces the notion that wealth acquisition entails dishonesty. Less than half agree that cheating is deterred by the fear of getting caught.

The most interesting answers are to the questions of the source of ethicality (Figure 3). There is a near parity of opinions on whether people are born to be ethical. In sharp contrast, a resounding majority (95%) believes that ethics is cultivated, with a quarter completely convinced. Adding these observations together, it appears that many respondents felt confused about where to look for ethical guidance and justification.

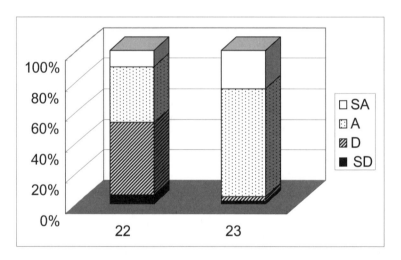

Figure 3. Are People Born to Be Ethical? 22-People are born to be ethical. 23-Ethics is cultivated. (A-Agree, SA-Strongly Agree, D-Disagree, SD-Strongly Disagree.)

2.3 China vs. the West: ethical or ethnical?

Respondents show unhesitant collective humility in assessing the Chinese reality. Led by a whole third of strong supporters, the largest "strongly agree" group in the entire survey, over 90% agree that as a

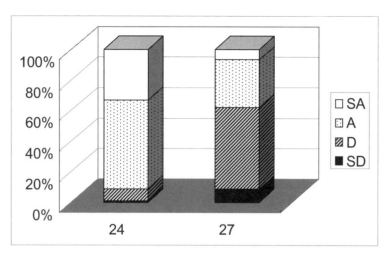

Figure 4. China and the West. 24-China has a long way to go before giving business ethics serious consideration. 27-Ethics is a tool for rich, developed nations to control and exploit developing nations. (A-Agree, SA-Strongly Agree, D-Disagree, SD-Strongly Disagree.)

nation China faces a long march towards regaining ethical leadership. Few doubt that China's development will benefit from ethical progress.

Noticeably, while most recognize the gaps between China-Asia and the west, nearly 40% support the notion that developed nations use ethics to control and exploit poorer countries (Figure 4).

2.4 *Kohlberg's model for moral development: being ethical means what?*

The most widely accepted model of moral development is the theory of cognitive moral development by psychologist Lawrence Kohlberg. This model, based on research on children's cognitive growth, identifies six sequential stages that individual development of ethical judgment goes through, namely (1) *punishment and obedience,* (2) *instrumental purpose and exchange,* (3) *mutual expectations, relationships, and conformity,* (4) *social system and conscience maintenance,* (5) *prior rights and social contract,* and (6) *universal rights, principles and justice* (Kohlberg, 1969).

Later, Kohlberg (1981, 1984) delineated the original six stages into three levels, which include the *pre-conventional,* the *conventional* and the *principled.* Accordingly, a person's early choice of the right is based on personal consequences. At the conventional level, expectations of others are at work. Few people reach the principled level, where moral justifications are independent of, indeed above and beyond, convention, authority, system, and society. There are two corollaries from this model. First, people develop their sense of morality through these successive levels and stages sequentially, namely from lower to higher or the pre-conventional to the principled. Second, moral developments do not all reach all six stages and all three levels.

The most interesting results from this survey reside in the answers to questions related to the Kohlberg cognitive moral development model. Near unanimous supports are given to the principled *basic rights, values and societal contracts* stage (5) and the *duties, responsibilities and social order* stage (4) definitions of ethics, receiving 99% and 98%, respectively, positive responses altogether, and both with a quarter "strongly agree" responses. The highest (6) stage of *universal rights, principles and justice* also receives extremely high approval, with overwhelming approval and a sizable "strongly agree" responses, and thus falls into the same category.

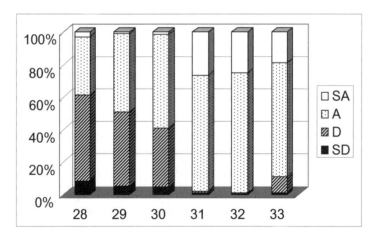

Figure 5. Kohlberg's Model for Moral Development. See Table 1 for survey questions. (A-Agree, SA-Strongly Agree, D-Disagree, SD-Strongly Disagree.)

In sharp contrast, the pre-conventional stage definitions receive, respectively, 51% (2) and 60% (1) negative responses and minimal, near zero "strongly agree" responses (Figure 5).

3. Discussion

The inherent complexities of globalization and hyper-competition are giving ethics a certain imperative impetus. Being active players in the world's marketplace has taught the more sophisticated members of China's business community that it is more conducive to sell products worldwide if a country adheres to international ecological standards, employment fairness, and ethical business practices. These issues are complex and multifaceted. They are as much issues of government-business relations as they are issues of ethics.

There can be little doubt that this is an area where China potentially has much to offer to the rest of the world, which is not only the aspirations of generations of Chinese visionaries from Sun Yat-sen onwards, but also the expectations of students of history in and outside Asia, eastern and western alike. Paradoxically, observers are both excited and simultaneously concerned by China's largely lone and steadfast pursuit of objectives under the modernization program. Few would dispute nonetheless that China's development is reaching a turning point where the economic and technological priorities are being supplemented by collective rethinking of cultural values, a process surely to rekindle needed discussion and debate, which started a generation ago and seem to be re-surfacing once again under the new socioeconomic climate.

Complexities are expected. Unlike neighboring Japan, which was transformed virtually overnight from a *Warring-State Age* like era to the modern industrial age, and unlike Singapore the tiny island state, which started the modernization process from a uniformly colonial background (Rohwer, 1996), China, with its enormous size and diversity and millennia long history, most of which saw the nation as the world's mightiest yet largely isolated economic and occasional military power, and as the self-styled flame keeper of heavenly righteousness, has just arrived at a stage where the national purposes are revisited and beginning to get disentangled at a critical time during a lengthy (nearly two centuries) and incessantly disrupted journey of national restoration.

The study presented here points to symptoms of a values system in transition. The inconsistencies and discrepancies themselves suggest complex processes that might have been responsible. To examine the often erratic patterns observed in this and other studies, and to explore possible underlying processes, it will be elucidating to place the discussion in the context of a general framework of cultural values, and in relevant historical perspectives.

3.1 The model of culture revisited and revised

There has been a steady flow of literature on the meaning and aspects of cultural values (e.g. Hall, 1959; Hofstede, 1980, 1991; various authors in Joynt and Warner 1985; Ohmae, 1990; various authors in Warner and Joynt, 2001). In his influential work, Trompenaars (1993) proposes a three-layered model of culture, which has been used as a teaching tool thanks to the model's simplicity (for example, in Hodgetts and Luthans, 1991).

The original model (Figure 6) consists of three spheres: the outer or "explicit artifacts and products" sphere, the middle or "norms and values" sphere, and the inner or "implicit basic assumption" sphere. Traveling from the outer to the inner layer, one experiences (1) observable realities, where prejudices arise from the symbolic artifacts, (2) common values and aspirations, where shared meanings of guides and priorities shape and maintain the very integrity of society, and (3) basic solutions to the challenge of physical survival, where fundamental cultural changes are driven by factors impacting the community's existence.

Figure 7 illustrates a revised model of culture based on Trompenaars's three-sphere metaphor. It replaces the three concentric spheres with five successive strata. There are two other noteworthy differences. The more obvious difference is that the sizes of the inter/lower and outer/top layers are reversed, and all layers are open rather than enwrapped in circles. The second and not so obvious difference is that the new model is more dynamic and formative, with a mechanistic focus, compared to the static, descriptive original model.

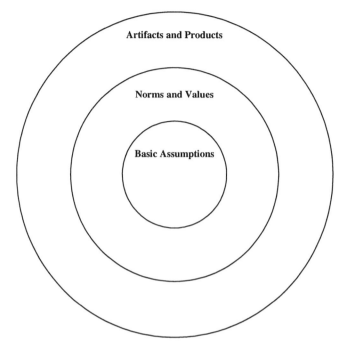

Figure 6. Trompenaar's 3-sphere Model of Culture

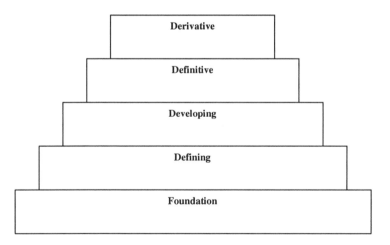

Figure 7. A New Model of Culture

The new model's five strata are "the foundation", "the defining", "the developing", "the definitive", and "the derivative" layers. The *foundation* and *derivative* layers largely correspond to Tromponaars's inter and outer spheres. The original middle or "norms and values" sphere is now differentiated into the *developing* and *definitive* strata, which seems to be already implied in Tromponaars's model. The *defining* layer is inserted to separate and accentuate the deliberate effort to identify common purposes. Following are brief descriptions of the five layers.

The Foundation Layer: Basic and fundamental challenges a nation must constantly face in order to survive.

The Defining Layer: Visionaries and leaders articulate national purposes and agenda to unify and motivate the people and to focus efforts and resources; philosophical and religious frameworks take roots.

The Developing Layer: Priorities, objectives, and solutions are contemplated, debated, clarified, and formulated; institutional instruments for maintaining social order begin to be constructed.

The Definitive Layer: Laws, customs, conventions, ethical criteria, social rituals, professional standards, business practices, behavioral guides, policy-optimization mechanisms and decision-making processes are well established and commonly accepted and followed.

The Derivative Layer: Behavioral patterns, attitudinal tendencies, and other explicit and observable cultural artifacts. This is the tip of the iceberg.

Even the proudest and most sentimental Chinese students will admit that the country is at a stage of redefining and re-constructing her priorities, societal norms and ethical conventions. Many questions are waiting for definitive answers. Clarity on issues, ranging from the basic and general to the specific and operational, would take time to be arrived at, and the process is bound to be intertwined with attitudes and reactions towards concepts from outside, given China's history for the past two centuries.

3.2 *China and the West: the Ti-Yong debate*

Not long ago, in answering interview questions from a Harvard Business Review (China edition) editor during a visit to Shanghai, the director of Harvard University's Center for East Asia Studies and author of *Japan as Number 1*, asserted that "the United States has little to learn from China," at least not yet (Yi, 2004). China today has been compared to Japan in the 1960's and 1970's, rapidly growing and in the mean time with questions on national purposes and priorities to be sorted out. Evidently most Chinese would agree that China has a lot to learn from the west, though many still do not feel completely comfortable with the thought of accepting foreign ideas directly and entirely.

In the current study, a sizable (37%) number of respondents question (6% strongly) the motive behind voices from developed nations advocating business ethics. In the mean time, few doubt that China lags behind in ethical practices, with a whole one third strongly supporting such a view. It would not be surprising that many Chinese students are tormented by the challenge to reconcile a commonly recognized fact (*i.e.* "China has a long way to go") and a frequently held and sometimes openly expressed sentiment (*i.e.* "But we should be the best"). This agony is very probably shared by considerable numbers of Chinese people today, transcending all socioeconomic, educational, and geographic boundaries.

Nationalistic pride and ethnocentrism would be convenient explanations, but beyond those sentimental factors, a persisting theme could also be recognized at work here: the *Ti* versus *Yong* debate that dates back to the earliest days when the empire was compelled by rapidly shifting circumstances to make tough choices on the national agenda (De Crespigny, 1992).

Simply put, *Ti* (pronounced "tea", with the third intonation) refers to the main body or framework of the culture. *Yong* (closest in sound to "yoong", fourth intonation) has to do with tools, applications, and practical and immediate uses. After repeated defeats by actually not so much superior foreign adversaries, particularly a newly westernized imperial Japan, the slogan "*Zhongxuewei Ti, Xixuewei Yong*" or "introducing some western techniques to serve the preservation and strengthening of the traditional Chinese cultural values" was coined by Late Qing reform-minded scholar-bureaucrats, in their desperate push to advance their renovation and restoration program. It was in part as a ploy to outmaneuver conservative mandarins and deflect the vicious "un-Chineseness" accusations from the latter, and in part out of the sincere belief that the only effective and practical prescription would be to pursue modernization without jeopardizing the nation's intellectual foundation. Even though the last hope to save the empire from downfall dashed with the dynasty's implosion, the *Ti-Yong* debate has lingered on, for well over one century, into the new millennium. Towards the end of his life, Deng Xiaoping (and even Mao Tsetung himself once) claimed to be faithful heirs to that pragmatist vision.

It is likely that a substantial number of Chinese, while desiring to see their country advance to the same level of technical and social development as leading western nations, remain sensitive to any attempt that would shake the faith in and question the validity of the nation's cultural foundation. From the perspective of those who still find modern business ethics education foreign and imposing, China simply deserves some respect for her historical supremacy that was lost during an invasion-ridden tumultuous period.

3.3 *Ethics characterized with Chinese characteristics*

It is not uncommon to observe such internal conflicts in contemporary Chinese thinking. Similar to the confusion observed regarding ethnic sentiment, a large number of respondents contradict themselves in identifying the come-about of ethical behavior. Ethics is considered a born character by nearly half of the respondents, who by and large immediately join the other half in asserting that ethics is by *nurture*.

Even more counter-intuitive is the finding of a resolute disregard of basic level meanings of morality while reaching for the higher, indeed loftier definitions. The discrepancy involves a (thin to dominating) majority.

Are the Chinese really that different? A closer look at the responses to the developmental model questions offers some further insights.

Stage 4, or the *duties, responsibilities and social order* stage, gets across-board approval and solid "strongly agree" responses. This is in line with the conclusion from research that most managers have achieved that level of moral development. The over 10% negative responses to Stage 6, or the stage of *universal rights, principles and justice,* separates it from Stage 5 the *basic rights, values and societal contracts* stage, which receives universal approval. The interpretation of this discrepancy could come from two different directions: cynicism and xenophobia.

Students all received the questionnaires without prior discussion of concepts in the Kohlberg model. Having not much time to ponder over the deeper meanings of the definitions, it is likely that a small yet distinct percentage simply find such words as "principles and justice" too far removed from the affair of making money, and the word "universal" could also strike a chord of sensitivity, for it could allude to the uncomfortable, (probably officially indoctrinated) thoughts of cultural invasion and western hegemony.

3.4 Priorities shaken at the foundation: flipped national purposes

The bigger questions, of course, are why the illogical mixing of nature and nurture as the origin of ethical values; and why the inversion of the pre-conventional and the principled definitions of ethics? The non-trivial nature of those questions warrants further exploration for deeper drivers.

Schizophrenic conflicts such as those discussed above could lead to frustration in those striving to understand certain Chinese attitudes and actions, especially when such efforts produce more bewilderment than clarity. The inconsistencies are hard to reconcile by applying conventional wisdom because the issues are rooted at the very foundation level in our structural metaphor, namely the model of culture. Most of the nation's multi-millennium history saw no precise identification of leading physical challenges and clear definition of national purposes until the mid-19th century, when China was dragged into the bigger world. The ensuing decades witnessed some desperate struggles to make sense of the situation and find the right direction for the nation. No sooner had Sun Yatsen articulated his vision than were the newly found national purposes placed, by various internal and external forces, on a long windy journey, during which China's priorities would be reversed at least once during every generation's life time.

Confusions and self-contradictions on certain cultural values, as evidenced by responses to questions on business ethics in this study, are mere outcrops of such reversals, which culminated during the mid-late 20th century. Contemporary Chinese, and working age citizens in particular, would have experienced two national priority reversals every decade early in their lives. A so frequently destabilized cultural foundation, despite the apparent continuity in the political system, left little time for defining and developing civil structures and processes, let alone the system of ethical values.

Many factors contribute to the renewed attention on business ethics, but the most powerful driving force evidently is the broad realization of the implications for social and economic interest. Proponents find ironclad cases in shocking tragedies such as the criminal Anhui's Fuyang powder milk incidences (resulting in dozens of infant fatalities), and in fraudulent scandals involving entire communities such as the infamy suffered by Guangdong's Shantou City, which spent years and invested heavily in repairing gravely tarnished city's reputation and seriously impaired commercial interests, and in rebuilding and regaining public trust and respect. The focus of discussion now is not only on issues of national scale, but also on the priorities and practices inside the communities and organizations.

3.5 *Entering an age of defining and developing*

Responses to the survey questions in Part 1 again point to the aftermath from a once impotent national purpose agenda that disabled the growth of an operational values system. Two sharply different organizational realities emerge from the composite snapshot based on those responses.

On one hand, the majority of respondents claim general acceptance, by their organizations, of the commonly perceived good practices in terms of business ethics, ranging from identifying stakeholders to balancing short-term profits and broader responsibilities and from executive agenda to organizational harmony. When it comes down to the operational level, however, the scorecard seems to be telling a different story. Issues with inadequacies regarding rules, policies, rewards, penalties, communication, employee promotion and retention, and supplier/contractor relations concern a respectable percentage of respondents. Lack of open discussion of ethical matters ranks the highest on the shortcoming list.

As China's preoccupation with economic growth deepens, ethics has become a focus of persisting public concern and incessant rhetoric by policy makers and opinion leaders for some time, even though, as a curricular subject, business ethics remains virtually absent from the country's management education programs. Indeed, the subject's propinquity to cultural values, ideological doctrines, nationalistic sentiments and political taboos still seems to interfere with potential focused effort to foster broader interest among academics, students, and executives.

Despite the current indecision and uncertainties, few would disagree that the towering cultural heritage of the Chinese nation could enormously enrich current discussion and development of business ethics. China's historical role as the cultural center of gravity among Asian countries could also point to the possibility of renewed leadership across China's sphere of influence in Asia and beyond. The diversity of Chinese communities across the globe, including those within China, provides plenty of opportunities for studying cross-cultural evolution of ethical values and business practices. And the vigorously developing Chinese business realities offer a fertile ground for research, education and training endeavors.

This study has revealed dynamic thinking towards business ethics amongst a new crop of current and future leaders and managers. It imparts the story of a people who has finally come out of a protracted age of incessant disruptions on an arduous journey towards modernity, a society that is striving to cast away long held qualms and regain self-confidence, and, indeed, a community that will delight itself and friends with handsome returns over investment in business ethics training and education.

Acknowledgement

I thank Professor Ilan Alon for having invited me to contribute to his book on an interesting subject, and for having rushed me to finish the writing within 10 days. Professor John R. McIntyre, co-editor of this book, offered stimulating comments during the preparation of the manuscript. Miss Jenny Yong Jiang of Waterville Inc. carefully compiled the survey data and prepared the figures from respondent results (though any possible errors and imperfections are entirely the author's responsibility). Finally, my sincere thanks go to my students, whose enthusiasm and participation are truly inspiring.

References

Brahm, L, ed. (2001). China's Century, the Awakening of the Next Economic Powerhouse. John Wiley & Sons (Asia) Pte Ltd.

Chen, S (2003). 袁岳：追求无形, Global Sources世界经理人 (September 2003), pp. 88-89.

Day, K (1997). Chinese Perceptions of Business Ethics, *International Business Ethics Review,* (Fall-Winter 1997), 4.

De Crespingy, R (1992). China This Century. Hong Kong: Oxford University Press.

Ferrel, OC, J Fraedrich and L Ferrell (2000). Business Ethics: Ethical Decision Making and Cases. Boston: Houghton Mifflin Company.

Hall, ET (1959). The Silent Language. New York: Doubleday.

Hodgetts, RM and F Luthans (2003). International Business: Culture, Strategy, and Behavior. The McGraw-Hill Companies Higher Education Group.

Hofstede, G (1980). Cultures Consequences: International Differences in Work-Related Values. Beverly Hills, CA, and London: Sage.

Hofstede, G (1991). Cultures and Organizations: Software of the Mind. London: McGraw-Hill.

Joynt, PD and M Warner (1985). Managing in Different Cultures. Oslo: Universitetsforlaget.

Kohlberg, L (1969). Stage and Sequence: The Congnitive Developmental Approach to Socialization. In *Handbook of Socialization Theory and Research,* DA Goslin (ed.), pp. 347-480. Chicago: Rand McNally.

Kohlberg, L (1981). Essays in Moral development: the Philosophy of Moral Development, Vol. 1. New York: Harper and Row.

Kohlberg, L (1984). Essays in Moral Development: the Psychology of Moral Development, Vol. 2. New York: Harper and Row.

Lewis, DJ (2001). Governance in China: the Present and Future Tense. In *China's Century*, L Brahm (ed.), pp. 234-243.

Li, X (2001). Creeping Freedoms in China's Press. In *China's Century*, L Brahm (ed.), pp. 386-402.

Ohmae, K (1990). The Borderless World. New York: McKinsey and Co Inc.

Rohwer, J (1996). Asia Rising. London: Nicholas Brealey Publishing.

Schell, O and D Shambaugh, ed. (1999). The China Reader: The Reform Era. New York: Vintage Books, a Division of Random House, Inc.

Smadja, C (2001). Dealing with Globalization. In *China's Century*, L Brahm (ed.), pp. 24-37.

Trompenaars, F (1996). Riding the Waves of Culture. London: Nicholas Brealey Publishing.

Warner, M and P Joynt (2002). Managing across Cultures: Issues and Perspectives. Hong Kong: Thomson Learning Press.

Yang, X (2001). A New Chapter in Constructing China's Legal System. In *China's Century*, L Brahm (ed.), pp. 218-233.

易学军（2004）. 如何名列世界第一, 哈佛商业评论 Harvard Business Review China (October 2004), pp. 32-36.

Chapter 5

Distance Learning Education in China

Jonatan Jelen

Mercy College

Ilan Alon

Rollins College

1. Introduction

"May you live in interesting times!" is a Chinese proverb that sounds much like a good-luck wish. China's membership in the WTO may just turn out to be such an ambivalent experience. Committed to a socio-politically cautious, deliberate, localized, and incremental absorption of market-economic structures into its system, beginning as early as in the 1980s, China initiated a multitude of concomitant internal reforms in support of matching up its infrastructure and competitiveness to Western standards of commerce. Particularly cognizant of the impact and leverage of education in this context, the overhaul of the education system, with particular emphasis on academic and higher education, has been and still is amongst the more pressing initiatives.

Amongst the various disciplines in turn, China is especially handicapped by a serious shortage of business leadership and a near-absence of post-capitalist management-style culture. Chinese Premier Zhu Rongji, for example, a driving force behind the nation-wide efforts to revamp the education system, specifically acknowledged that China needs 1.5 million MBAs over the next 10 years. Other estimates are in the millions (Southworth 1999). And even if a 2001 Gallup survey more modestly estimated the number at 350,000, it remains that this demand by far exceeds the most optimistic capacity estimates of Chinese universities' business programs despite the explosive proliferation of proprietary MBA education during the 1990s, given the over 284,000 state owned enterprises (SOEs), more than 428,000 joint ventures or foreign-owned corporations and about 2,000,000 private or township enterprises in the country (Chinese MBA Website 2002). But quantity is not the only issue. Of major concern is the different nature and "quality" of Chinese business education with it limitations and shortcomings in terms of tradition, content, delivery, pedagogy, and competitiveness.

This new context has not gone unnoticed by U.S. business education providers. Pressured by domestic market maturity, dwindling subsidies, and a slow economic growth at home, and in helping China fill the void, domestic Universities recognize a tremendous opportunity for expansion into this extremely populous and vibrant of markets and are ready to respond.

U.S. Business Education in particular lends itself well to this type of export: It is the US crown jewel of strategic competitiveness; it is held in high regard throughout the world as demonstrated by the many foreign students and graduates of U.S. Business Programs; it is portable across nations and increasingly universal; it is politically unobtrusive and almost inconspicuous; and it is a substantial source of revenue for US-based universities.

However, differences in culture, tradition, philosophy, and socio-politico-economic infrastructure will certainly bring about challenges for American and other Western providers of Business Education internationally. Providers of Business Education to China or the services to restructure Chinese Business Education locally will have to take into account idiosyncrasies of tradition, culture, and environment in formulating their solutions and offerings. Thus the question is not only one of "adoption" of let's say US-based Western Business Programs by Chinese students and institutions, but also one of appropriate and relevant levels of "adaptation" of such programs.

In this article, we take the position that China's interests could probably be served, at least partially, with the adoption of Continental-European and Anglo-Saxon business education models by students and institutions respectively. In this context we will explore four strategies employed by foreign and domestic universities in China: (1) education of Chinese students in the U.S. (2) local education of Chinese students; (3) adaptation and reconfiguration of Chinese universities' business education departments; and (4) Distance Education provided to China from overseas, the U.S. for example. Subsequently, a framework is developed for the analysis of possible deployment by the U.S. education industry, and to assess educational competencies and capabilities towards a proper response to the ambitious Chinese educational effort. To that effect, we discuss the following questions:

(1) Is the Chinese learner receptive to Distance Education?
(2) How capable is the Chinese infrastructure to accommodate this paradigm?
(3) How can the market be penetrated?
(4) What adaptations need to be implemented?

The paper ends with a brief conclusion which attempts to discuss the applications and implications of these educational and technological innovations.

2. Traditional Paradigms of Educational Transfer

Generally, three mainstream paradigms were established since 1978 in China to deliver educational content and expose the Chinese to Western methods:

(1) Attracting Chinese students to study in the U.S.
(2) Direct presence in the Chinese market
(3) Reconfiguration Chinese business education

We will discuss each in this section.

2.1 *Attracting Chinese students to study in the U.S*

One powerful approach to the Chinese market is to attract more Chinese students and accommodate them in the domestic business school market. This is certainly not a novel approach, but is one adopted by many U.S. universities who have experience with international students. The Chinese students, in particular, are able to score highly on the standardized entrance examinations, such as the GMAT, and can improve the admittance profile and subsequent ranking of U.S. schools.

U.S. colleges and universities traditionally have been accommodating an increasing numbers of foreign students. But, with respect to China, this approach could enjoy renewed interest. Chinese GDP growth has been robust and accelerating for two decades and, thus, an increasing proportion of the future management elite can actually afford overseas education. Recent research suggests that China has sent over 320,000 students to study overseas in 103 countries from 1978 to 1998 (Shen 2000), and currently around 50,000 Chinese students study abroad every year (Yi 2001). This number is increasing at 20 percent annually *(People's Daily* 2001). English-speaking countries account for approximately 75 percent to 80 percent of Chinese students abroad and the top four destination countries favored by prospective Chinese students are the United States, Canada, the United Kingdom and Australia (Böhm & King 1999).

China's share of the total international students in these host countries has increased significantly in recent years. In the United States, United Kingdom and Australia, Chinese students make up more than 10 percent of all international enrollments. Thus, China has become the number one source country for these host countries. Of these Chinese students, about 30 to 40 percent are enrolled in business courses (Böhm & King 1999; Economist 2003).

Albeit cognizant of the new realities, with some relevant exceptions, traditional U.S. colleges and universities increasingly need an injection of a fresh student population following domestic saturation and the end of the Baby Boom impact. Originally conceived as regional monopolies, with little incentive for efficiency and effectiveness, universities are preoccupied with fund raising, campus building, and structures that barely accommodate the occasional self-selected foreign students. This happens with the usual administrative snags in registration, payment, and visa application processes, let alone large numbers of foreign students in a coordinated fashion. Due to the war on terrorism, attracting foreign students has been exacerbated by the recent immigration restrictions including additional interaction with the INS successor organization "USCIS".

But as a politician would say: "There are no problems, just new challenges and opportunities." We see this new complexity best addressed via specialization, performed by a new type of "education intermediary" that will "package" cohorts of students by undertaking the necessary marketing and administrative processing, evaluation, and acculturation efforts. As an example, such intermediation could be established on terms whereby the University stipulates profit sharing with the intermediary "outsources" a certain selection of core course to be taught by the educational intermediary in an effort to consolidate the foreign students into economically viable cohorts, and prepare them for the typical interactive environment in business schools' advanced courses and seminars. Such courses can then be integrated via traditional waivers or recognized directly if taught with the requisite quality. In other words, universities can deliver course content in the foreign country, say China, and admit the students to the latter part of the curriculum to the home country to receive a diploma. However attractive, it remains a "physical" environment, with all its ancillary constraints especially with respect to the students' financial endowment, and logistics related to the students' housing, work, family, etc.

Alternatively, the host institution can work out a matriculation agreement with the home institution which will be used as a contractual framework for a dual degree program delivered entirely in the host market. To do that, the University may need to develop a present in the host market, discussed below.

2.2 Direct presence in the Chinese market

Some of the renowned and endowed institutions have ventured down a more progressive path. For example, Fordham University's graduate business education entity (to name but one for its first-mover ambitions) maintains its "Beijing MBA" (BiMBA) in its entirety in China. This is the first foreign MBA degree in Beijing to be approved by the Chinese government. According to he Fordham's website (www.bimba.org), "[t]he goal of the Beijing International MBA is to provide world-class graduate business education for exceptional students and executives in China as well as for a small group of foreign students".

Profiles of entering students, both full- and part-time, are comparable to entering classes of top U.S. business schools. With all courses in the BiMBA program taught in English, it is possible for students from participating consortium schools like Fordham to attend a semester in Beijing for credit toward their MBA. In this way, the Beijing program supports the internationalization of the university's curriculum. Currently, student population at BiMBA is about 250, a substantial increase from the 80 students enrolled in its first class two years ago. Further, this year marked a special occasion in the program's development, with 22 members of the first BiMBA graduating class traveling to New York to participate in Fordham's diploma ceremonies. In a separate but related development, Fordham has agreed with the China Institute to create a pilot language program in Mandarin Chinese tailored to faculty who are planning to teach in Beijing and to students who wish to spend a semester at BiMBA."

Such comprehensive and involved efforts remain, however, the domain of the well endowed universities of the world. It may be true that the financial and administrative efforts of such an implementation are commensurate with the prestige and positioning that the school will enjoy in the long run, but rarely are such resources readily available. Though we certainly do not dismiss this strategy, we consider that it may not be generalizeable enough to benefit the average American college.

We would also point out that there is a significant difference between credible, renowned programs and the "hundreds of foreign involved MBA education or training programs [...] currently running in Mainland China, either permitted by the Chinese central government or in collaboration with regional authorities (Shi 2000)" according to Peng (2003). Peng (2003) further suggests that "[a]s the Chinese central government maintains strict control over foreign degrees being offered in China, a common way to tap into the market is to build alliances with local Chinese educational institutions. Other alternatives include cooperating with major multinational companies in China which have an immediate demand to train their local Chinese employees or selling courses over the Internet with assistance of a local agent to recruit and administrate students."

2.3 *Reconfiguring Chinese business education*

The most robust but also the most intensive approach is the direct investment into a distinct and specific Chinese academic business education culture. This, however, is a discussion that needs to include additional sociological and political considerations as it goes at the very core of Chinese management education traditions. For the three post-world-war decades, a command and planning model became ingrained as China's economic systems that reduced the enterprise entity to a mere production unit in the national economic system (Newell 1999). Western management theories introduced in the late 1890s were gradually replaced by Soviet-style socialist and Marxist ideology and didn't survive except for isolated instances such as at Shanghai Jiaotong University (Li & Maxwell 1989). In fact, Wang (1987) notes that such subjects as organizational behavior or Western style market economics were considered antisocialist and, understandably, were not allowed to be taught in Chinese higher education institutions before 1978 (Wang 1987).

Chinese higher education institutions emulated the Soviet structure of three types of institutions, i.e. comprehensive universities, technological institutes, and financial and economic colleges (Borgonjon & Vanhonacker 1994; Shi 2000) which map to three streams of management education philosophy. At comprehensive universities, management education focused on macro level issues to incorporate Marxist economics and socialist theory (Zhao 1997). A second stream stressed industrial management engineering (at technological institutes), largely influenced by Taylorian scientific management theory and emphasized quantitative methods (Shi 2000). The third stream with a financial management emphasis was delivered at specialized financial and economics colleges, catering to book-keeping requirements for the central-planned socialist economy (Wang 1987). Only after the open door policy following 1979, were more qualitative courses introduced, such as strategic management, marketing, human resource management, and management information systems. Interestingly, but expectedly, these patterns also coincided with the dominant ideologies of the day.

While the Cultural Revolution (1966-1976) stressed Marxist and socialist ideas, Taylorism became popular after 1979, allowing for improving production efficiency without threatening socialist ideology, yet allowing for quick economic reform (Borgonjon & Vanhonacker 1994). Traditional Chinese management education was thus biased towards a quantitative approach, away form a people oriented one, as observed by many Western scholars (for example, Borgonjon & Vanhonacker 1992; Branine 1996; Warner 1992).

The post-1979 dramatic economic transition, however, demanded unprecedented levels of new managerial competence, evolving from bureaucratic order-takers to innovative entrepreneurs (Newell 1999), as state owned enterprises (SOE) were gradually transformed from 'government production units' to independent economic entities with increased decisional autonomy, in-flow of FDI via numerous joint ventures rapidly increased, and thousands of private and rural (collectively-owned) enterprises have emerged with only limited policy guidance from local governments. Fan (1998) use a vivid metaphor to describe the new attitude towards this competitive, uncertain, and unpredictable environment: A Chinese manager felt like "a non-swimmer being suddenly plunged into the 'sea of market' by the force of reform [...] rushed in desperate search for new management concepts and techniques". (Fan 1998, p. 203)

In response, the Chinese government implemented several management training schemes throughout the 1980s by taking a 'look West' approach (Borgonjon & Vanbonacker 1994). Among them, two are important in terms of influencing the development of Chinese MBA education. The first was a cooperative management training agreement between the Chinese government and the United States' Department of Commerce in 1984, culminating in the establishment of the National Center for Industrial Science and Technology Management Development in Dalian (Fischer 1999; Li 1996). This Dalian-based program provided MBA courses from the State University of New York at Buffalo complemented by the then Dalian Institute of Technology for China-specific aspects (Li 1996). The second program was sponsored by the European Commission and the China Enterprise Management Association, with the China Europe Management Institute (CEMI) in Beijing in 1984 (Fischer 1999). This second Sino-Foreign program recruited both MBA and EMBA students, and drew teaching faculty from leading business schools across Europe through the network of the European Foundation for Management Development (EFMD) (Southworth 1999).

Although ostensibly successful these two international cooperative projects had distinct destinies. After 10 years and after graduating 241 MBA candidates propelled to high profile positions in the Chinese government (Li 1996), the Sino-US program folded due to the American government's inability to maintain its involvement (Fischer 1999). The Sino-European program on the other hand, after graduating 236 Chinese managerial personnel during it initial operation from 1984 to 1994 (Wang 1999) was relocated in September 1994 to Shanghai and renamed to China Europe International Business School (CEIBS), now a joint venture of the European Union Committee and the Shanghai Municipal Government with its proper facilities on the Pudong campus of Shanghai Jiaotong University (Southworth 1999). CEIBS is now a leading international MBA education institute in Mainland China, and was ranked the 43th worldwide as well number one in Asia for its English MBA programs (Economist Intelligence Unit 2002).

These two initiatives are credited with laying the foundation for subsequent proper Chinese efforts.

Deng Xiaoping's pragmatism and the dynamism of the new Chinese economy of the 1980s (Clarke 1999) triggered an urgent need for Chinese managers (Borgonjon & Vanhonacker 1994). Consequently, a series of developments resulted in Chinese domestic MBA programs since the late1980s (Shi 2000; Wang 1999; Zhao 1997). Initial progress to develop Chinese domestic MBA education was made in 1988 when a number of management professors were assembled by the national Academic Degrees Committee (ADC) to conduct a feasibility study with respect to MBA education in Chinese universities (Li 1996). Consequently, a task force was set up in 1989 to formulate a working plan regarding training objectives, admission criteria, course structure, teaching methods and degree conferment of MBA programs to be provided in Chinese universities (Shi 2000). Then in 1990, a national decree was issued by the State Council to legislate setting up MBA programs on a trial base in selected Chinese universities (Zhou 1998).

Formal MBA education started in the early 1990s in Mainland China. In 1991, a National MBA Coordination Group was organized to implement trial MBA programs and nine universities were authorized to offer experimental MBA programs with a total of 86 intakes (Wang

1999). An additional seventeen universities were added to the initial group, totaling 26 universities eligible to offer MBA education in China in 1993. As Chinese higher education institutes were still lacking the necessary expertise and teaching materials for MBA education, many of these experimental universities sought assistance from their Western counterparts: Nanjing University partnered with the University of Missouri-Columbia, Qinghua was assisted by the University of Western Ontario, and Beijing University cooperated with Fordham University. The Chinese MBA providers simply emulated Western curricula (Shi 2000).

To ensure the quality of these national MBA programs, a National MBA Guiding Committee was set up in 1994 to replace the previous National MBA Coordination Group (Zhou 1998) to standardize screening, admissions, and examinations practices (Shi 2000; Li 1996). In 1995, thirty more universities were approved to offer MBA programs (Shi 2000). A mandatory national MBA entrance examination system called GRK and modeled after the GMAT was established in 1997 (Zhao 1997). In addition, efforts were made to compile case materials that were specific to the Chinese business context (Wang 1999). With this increase of officially authorized MBA programs (62 currently), the annual enrollment of MBA students in Chinese universities has grown from 86 in 1991 to about 15,000 in 2002 (People's Daily 2002).

Peng (2003) estimates that the annual intake of MBA students will need to be expanded to around 30,000 by 2006 and he concludes that "[m]anagement education in Mainland China has evolved from a political-ideology-dominated model to an economic-function-oriented approach. In particular, the rapid business growth brought about by economic reform and the open door policy has created an unsatisfied demand for professional managers. Differing from those earlier pure policy implementers required in the central command system, the professional managers demanded for the free economy should, first of all, understand the underlying mechanism of a market economy. Furthermore, they should be able to utilize available resources to maintain sustainable corporate development in a dynamic competitive environment. To meet the demand for such professional managers, Western style MBA education was imported into China in the early

1980s and Chinese MBA education has experienced a dramatic growth in the last decade of the twentieth century." (Peng 2003, p.23)

3. Internet Mediated Distance Education in China

There is opportunity for Internet-mediated distance education models to be employed in China. The maturing of the Internet to a ubiquitous medium for learning, business, and lifestyles has also spurred an explosive proliferation of distance learning offerings in Business, especially due to the "Internet-readiness" of the content. But while we may consider the paradigm ubiquitous in the West, it may not enjoy the same acceptance level elsewhere (Shive, 2000). A careful analysis of the antecedents and success factors of Internet-mediated Distance Education to foreign students is paramount for the evaluation of this medium in the Chinese context. Four factors are evaluated herein:

(1) The Receptiveness of Chinese Students to Distance Learning
(2) Infrastructure Considerations
(3) Market Penetration Strategies
(4) Necessary Adaptations of Delivery, Content, and Pedagogy for the Chinese Market

3.1 *The receptiveness of Chinese students to distance learning*

From a historical perspective, the United States of America has advocated that Distance Learning (DL) models of education. These were put into place to help disadvantaged students and working students to reach higher academic qualifications. In China, the model has a significant advantage over other modes due to the increased sophistication of the market and the gap that exists between needed educational services and their supply.

Indeed, "Dual Mode" correspondence-based learning started the "first generation of long-distance education" [Yuhui 1988] as early as 1953 at the People's University of China. By 1997, this first generation mode was implemented in 635 conventional universities via their correspondence education divisions/schools, which provide for printed course materials, correspondence tutorials (assignments marking), compulsory face-to-face tutorials, and regular semester-end convocations.

The second generation was marked by the predominant use of the 'new broadcast media'. Indeed, China was one of the first countries to use radio and television for higher-educational purposes with the opening of its first Radio and Television University in 1960. In a phased approach, a first group of Metropolitan TV Universities also emerged in 1960. Though interrupted by the 'Cultural Revolution' (1966-76), these original initiatives experienced heightened interest after 1976, especially as a consequence of the Open Door policy. This socialist modernization project called for an extensive qualified work force. Although the general level of primary and secondary education in China was higher than in most developing countries, admission of students to higher education institutes was relatively limited.

In 1975, the enrolment rate in China's higher education was less than 2 per cent, whereas in ninety-two other developing countries the rate was over 4 per cent. The number of college and university students constituted a mere 0.7 per cent of China's adults above the age of 25. The number of qualified technicians and engineers accounted for only 2.5 per cent of the country's work force in state-owned enterprises and institutes. A turnaround could not be accomplished by relying solely on conventional colleges and universities within a short timeframe. This led to the founding of the National Radio and Television University in February 1978, subsequently culminating in the establishment of the National Radio and TV Universities system in 1979. A Central Radio and Television University (CRTVU) was set up in Beijing supported by a system of initially 28 provincial radio and television universities (PTVUs), 279 prefectural/civic branch schools and 625 district/county work stations.

In October of 1986, TVU teaching programs began to be transmitted by satellite every evening from 4.50 to 11 p.m. Forty-nine teaching hours of transmission time was thus added to thirty-three teaching hours per week via this microwave network. All these changes have provided new opportunities for TVUs to develop and expand. [For a comprehensive discussion of the Chinese DL in higher education up to 1988, see Yuhui 1988.]

We interpret this level of exposure and length of experience of the Chinese learner to Distance Education and non-traditional forms of delivery as a potential proxy for evidence of robust acceptance and receptiveness levels for today's Internet-mediated Distance Education, especially when considering the quickly evolving imaging technologies and video-conferencing possibilities due to rapid expansion of bandwidth, throughput, and capacity.

3.2 Infrastructure considerations

With respect to China's digital infrastructure the following milestones are ample evidence of its capability and quality (Ji'an 2001): At the end of 1994, sponsored by the former Education Commission of PRC, Tsinghua and other 9 universities, China completed the China Education and Research Network (CERNET) Pilot Project, the first TCP/IP-based public computer network in China. CERNET consists of a nationwide-backbone, regional networks, provincial networks, and campus networks, providing high speed transmission covering 30 main Chinese cities. The system is controlled by various ministries of the government allowing some room for private-sector participation with ChinaNet and China GBN (Tan 1999).

In 1996, Wang Dazhong, President of Tsinghua University, had the lead in advocating Distance Learning. In 1997, Hunan University, through cooperating with Hunan Telecom, established China's first on-line university. In 1998, Tsinghua University launched the on-line master programs. In September of the same year, the Ministry of Education officially entitled Tsinghua University, Beijing University of Post and Telecommunications, Zhejiang University and Hunan University as the first batch of educational institutions to pioneer the digital era of Distance Learning. August 1999, Beijing University and the Central Broadcast and TV University were added to the list. In 1999, the Ministry of Education promulgated the "Comments on Developing Advanced Distance Learning in China", stipulating guidelines, aims and tasks of Distance Learning in China. As it reads, the mandate for Distance Learning development focuses on "overall planning, demand driving, expanding deregulation and improving quality".

Another significant milestone was reached in December of 2000 as the "CERNET High-speed Backbone Project" was completed. In support, the Ministry of Education had released in July of 2000 the Provisional Administration Methods for Educational Website and On-line Schools, stipulating the jurisdiction of the Ministry over educational websites and Internet-based schools. The Ministry also granted Distance Learning licenses to Tsinghua and another 14 universities, and expanded the pioneer list to include 31 universities and colleges. It also promulgated the "Several Comments on Supporting Some Universities and Colleges to Set up Internet Education Schools and Pioneer Distance Learning" granting the 31 universities and colleges substantial autonomy in their Distance Learning initiatives, allowing them to set admissions criteria and determine the admission quota, to offer programs outside the subject catalogue, and to award degree certificates statutorily recognized for example.

In July of 2000, the 31 pioneers formed a consortium named "Coordination Team for Advanced Distance Learning in Higher Education", with the objective of enhancing inter-pioneer communication and cooperation and facilitating sharing and leveraging of educational resources. In October the China Advanced Distance Learning Satellite Broadband Multimedia Transmission Platform got into operation, allowing simultaneous transmission of video and multimedia channels at different rates. Moreover, the Internet access service provided by the platform enables high-speed interconnection with CERNET, forming a satellite-land consolidated bi-directional education network. Operation of this platform thoroughly changes the situation of the initial one-way transmission over the satellite TV network in China.

According to the latest estimates by the Ministry of Education the 31 pioneering institutions have accommodated nearly 190,000 degree seeking students. This vast infrastructural effort clearly demonstrates China' capabilities and readiness for interactive multimedia delivery of programs designed in the West.

3.3 Market penetration strategies

Potential Western providers of Distance Education to China must take note of market structural and cultural idiosyncrasies. The American model is characterized by private and competitive initiative, dominated by concerns for organic growth, and motivated predominantly by *effectiveness* concerns. And to maintain the parallel, in e-Commerce terms, it is a quest for *richness*. The Chinese model is grounded in the central planning tradition and culturally motivated by the concerns of a very large collectivist society for universal access to education and thus exploits the *efficiency* paradigm of Distance and Virtual Learning and, consequently the *reach*-paradigm of e-Commerce. This implies that the Chinese market cannot be approached the same way as the domestic market.

The cultural paradigm of collectivism demands level of large-scale cooperation and collaboration with the political superstructure just as much as at individual institution level. Traditionally, to enforce intimate level of cooperation, the Chinese economy has accommodated foreign investment only in form of joint ventures with equal ownership. This leaves little room for incremental and experimental small-scale partnerships, but requires potential providers to immediately demonstrate capacity for large coverage. This commoditization and liberalization of education requires careful unbundling and outsourcing of some aspects of the education process as well as the integration of partners from business and industry. While most college faculty knows how to "chalk-and-talk", the design and production of effective learning tools and activities in an online environment is a distinct skill. Teamwork between content specialists, curriculum designers, and online technicians form both cultures will be necessary, but can complicate the process and progress significantly (Shive 2000). While there is no magic solution to an endeavor of such ambitious magnitude, we advocate a multi-dimensional strategy that begins with partnership building as a distinct milestone long before content and delivery are considered.

3.4 Necessary adaptations of delivery, content, and pedagogy for the Chinese market

From an American perspective, what the e-Commerce revolution was for Business, Distance Learning was for Education! A fast-paced revolution atop a rather inert body of knowledge issued from several hundred years of evolution and centered on "talk-and-chalk" technology. But, analogous to Peter Drucker's vision in 'The Post Capitalist Society" of Management as a practiced but widely un-conceptualized discipline, in the now almost typical pattern for technological change, Distance Learning has come without much warning and is being practiced without much preceding theoretical development. Especially in the U.S. it is still treated as a phenomenon, with all its experimental characteristics.

As such, it cannot be leveraged to serve the Chinese market. The demands and the size of the Chinese market require standardization, quality control, and the recognition that course production is no longer the private preserve of individual faculty members. Ironically, this approach seems to have failed in the U.S. market as demonstrated by some recent divestments from NYU, Columbia, and other reputable institutions that couldn't recapture the initial investment into large-scale course-design. Finally, what attracts students to the American market is the very experience of the program delivered by English speaking faculty.

It will be important to recognize that Distance Education to China pedagogically involves more than posting asynchronously to bulletin boards and synchronous face-less chatting. Pedagogically then, we conjecture that the crucial success factor will be to evolve our own Distance Learning into Internet mediated video conferencing, the mode that made Distance Education in Chine successful in the first place. This in turn requires us to first and foremost review and revise our own distance learning models. Even if the Management Discipline so naturally seems to lend itself to face-less Distance Learning for the Western market, it remains that its mission expands when provided to China. It must stimulate more than just descriptive and analytical outcomes, it must become generative for an entire culture to change.

4. Conclusions and Discussions

This paper discusses approaches that can be used by educational institutions to penetrate foreign markets and capitalize on the market potential overseas. In this context, the authors advocate an internet-based computer-mediated approach to distance education that can work either standalone or in combination with traditional instruction to help bridge the space and time constraints of global markets. Clearly the potential of internet-mediated distance education goes beyond teaching via the internet within the interstate/inter-nation boundaries or within one discipline. A number of examples from the literature can be used to illustrate the broad range of potential applications and implications of these new technologies across the globe:

- *International marketing education:* Alon and Cannon (2000) showed how international internet-based experiential exercises enhance student learning in the domestic learning of international marketing by linking student teams around the world.

- *E-marketing:* Granitz and Greene (2003) pointed to the e-marketing capabilities of distance education including personalization, community, disintermediation, consumer tracking, enhance customer service, and mixing bricks and clicks.

- *Information technology management:* Loebbecke and Wareham (2003) offer a structured framework for strategic planning using information, communication and media technologies.

- *Economics:* Leamer and Stoper (2001) analyze the economic geography that changes as a result of internet mediated transfers of knowledge. Their results show that in fact the internet causes additional agglomeration of economic activity.

- *Library:* Lyman (1996) discussed the concept of a digital library that can balance the needs of markets and polity as well as intellectual property and the public interest.

- *Educational policy:* Selwyn and his colleagues (2001) claimed that internet mediated education can help overcome the social exclusion in education and lifetime learning practices. Johnson (1997) provided an overview of legal, cultural and technological issues surrounding the effort to develop an international model of distance learning that can be used in both developed and developing nations.

- *Early childhood education:* Ludlow (2003) examined how the use technology-mediated instruction to offer initial certification training and staff development activities to prospective and practicing teachers, and therapists, enabling internationalists to enroll in at a West Virginia University to complete the program.

As one can see from the above examples, Internet-mediated distance education has the potential to revolutionize traditional models of education, learning, teaching, and sharing information. While cultural, linguistic, legal/governmental and infrastructural differences still exist between countries, the present article shows how one may overcome these difficulties to create value for societies and educational institutions alike. There is pent-up demand for Western style education in emerging and transitioning markets that can fulfill the educational objectives of both these countries and the institutions that serve them in more ways that are currently perceived.

It is possible, for example, that delivering (English) language education by broadband video conferencing is a compelling topic across disciplines and that the market for this includes China as well as other developing countries. Conversely, an American student maybe able to leverage the Internet and instructors in China to learn Chinese language, culture, history, etc. Such efforts maybe cost efficient and effective educational tool. While we are not aware of such efforts in China, we hope that educational policy makers, university entrepreneurs, and supporting businesses will continue to break grounds in this area.

References

Alon, I and Cannon, N. (2000), "Internet-based experiential learning in international marketing: the case of Globalview.org," *Online Information Review*, 24 (5), pp. 349-356.

Anonymous 2002, 'MBAs Lose Perspective,' *Far Eastern Economic Review*, vol. 164, no. 21, May 30, pp. 24.

Berrell, M, Wrathall, J & Wright, P 2001, 'A Model for Chinese Management Education: Adapting the Case Study Method to Transfer Management Knowledge,' *Cross Cultural Management*, vol. 8, no. 1, pp. 28-44.

Biggs, J 1994, 'Asian learners through Western eyes: an astigmatic paradox,' *Australian and New Zealand Journal of Vocational Educational Research*, vol. 2, part 2, pp. 40-63.

Böhm, A & King, R 1999, *Positioning Australian Institutions for the Future: An analysis of the international education markets in the People's Republic of China*, IDP Education Australia, Sydney.

Bond, M H 1992, *Beyond the Chinese Face – Insights from Psychology*, Oxford University Press, Oxford.

Borgonjon, J & Vanhonacker, W R 1994, 'Management training and education in the People's Republic of China', *The International Journal of Human Resource Management*, vol. 5, no. 2, pp. 327-356. — & — 1992, 'Modernizing China's managers', *The China Business Review*, September-October, pp. 12-18.

Branine, M 1996, 'Observations on training and management development in the People's Republic of China', *Personnel Review*, vol. 25, no. 1, pp. 25-39.

Cai, F & Wang, M 2002, 'How fast and how far can China's GDP grow?' *China & World Economy*, vol. 10, no. 5, pp. 9-15.

Chan, S 1999, 'The Chinese learner – a question of style', *Education + Training*, vol. 41, no. 6/7, pp. 294-304.

Chen, K & Jefferson, G H 1992, 'Lessons from China's economic reform,' *Journal of Comparative Economics*, vol. 16, no. 2, pp. 201-226.

Chen, R 1997, 'The quality of managers and the quality of MBA education', *Academic Degree and Graduate Education*, issue 5, pp. 53-56 (in Chinese).

Chinese MBA Website 2002, 'China will speed up its development of MBA education', Retrieved December 18, 2002, from <http://www.mba.org.cn/news/old1205/704.html>, (in Chinese).

Clarke, T 1999, 'Economic growth, institutional development and personal freedom: the educational needs of China,' *Education + Training*, vol. 41, no. 6/7, pp. 336-343.

Dacko, S G 2001, 'Narrowing skill development gaps in marketing and MBA programs: the role of innovative technologies for distance learning,' *Journal of Marketing Education*, vol. 23, no. 3, pp. 228-240.

Economist 2003, 'Western promise: Chinese students are flooding in to British universities,' *The Economist*, vol. 366, issue 8317, March 29, p. 53.

Economist Intelligence Unit 2002, 'Which MBA?' Retrieved May 18, 2003, from <http://mba.eiu.com/index.asp?layout=2002rankings>.

Fan, Y 1998, 'The transfer of Western management to China,' *Management Learning*, vol. 29, no. 2, pp. 201-221.

Fischer, W A 1999, 'To change China redux: a tale of two cities,' *Education + Training*, vol. 41, no. 6/7, pp. 277-285.

Fordham University BiMBA Website, Retrieved July 31, 2003 from <http://www.bimba.org>,

Frazer, A J 1999, 'A scouting report on training options,' *The China Business Review*, vol. 26, no. 1, pp. 44-47.

Granitz, Neil and Greene, C.S. (2003), "Applying e-marketing strategies to online distance learning," *Journal Of Marketing Education*, 25, no. 1, pp. 16-30.

Haight, G T & Kwong, K K 1999, 'Future of the MBA in China', *Business Forum*, vol. 24, nos. 1/2, pp. 33-36.

Howe, W S & Martin, G 1998, 'Internationalisation Strategies for Management Education,' *Journal of Management Development*, vol. 17, no. 6, pp. 447-462.

Jaeger, A 1990, 'The Applicability of Western Management Techniques in Developing Countries: A Cultural Perspective,' in A. Jaeger and R. Kanungo (eds), *Management in Developing Countries*, Routledge, London.

Jennings, R 2001a, 'China embraces the MBA,' *Far Eastern Economic Review*, vol. 164, no. 28, p. 61. — 2001b, 'MBAs in China: Is the demand being met?' *China Staff*, September, pp. 6-8.

Ji'an, L, 'Advanced Distance Learning', China Education Daily, Retrieved August 30, 2003, from <http://www.edu.cn/20010830/200786.shtml>

Johnson, Andrea L (1997), "Distance learning and information technology: Working towards an international model," *Law Technology*, 30 (4), pp. 1-29.

Leamer, E., Storper, M. (2001), "The economy geography of the Internet age," *Journal of International Business Studies*, 32, no. 4, pp. 641-665.

Li, G & Maxwell, P 1989, 'Higher business education in China', Working Paper 4-89, Curtin Business School, Curtin University of Technology, Australia.

Li, S 1996, 'MBA: fast-track to success,' *Beijing Review*, April 8-14, pp. 17-20.

Lin, J Y & Cai, F 1996, 'The lessons of China's transition to a market economy,' *CATO Journal*, vol. 16, no. 2, Fall, pp. 201-232.

Liu, Z 1998, 'Earnings, education, and economic reforms in urban China,' *Economic Development and Cultural Change*, vol. 46, no. 4, pp. 697-725.

Loebbecke, C and Wareham, J. (2003), "The Impact of eBusiness and the Information Society on 'STRATEGY' and 'STRATEGIC PLANNING': An Assessment of New Concepts and Challenges," *Information Technology And Management*, 4, no. 2-3, pp. 165-182.

Ludlow, B. (2003), "An international outreach model for preparing early interventionists and early childhood special educators," *Infants and Young Children*, 16, no. 3, pp. 238.

Lyman, P. (1996), "What is a digital library? Technology, intellectual property, and the public interest," *Daedalus*, 125, no. 4, pp 1-33.

Martinsons, M G & Martinsons, A B 1996, 'Conquering cultural constraints to cultivate Chinese management creativity and innovation,' *Journal of Management Development*, vol. 15, no. 9, pp. 18-35.

Mooney, P 2000, 'China Plans to Expand Distance Education in Western Regions,' *The Chronicle of Higher Education*, July 13, 2000.

Morrison, W M 2002, *Issue Brief for Congress: China's Economic Conditions*, Foreign Affairs, Defense, and Trade Division, American Congress, updated May 29.

Newell, S 1999, 'The transfer of management knowledge to China: building learning communities rather than translating Western textbooks?' *Education + Training*, vol. 41, no. 6/7, pp. 286-293.

Network of Chinese MBA 2002, 'National MBA Guiding Committee,' Retrieved December 4, 2002, from <http://www.mba-a.com/mba05.asp>, (in Chinese).

Newton, A & Subbaraman, R 2002, *China: Gigantic Possibilities, Present Realities*, Lehman Brothers. *People's Daily* 2002, 'China will speed up development of MBA education, the planned recruitment for 2002 is 15,000', 12 May, (in Chinese).

2001, 'Hot and cool thinking over studying abroad – reflections on China international higher education exhibition tour 2001,' 18 February, (in Chinese).

Peng, Z 2003, 'Development of MBA Education in China: Opportunities and Challenges for Western Universities', The International Journal of Business and Management Education, Volume 11, No. 1, 2003

Redding, G 1990, *The Spirit of Chinese Capitalism*, Walter de Guyter, New York, NY.

Ribeiro, T 2002, 'China seeks growth,' *The Banker*, August, p. 82.

Selwyn, N, & Gorard, S, & Williams, S. (2001), "Digital divide or digital opportunity? The role of technology in overcoming social exclusion in U.S. education," *Educational Policy*, 15, no. 2, pp. 258-277.

Shen, L 2000, 'Thirty-two hundred thousands study overseas in twenty years,' *Life Daily*, 6 January, Study Abroad Information Section, (in Chinese).

Shi, Y 2000, 'A status report on MBA education in China,' *International Journal of Educational Reform*, vol. 9, no. 4, pp. 328-334.

Shive, G 2000, 'Distance Learning in a Digital Era: Implications for Sino-American Educational Exchanges', Retrieved Oct 13, 2003, from <http://www.chinaonline.com/commentary_analysis/intrelations/currentnews/secure/edusample.asp>

Southworth, D B 1999, 'Building a business school in China: the case of the China Europe International Business School (CEIBS),' *Education + Training*, vol. 41, no. 6/7, pp. 325-330.

Stevenson, H W & Lee, S Y 1996, 'The academic achievement of Chinese students,' in *The Handbook of Chinese Psychology*, ed. M. H. Bond, Oxford University Press, Hong Kong, pp. 124-142.

Tan, Z., & Foster, W. & Goodman, S. (1999), "China's state-coordinated Internet infrastructure," *Association For Computing Machinery. Communications of The Acm*, 42, no. 6, 44-52.

Thompson, E R 2000, 'Are Teaching Cases Appropriate in a Mainland Chinese Context? Evidence From Beijing MBA Students,' *Journal of Education for Business*, vol. 7, no. 1, pp. 108-112.

UNCTAD (2002), 'UNCTAD Predicts 27% Drop in FDI inflows This Year: China may outstrip U.S. as world's largest FDI recipient,' TAD/INF/PR/63, 24/10/02, Retrieved May 1, 2003 from
http://www.unctad.org/Templates/Webflyer.asp?docID=2832
&intItemID=2068&lang=1>.

Wang, Z 1987, 'Management education in China: retrospects and prospects', Management Paper No. 5, Graduate School of Management, Monash University, Australia.

Wang, Z M 1999, 'Current models and innovative strategies in management education in China', *Education + Training*, vol. 41, no. 6/7, pp. 312-318.

Warner, M 1993, 'Human Resource Management with Chinese Characteristics,' *International Journal of Human Resource Management*, vol. 4, no. 1, pp. 45-65. — *1992, How Chinese Managers Learn, Macmillan, London.*

Yi, Y 2001, 'Promotion war in hot for international education market,' viewed 1 July 2001, <http://abroad.netbig.com/head/h1/456/20010629/105509.htm>, (in Chinese).

Yuhui, Z 1988, 'China: Its Distance Higher-Education System,' *Prospects*, vol. 18, no. 2, pp. 217-28.

Zhao, S 1997, 'MBA graduate education in the People's Republic of China', *Journal of the Australian and New Zealand Academy of Management*, vol. 3, no. 1, pp. 59-66.

Zhou, W 1998, 'MBA education in China', *Journal of Higher Education in Jiangshu*, issue 3, pp. 64-66 (in Chinese).

II. Pedagogical Issues in China

Chapter 6

Teaching Students from Confucian Cultures

Romie F. Littrell
Auckland University of Technology

1. Introduction

Students and teachers bring with them the beliefs and expectations about schooling they have formed from their own life experiences. They also bring their language and their beliefs about education based on their native culture. This will, of course, lead to problems when the teacher and students are generally unfamiliar with the culture of the other, and are unaware of the cultural accommodations they must make.

The chapter will include a brief discussion of Confucianism, a discussion of East Asian learning styles, review of some theories of measuring cultures, and some prescriptions concerning practice.

Confucianism has had a major influence on Chinese life for two thousand years, so an understanding of the influence of Confucianism is essential for successful teaching in East Asia. In light of the China theme of this book, Confucian cultures will be discussed, with the majority of the information dealing with China.

2. Confucianism

The most important figure in North Asian civilization is unquestionably Confucius (Little and Reed, 1989). The Confucian philosophy of life has had strong influence for more than two thousand years on the cultures of China, Vietnam, Korea, and Japan.

Of interest in this chapter is Confucius' emphasis upon respect for education. Confucius emphasized by example and in his teaching the importance of education and self-cultivation in the service of the community and to achieve good government. His teachings have contributed to the development of a tradition of a ruthlessly competitive education process as a preparation for the holding of high office and as qualification to enter the bureaucracy. This kind of bureaucracy has governed China and continuously recorded this experience over several thousand years, in a manner unknown in the rest of the world. However, this respect for education is linked with a tradition of unquestioning obedience to superiors, teachers, parents, and a reverence for antiquity.

The resilience of the Confucian way of life in China can be seen in the results of "The Great Proletarian Cultural Revolution", a movement launched in 1966 to remold Chinese society and return to Communist ideals. It resulted in disaster, quickly degenerating into a power struggle between Mao Zedong, Chairman of the Communist Party, and his rivals. For many it resulted in a loss of tradition, a loss of their career, loss of hope and loss of trust. Many people lost their lives. A tenet of the revolution was elimination of the "Four Olds",

- Old ideas
- Old culture
- Old customs
- Old habits

Confucianism was adopted as China's guiding principles for the nation during the Han Dynasty (250 B.C. – 0, Christian/Gregorian calendar, used hereafter). During the Tang Dynasty (618-906), the Confucian Classics became the basis for the great civil service examinations that provided magistrates and bureaucrats (the "Mandarins") for the Chinese government.

Confucianism became the state ideology of Korea during the *Choson* Dynasty in Korea in 1392. The influence is still considerable.

Confucianism was introduced into Japan via Korea in the year 285. Confucianism was also become an integral part of the warrior or *bushido* culture.

Confucianism was introduced into Vietnam in the first century, during the Chinese domination. However, it was after Vietnam achieved independence from China that Chinese influence and Confucianism became important. As a political philosophy favorable to the monarchy, Confucianism was promoted and supported by the government. Vietnam was considered a Confucian state until the mid nineteenth century. In Vietnam official support of the Confucian system of philosophy lost prominence in more recent history, but its practice is still common among government bureaucrats and leaders.

The mythology that determines the reputation of Confucius today is, of course, largely the product of his long history of influence in China. The writings that are ascribed to him or his influence have set parameters that have been the dominant philosophical, social, and political force in the evolution of Chinese civilization.

Sometimes noted for denigrating engaging in commerce, Confucius himself stated, "Wealth and high station are what men desire" (*Analects*, IV: 5), however, later Confucians turned warnings against succumbing to the *temptation* of profit into a *condemnation* of profit, which meant that their influence was often turned against the development of Chinese industry and commerce. Thus, neo-Confucians themselves were perfectly happy to seek "wealth and high station," while stifling the ability of other Chinese to produce wealth. Over time, this became a debilitating influence in Chinese history. A more detailed discussion of Confucius and commerce is available in Lu (2003).

Despite the hold of Confucianism on China, significant influences of the particular implementation of communism in China do exist. A useful discussion of some of the issues is available in Li (2004).

The influence of Confucianism may be waning, as Egri and Ralston (2004), in a study of Chinese managers in three age cohorts of "less than 41 years", "41–51 years", and "older than 51 years", reported younger managers to be higher in individualism values, lower in collectivism values, and lower in the values of Confucianism, with the differences significant a $p < 0.05$ or better.

3. East Asian Learning Styles

Reid (1997) and Peacock (2001) carried out studies indicating that lecturer-student mismatches in teaching and learning styles cause learning failure, frustration and demotivation.

Significant study of learning styles across cultures began in the 1980s in the USA, driven by teachers of English to speakers of other languages. If you are not familiar with "learning styles", a useful textbook is Reid (1998), and "Learning styles and pedagogy in post-16 learning: A systematic and critical review" is available for download at no charge. This report critically reviews the literature on learning styles and examines in detail thirteen of the most influential models. The report concludes that results of assessment are a function of which instrument is chosen. The implications for teaching and learning in tertiary are serious and should be of concern to learners, teachers and trainers, managers, and researchers in education, the website is: http://www.lsda.org.uk/files/PDF/1543.pdf.

As noted above, Egri and Ralston (1999) have demonstrated significant generational differences in individualism, collectivism, and the influence of Confucianism. However, the long influence of a stable cultural milieu in East Asia, with major international interactions being between neighboring countries, has led to a unique cultural cluster in East Asia, which has in turn led to a particular learning style on the part of students from the area. In theory, there exist as many learning styles as there are learners, but national groups have proven to demonstrate similarities. Various theorists have defined several schemes of classifying learning styles.

Montgomery (2004) comments that she used the Canfield learning styles inventory (www.tecweb.org/styles/canfield1.html) when teaching Economics in English in China. The inventory was developed for K-12 and then turned into a college level curriculum tool in the USA. "It is such a foreign way to look at learning (in China) that it generates a great deal of discussion about cultural differences."

Rao (2001) and Clenton (1999) have provided excellent discussions of the many student learning styles observed in East Asia. Teaching in most East Asian countries is traditionally dominated by a teacher-centered, book-centered method and an emphasis on rote memory (Liu & Littlewood, 1997). These traditional teaching approaches have resulted in a number of common learning styles in East Asian countries.

3.1 *Introverted learning*

For this style, knowledge is something to be transmitted by the teacher rather than discovered by the learners; the students receive learning from the teacher rather than interpret it. Harshbarger et al. (1986) reported Japanese and Korean students are often quiet, shy and reticent in classrooms. They dislike public touch and overt expressions of opinions or displays of emotions, indicating a reserve that is the hallmark of the Western definition of introverts. Chinese students likewise name "listening to teacher "as their most frequent activity in senior school classes (Liu & Littlewood, 1997). All these claims are supported by Sato (1982); she compared the participation of Asian students in classroom interaction with that of non-Asian students. Sato found that the Asians took significant fewer speaking turns than did their non-Asian classmates (36.5% as opposed to 63.5%). Asian students are reluctant to "stand out" by expressing their views or raising questions, particularly if this might be perceived as expressing public disagreement (Song, 1995).

3.2 *Closure-oriented style*

Closure-oriented students dislike ambiguity, uncertainty, or fuzziness; to avoid these, they will sometimes jump to hasty conclusions from incomplete information. Sue and Kirk (1972) found Asian students to be autonomous, more dependent on authority figures, and more obedient and conforming to rules and deadlines. Harshbarger et al. (1986) noted that Korean students insist that the teacher be the authority and are disturbed if this does not happen. Japanese students often want rapid and constant correction from the teacher and do not feel comfortable with multiple correct answers.

3.3 *Analytic and field-independent*

Analytic learners are sequential, orderly and organized, and focus on details and tend to formulate plans. If you are "field independent," you will be able to focus on the relevant details and not be distracted by unnecessary details. Field dependence means being "holistically oriented", going from the big picture to the detail. Generally, field independent learners are better at spatial tasks, math, and science. Individuals with an analytical learning style tend to focus on sequential details rather than the overall structure. People with a relational (global) learning style tend to relate all of the information to the overall structure and focus on the interactions involved. Oxford & Burry-Stock (1995) state that the Chinese, along with the Japanese, are often detail-and precision-oriented, showing some features of the analytic and field-independent styles. They have no trouble picking out significant detail from a welter of background items and prefer learning strategies that involve dissecting and logically analyzing the given material, searching for contrasts, and finding cause-effect relationship.

3.4 Visual learning style

Reid (1987) found Korean, Chinese and Japanese students to be visual learners, with Korean students ranking the strongest. They like to read and obtain a great deal of visual stimulation. For them, lectures, conversations, and oral directions without any visual backup can be very confusing and anxiety producing. This visual learning style stems from a traditional classroom teaching in East Asia, where most teachers emphasize learning through reading and tend to put a great deal of information on the blackboard. The perceptual channels are strongly visual (text and blackboard), with most auditory input closely tied to the written.

3.5 Concrete-sequential

Students favoring this learning style are likely to follow the teacher's guidelines to the letter, to be focused on the present, and demand full information rather than drawing their own conclusions. They prefer learning materials and techniques that involve combinations of sound, movement, sight, and touch that can be applied in a concrete, sequential, linear manner. Oxford & Burry-Stock (1995) found that Chinese and Japanese are concrete-sequential learners, and use a variety of strategies such as memorization, planning, analysis, sequenced repetition, detailed outlines and lists, structured review and a search for perfection. Many

Korean students also prefer situations where they have rules to follow (Harshbarger et al, 1986), indicating a concrete-sequential style.

3.6 Thinking-oriented and reflective styles

These styles are closely related to visual, concrete-sequential, analytic and field-independent. Nelson (1995) found Asian students to be more overtly thinking-oriented than feeling-oriented. They typically base judgment on logic and analysis (rather than on feelings of others), the emotional climate, and interpersonal values. Compared with American students, Japanese students, like most Asians, show greater reflection (Condon, 1984), as shown by the concern for precision and for not taking risks in conversation (Oxford et al, 1992). Typical is "the Japanese student who wants time to arrive at the correct answer and is uncomfortable when making a guess" (Nelson, 1995, p.16). The Chinese students have also been identified to posses the same type of thinking orientation by Anderson (1993).

The generalizations made above about learning styles in East Asia do not apply to every representative of all East Asian countries; many individual exceptions of course exist. Nevertheless, these descriptions do have a basis in research. Worthley (1987, in Rao, 2001) noted that while diversity within any culture is the norm, research shows that individuals within a culture tend to have a common pattern of learning and perception when members of their culture are compared to members of another culture.

Comparison of East Asian learning styles with those of students from other cultures will indicate differences, and understanding and accommodating the differences should be a goal of a dedicated teacher. There is no clear evidence that any one style is generally better than another for efficient and effective learning, and cannot alter how we prefer to learn. Accommodation is the responsibility of the lecturer.

4. Cultural Differences in Discourse

Taylor (1990, chapter III) points out that in addition to learning style differences between cultural groups, variations also exist in the rules for general discourse in oral communication. Teachers and students will naturally follow the assumptions and rules from their respective cultures. Discourse rules govern such aspects of communication as:

- Opening or closing conversations;
- Taking turns during conversations;
- Interrupting;
- Using silence as a communicative device;
- Knowing appropriate topics of conversation;
- Interjecting humor at appropriate times;
- Using nonverbal behavior;
- Expressing laughter as a communicative device;
- Knowing the appropriate amount of speech to be used by participants;
- Sequencing of elements during discourse.

A careful review of these aspects of communication by a lecturer will lead to the conclusion that practically everything one does in a classroom can lead to cross-cultural misunderstandings.

5. Matching Teaching Styles with Learning Styles

An imperfect tool (English only), but providing instant feedback, is available on the Internet, providing a limited set of styles, is the learning styles diagnostic developed in the USA by Barbara A. Soloman and Richard M. Felder at North Carolina State University in Raleigh, North Carolina, USA, at http://www.engr.ncsu.edu/learningstyles/ilsweb.html

From this tool you can get some idea about your learning styles, which will affect your teaching, as can your students. Ideally, you need the assessment of the various styles of your students prior to developing course materials. The general recommendation for solving the problem of lack of knowledge concerning styles is to design the course to use techniques that support ALL learning styles. Which, given enough time and money, is a wonderful idea. If you don't have enough time and money, consider the following suggestions from a panel session at the March 1999 National Meetings of the American Association of Higher Education, paraphrased and organized by McKinney (2004). McKinney provides examples of how teacher's teaching style can be matched with students' learning style in East Asian settings. She obtained the ideas from literature review; responses to a questionnaire sent to selected overseas students in the USA from Japan, Korea and China in Australia; and her teaching experience in China:

5.1. Diversity in design, structure, and strategies of the course

McKinney (2004) suggest some techniques for accommodating a variety of student learning styles in class:

- Have your students take surveys of their learning styles and adjust the class to who they are, or provide more options based on the diversity of styles;
- Use several diverse forms of assessment (oral exams, take-home exams, essay exams, portfolios, projects, group work, journals, group quizzes, performances, presentations, creative writing, poster sessions, etc.);
- Give students background knowledge tests (pretests) and adjust material or provide alternative learning sequences;
- Use multimedia, broadly defined: text, audio, video, overheads, computers, discussion, group work, lecture, poetry, music, art, touch to present material;
- Present verbal material in more than one way and use many examples;
- Make use of technology to vary modes of learning, and for asynchronous learning
- Recommend or require diverse out-of-class learning opportunities.

Identifiable learning styles exist for students in most East Asian societies. A native Western-educated and experienced lecturer engaged in teaching East Asian students is likely to confront a teaching-learning style conflict. Such style differences between students and teachers consistently and negatively affect student performance (Wallace and Oxford, 1992). Matching appropriate teaching approaches with students' learning styles can increase motivation and achievement (Brown, 1994).

6. Chinese School Class Organization

Chinese students, in the past, and in many cases today, are grouped into classes with no concern for ability, and the grouping may remain relatively stable from lower grades through university level education. These class groups may take all their classes together and stay together throughout their educational career. A "Class Manager" is usually elected by the class or appointed by the university. The Class Manager is responsible for managing communications between the students, the departments, the instructors, and the school administration. He or she will take attendance in classes and report to the instructor, arrange and supervise study periods, plan class outings, and organize and supervise most class activities. There may be co-managers, a male and a female. There is no consistent relationship between being a class manager and academic achievement; other factors are influential. The class manager may change from time to time.

A long tradition in this environment is for the better students in the class to tutor and assist the weaker students in the class. This could include assisting the weaker students during examinations at the university.

In schools in Western cultures the intent of an examination is to measure the knowledge of the individual. In China you may be surprised to see that assisting classmates on examinations, what is called "cheating" in schools in Western cultures, may be ignored or tolerated in Chinese schools. Many consider it a duty for those with greater ability to assist those with less ability, even on exams. If the college group is based upon the middle school attended, this assistance may have been going on for ten or more years. If the lecturer wishes to impose Western standards in class, this should immediately be made clear to the students orally and in writing.

Montgomery (2004), a teacher fluent in Chinese and English, related experiences with the behavior of freshman through senior level Chinese students in Economics classes taught in English. She coins the phrase "lateral learning" to describe in-class learning and for behavior in in-class quizzes. When she would ask a question about the assigned reading and pause, waiting for a volunteer to answer, instead of one person raising their hand immediately, the students often talked about it first among neighbors in their row. There was a quick, informal agreement process in each row; then the best speaker among them would answer. If she called on people to answer directly they most often said they did not know and that she should ask someone else, usually identifying the best speaker.

Quizzes were difficult because in the "lateral learning" approach students would debate the quiz answers aloud despite rules against this. They were busy looking at each other's papers and didn't seem at all embarrassed about it if she told them that was not allowed. Finals and major mid-term tests were highly structured and closely monitored by the Chinese university staff and although some cheating occurred, not very much.

Montgomery (2004) comments,

> "I think for all of the emphasis on teachers as sacred cows in China, the English teachers need to be a lot more sensitive to the structural issues they are facing and adapt to them. I don't think the University I taught in had a clue about what I saw there – they are too embedded in the culture to rethink how to make the English-language classes more effective – "more effective" to me became allowing students the chance to talk more among themselves and self-correct. They learn this process early on.
>
> "I also observed these informal, lateral classroom structures in the local elementary school where my (Chinese-speaking) daughter attended school. They are extremely crowded conditions and only one or two teachers per 50+ kids. The desks can't be moved into groups so all kids face forward. But the learning is still "lateral" – by that I mean they check in with each other in the rows, usually five of them. The teacher walks up and down rows if she can or skirts the classroom when there is not enough room.
>
> "The thinking and correcting goes in a lateral fashion among those who find the answer first and pass it through

the rows. This helps the teacher too. The students then ask each other questions. If they still don't get it students gather around the one who doesn't get it and help him/her until they do understand. The classrooms are quite noisy and chaotic at times But they sure learn math don't they.

"In the USA (for certain classes) we might put four desks together and have students work in these modules to come up with answers. In China, there is simply not enough classroom space.

"Needless to say, after re-entry to the USA, students in my daughter's class were shocked when she would lean over both sides of her desk and ask what answers they got! They accused her (rightly so in our culture) of cheating. She felt totally left out of the learning process."

7. Comparisons of Values

Chart 1

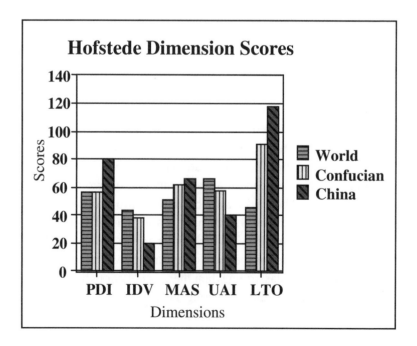

Hofstede (1994) has pointed out,

> "Values represent the deepest level of a culture. They are broad feelings, often unconscious and not open to discussion, about what is good and what is bad, clean or dirty, beautiful or ugly, rational or irrational, normal or abnormal, natural or paradoxical, decent or indecent. These feelings are present in the majority of the members of the culture, or at least in those persons who occupy pivotal positions."

There is considerable support for the belief that the behavior of people coming from a country will be shaped for the most part by the same values and norms as their compatriots (Hofstede, 1991; Smith and Bond, 1998). Also, it is important to point out that culture is not the only factor influencing human behavior. General dimensions of culture can be established at a culture level, but they may not necessarily be reflected in the behavior of each individual from that culture. In other words, using data from one level of analysis (such as the culture level of analysis) at another level of analysis (the individual level) is inappropriate. This type of error is labeled an "ecological fallacy" by Hofstede (2003, 1991). Culture-level analysis always reflects "central tendencies...for the country" (Hofstede, 1991, p.253). It does not predict individual behavior.

The ITIM Culture and Management Consultants website (www.itim.org) provides the currently available dimension scores and discussions of their meanings and relationships. On their website http://www.geert-hofstede.com/, one can select the China link, to http://www.geert-hofstede.com/hofstede_china.shtml

Looking at Chart 1, we see that even among Confucian Asian cultures China is somewhat unique.

7.1 Hofstede: A national cultural values at school

Concerning values and education, Hofstede (2002) has conveniently provided us with charts, see Table 1, defining a few critical descriptions of the expectations of members of cultures having higher and lower scores on the original four value dimensions for various social milieu.

Table 1. Hofstede's (2002) descriptions of expected behaviors as a function of cultural value scores and environment.

Small Power Distance Societies	Large Power Distance Societies
In the family:	
1. Children encouraged to have a will of their own 2. Parents treated as equals	1. Children educated towards obedience to parents 2. Parents treated as superiors
At school:	
1. Student-centered education (student initiative) 2. Learning represents impersonal "truth"	1. Teacher-centered education (order) 2. Learning represents personal "wisdom" from teacher (expert, guru)
At work place:	
1. Hierarchy means an inequality of roles, established for convenience 2. Subordinates expect to be consulted 3. Ideal boss is resourceful democrat	1. Hierarchy means existential inequality 2. Subordinates expect to be told what to do 3. Ideal boss is benevolent autocrat (good father)
Collectivist Societies	**Individualist Societies**
In the family:	
Education towards "we" consciousness Opinions pre-determined by group Obligations to family or in-group: - Harmony - Respect - Shame	Education towards "I" consciousness Private, personal opinions expected Obligations to self: - Self-interest - Self actualization - Guilt
At school:	
Formal learning is for the young only Learn how to do	Education can be lifelong Learn how to learn
At work place:	
Value standards different for in-group and out-groups: particularism Other people are seen as members of their group Relationship prevails over task Moral model of employer-employee relationship	Same value standards apply to all: universalism Other people seen as potential resources Task prevails over relationship Calculative model of employer-employee relationship

Feminine Societies	Masculine Societies
In the family:	
1. Stress on relationships 2. Solidarity 3. Resolution of conflicts by compromise and negotiation	1. Stress on achievement 2. Competition 3. Resolution of conflicts by fighting them out
At school:	
1. Average student is norm 2. System rewards student's social adaptation 3. Student's failure at school is relatively minor accident	1. Best students are norm 2. System rewards student's academic performance 3. Student's failure at school is disaster, may lead to suicide
At work place:	
1. Assertiveness ridiculed 2. Undersell yourself 3. Stress on life quality 4. Intuition	1. Assertiveness appreciated 2. Oversell yourself 3. Stress on careers 4. Decisiveness
Weak Uncertainty Avoidance Societies	**Strong Uncertainty Avoidance Societies**
In the family:	
1. What is different is ridiculous or curious 2. Ease, indolence, low stress 3. Aggression and emotions not shown	1. What is different is dangerous 2. Higher anxiety and stress 3. Showing of aggression and emotions accepted
At school:	
1. Students comfortable with: 2. Unstructured learning situations 3. Vague objectives 4. Broad assignments 5. No time tables 6. Teachers may say "I don't know"	1. Students comfortable with: 2. Structured learning situations 3. Precise objectives 4. Detailed assignments 5. Strict time tables 6. Teachers should have all the answers
At work place:	
1. Dislike of rules, written or unwritten 2. Less formalization and standardization	1. Emotional need for rules, written or unwritten 2. More formalization and standardization

In Hofstede (2002), the five dimensions of national cultures were related to expectations of behavior.

1. Expectations of Inequality can lead to reticence of students to interact with lecturer:
    Less interaction: Large Power Distance
    More interaction: Small Power Distance

2. Reaction to the unfamiliar can influence openness to new ideas and new ways of doing things:
    Fight: Strong Uncertainty Avoidance
    Tolerate: Weak Uncertainty Avoidance

3. Relation with in-group can affect the perception of the lecturer as and insider or outsider, and determine attitudes toward assisting other students:
    Loose relationship: Individualism
    Tight relationship: Collectivism

4. Emotional gender roles might affect attitudes toward male and female lecturers and fellow students:
    Different: Masculinity
    Same: Femininity

5. Need gratification:
    Later: Long Term Orientation
    Now: Short Term Orientation

Chinese practices that arise out of their national cultural value of high Power Distance are as follows:

- Inequalities are expected, accepted, and desired
- Less powerful subordinates should be dependent on the powerful superiors who must protect them and take care of their careers and welfare
- Parents, teachers, bosses, must all be obeyed (and not questioned).
- Age brings seniority in the firm or organization
- The ideal boss is a benevolent autocrat, parent

- Privileges for managers are expected and popular
- Subordinates expect to be told what to do

Lecturers experienced in working in low Power Distance cultures, and who expect students to engage in considerable amounts of interaction and give-and-take in the classroom, will need to carefully plan and nurture development of the interaction. Using the traits of "expecting to be told what to do" and "obeying and not questioning superiors" the lecturer can lead the class to develop student-teacher oral interaction, perhaps even to the point of questioning the validity of the opinions expressed by the lecturer.

7.2 Placing yourself in context

After becoming familiar with the definitions of Hofstede's value dimensions one can fairly accurately place oneself on the continua. However, actually using the instrument to place yourself is far more valid and reliable. Differences in your values and the expected values of students from a Chinese culture can provide guidelines for explaining your approach to teaching vs. their approach to learning. It can also help you design instruction.

7.3 Shalom Schwartz' cultural values system

The work of Shalom Schwartz considers relations of cultural value emphases to national differences in the importance of values or goals. Schwartz' (1992, 1994a, 1994b) basic contention is that the types of goals whose pursuit is encouraged and rewarded, rather than discouraged and sanctioned, depend in part on the prevailing cultural value emphases in a society. Moreover, other things being equal, the goals chosen by teachers to motivate students will be more effective if they are compatible with prevailing cultural emphases. No one type of goal setting is likely to be the most effective across all cultures.

Correlations between these measures and Hofstede's indicate that although these new measures may have some advantages, Hofstede's data is more dependable than many had thought.

Ralston's China and Vietnam studies (Ralston et al., 1993, 1996, 1997, 1999a, 1999b, Egri and Ralston, 2004) employing the Schwartz Value Survey to assess managerial values are by far the most thorough and significant work in the study of differences between values of managers in East Asia and other national cultures. Results from studies yielding comparisons across several years between Chinese managers and US and Hong Kong Managers should be reviewed. The differences found are consistent with Hofstede's characterizations presented and discussed above.

7.4 *Expectations of "Western" lecturers*

Another difference in East Asian and Western students is the collection of environmental actors that transmit values. Astill, Feather, and Keeves (2002) from a study of 12th year Australian high school students showed that sex of student, language background, the religious involvement of the student, parental social position and the values held by parents and peer groups had much greater effects upon the students' values than the schools and their teachers. From this study it is evident that to be maximally effective, teachers of culturally distant and diverse students must consider differences between the lecturer's values and those of the students. Contrasting this finding with the Confucian philosophy and East Asian classroom practices noted above, the expectations of Confucian culture students and "Western" lecturers can be at odds.

8. A Prescription

Frequently lecturers from tertiary institutions do not have formal education in methods of teaching. Under the best of circumstances, with intelligent students and lecturers dedicated to teaching and learning, this lack is not an issue in performance in the classroom. However, with a lecturer and students from two or more different cultural backgrounds, one or the other operating in a second language, good teaching technique can go a long way in making life easier for everyone.

Chalmers and Fuller (1996) and the *Teaching and Educational Development Institute* of Australia, www.tedi.uq.edu.au indicate that for maximum student learning and retention, approximately only 50 percent of the material presented in any lecture should be new. The rest of class time should be devoted to material or activities designed to reinforce the material in students' minds. Chalmers and Fuller specify processes to follow:

1. Provide a preview of information prior to an explanation
2. Organize information within a step-by-step lesson sequence
3. Assess student learning when information is being given, actively and frequently
4. Signal transitions between information; the key is to make the transition explicit
5. Use multiple examples to illustrate information points (obtain student feedback to see if the examples are understood.
6. Stress important points during explanations
7. Provide for brief pauses at appropriate times during the lecture (Research suggests that the amount of notes a student takes correlates positively with achievement); teachers talk at a rate of 120-240 words per minute, many students are only capable of taking notes at a rate of 20 words per minute. In addition, one study (Ruhl et al. 1987) demonstrated that pausing periodically for as much as two minutes so that students could compare notes, led to a significant increase (both statistically and educationally) in both short-term and long-term recall.
8. Eliminate additional unexplained content nonessential to current explanation
9. Review information frequently

Carefully designing classroom processes and procedures will facilitate learning in cross-cultural, multi-lingual situations by providing a more structured environment for both lecturer and students.

9. Conclusions

Many tertiary educators already have considerable experience dealing with culturally diverse groups of students, due to the explosive growth of export education in developed and developing countries. Nonetheless, the situation is changed when the educator is asked to perform in a country with a high cultural distance from the home country. Careful planning and execution of classroom education is of particular importance, and should include:

- As thorough a study as possible of the history, sociology, psychology, anthropology, legal systems, and business practices of the culture in which the educator will work to develop an awareness of differences
- A thorough understanding of the culture and value *differences* between the educators home country and the country in which the education will be delivered; a presentation and discussion of these differences at the beginning of the course is helpful to everyone
- Specific knowledge of the variety of learning styles that may be common to students in the cultural environment in which the educator is working
- Thoughtful design and delivery of classroom instruction that takes multiple learning styles into consideration
- Focus on the delivery rate of speech, with frequent feedback checks from students
- Adjustment of expectations as to what can be taught and read in the time schedule of the course, compared to the educator's home country
- From personal experience teaching in China, the author has found performance on assessments in English to be improved when reading material to be studied is available in both English and Chinese; quite a number of publishers provide both English and Chinese translations of popular textbooks; the University of Western Ontario, for example, produces some case studies in multiple languages
- When designing content for delivery in China, Chinese branding and images need to be considered when constructing case studies or using examples. The People's Daily newspaper website http://english.peopledaily.com.cn/, publishes articles on Chinese brands, and the annual top-ranked brands report. Publication of

case studies of Chinese businesses is growing, with many available from the University of Hong Kong, the University of Western Ontario Ivey Business School, Harvard Business School, and the European Case Clearing House at Cranfield University in the UK.

We use averages, generalizations, summaries and such to create categories that we can comprehend and remember. However, individual behavior is in response to a unique set of genetic, learning, and contingency factors. The competent educator is one who can quickly and effectively adapt to changing information.

Endnotes

[1] Schwartz and Ros (1995) discuss cultural level value differences between US, East Asian, and European teachers and students. The relationships in the article are rather complex, and their analysis is beyond the scope of this chapter. The findings concerning relative values across the three regions do not differ from those discussed above.

References

Allport, GW, PE Vernon and G Lindzey (1970). *Manual for the study of values*. Boston: Houghton Mifflin.

Anderson, J (1993). Is a communicative approach practical for teaching English in China? Pros and cons. *System*, 21(4), 471-480.

Astill, BR, NT Feather, and JP Keeves (2002). A multilevel analysis of the effects of parents, teachers and schools on student values. *Social Psychology of Education*, 5 (4), 345-363.

Brown, H (1994). *Principles of language learning and teaching*. Englewood Cliffs, NJ: Prentice Hall Regents.

Chalmers, D and R Fuller, (1996). *Teaching for learning at university*, London: Kogan Page.

Clenton, J (1998). Learning styles and the Japanese, MA dissertation. University of Sussex Language Institute,

Clenton, J (1998). Learning Styles and the Japanese, MA dissertation. University of Sussex Language Institute, http://www.sussex.ac.uk/langc/skills/LearningStylesJapanese.pdf, [accessed 1 October 2004] and in Rao, Z (2001) Matching Teaching Styles with Learning Styles in East Asian Contexts. *The Internet TESL Journal*, VII(7), http://iteslj.org/Techniques/Zhenhui-TeachingStyles.html [18 September 2004].

Condon, J (1984). *With respect to the Japanese*. Yarmouth, ME: Intercultural Press

Duan, X-R (2003). Chinese higher education enters a new era. *Academe*, 89(6), 22.

Egri, C and D Ralston (2004). Generation cohorts and personal values: A comparison of China and the United States. *Organization Science*, 15(2), 210-230.

Friesner, T and M Hart (2004) A Cultural analysis of e-learning for China. *Electronic Journal of e-Learning*, 2(1), 81-88.

Harshbarger, B., T Ross, S Tafoya, and K Via (1986). Dealing with multiple learning styles in the ESL classroom. Symposium presented at the Annual Meeting of Teachers of English to Speakers of Other Languages, San Francisco, CA.

Hedberg, J and I Brown (2002). Understanding cross-cultural meaning through visual media. *Educational Media International*, 39(1), 23-30.

Hofstede, G (1994). The Business of international business is culture. *International Business Review*, 3(1): 1-14.

Hofstede, G (1996). *Cultures and organizations: Software of the mind*. London: McGraw-Hill.

Hofstede, G (2002) Europe: Strengths and pitfalls of diversity. *2nd International Conference on Human Resource Management in Europe Trends and Challenges*, Athens University of Economics and Business, Athens, October 17. http://www.mbc.aueb.gr/hrconference/application.htm [21 June 2003].

Hofstede, G (2003) *Culture's consequences: Comparing values, behaviors, institutions and organizations across nations*, 2nd edition, Newbury Park, CA: Sage.

Hofstede, G (2004a). A summary of my ideas about national culture differences. http://feweb.uvt.nl/center/hofstede/page3.htm, (accessed 24 September 2004).

Hofstede, G (2004b). Private communication.

Hofstede, G. (2001). *Culture's consequences: Comparing values, behaviors, institutions, and organizations across nations. Second edition*. Sage. Beverly Hills. http://www.abdwebsite.com/2001proceedings/01pSmotherman-Kooros.pdf, [accessed 17 August 2003].

http://www.cat.ilstu.edu/teaching_tips/handouts/support.shtm l [16 September 2004].

http://www.sussex.ac.uk/langc/skills/LearningStylesJapanese.pdf, [accessed 1 October 2004].

Kumar, K and MS Thibodeaux (1999). Differences in Value Systems of Anglo-American and Far Eastern Students: Effects of American Business Education. *Journal of Business Ethics*, 17(3), 253-262.

Li, Shaomin (2004). Why Is Property Right Protection Lacking in China? An Institutional Explanation. *California Management Review*. 46(3): 100-115.

Little, R and W Reed (1989). *The Confucian renaissance*. Sydney: The Federation Press.

Liu, NF and W Littlewood (1997). Why do many students appear reluctant to participate in classroom learning discourse? *System*, 25(3), 371-384.

Lu, L (2003). "Influences of Confucianism on the market Economy of China," In *Chinese Culture, Organizational Behavior and International Business Management*, I Alon, (ed.), Westport, CT: Preager.

McKinney, Kathleen (2004). Center for the advancement of teaching, Illinois State University.

Montgomery, E (2004). Ph.D. student at the Fielding Graduate Institute, California, private communication.

Nelson, G (1995). Cultural differences in learning styles. In Reid, J. (ed.), *Learning styles in the ESL/EFL classroom, 3-18*. Boston, MA: Heinle & Heinle.

Olivas-Lujan, MR, A-W Harzing, and S McCoy (2004). September 11, 2001: Two quasi-experiments on the influence of threats on cultural values and cosmopolitanism, *International Journal of Cross Cultural Management*, (4)2: 211-228.

Oxford, RL and JA Burry-Stock (1995). Assessing the use of language learning strategies worldwide with ESL/EFL version of the Strategy Inventory for Language Learning (SILL). *System*, 23(2), 153-175.

Oxford, RL, ME Hollaway, and D Murillo (1992). Language learning styles: research and practical considerations for teaching in the multicultural tertiary ESL/EFL classroom. *System*, 20(4), 439-445.

Peacock, M (2001). Match or mismatch? Learning styles and teaching styles in EFL International Journal of Applied Linguistics, 11(1), 1-20.

Ralston, DA, DH Holt, RH Terpstra and K-C Yu (1997). The impact of national culture and economic ideology on managerial work values: A study of the United States, Russia, Japan, and China. *Journal of International Business Studies*, 28, 177 – 207.

Ralston, DA, DJ Gustafson, FM Cheung and RH Terpstra (1993). Differences in managerial values: A Study of U.S., Hong Kong and PRC managers. *Journal of International Business Studies*. 24, 249 – 275.

Ralston, DA, KC Yu, X Wang, RH Terpstra, and W He (1996). The cosmopolitan Chinese manager: Findings of a study on managerial values across the six regions of China. *Journal of International Management*, 2, 79-109.

Ralston, DA, NV Thang and NK Napier (1999a). A comparative study of the work values of North and South Vietnamese managers. *Journal of International Business Studies*, 30(4), 655-673.

Ralston, DA, Ralston, CP Egri, S Stewart, RH Terpstra, K Yu (1999b). Doing business in the 21st century with the new generation of Chinese managers: A study of generational shifts in work values in China. *Journal of International Business Studies*, 30, 415 – 427.

Rao, Z (2001) Matching teaching styles with learning styles in East Asian contexts. *The Internet TESL Journal*, VII(7), http://iteslj.org/Techniques/Zhenhui-TeachingStyles.html [18 September 2004].

Reid, J. (1987). The learning style preferences of ESL students. *TESOL Quarterly*, 21(1), 87-111.

Reid, JM (1998) *Understanding learning styles in the second language classroom*, Upper Saddle River, NJ: Pearson Education.

Sato, C. (1982). Ethnic styles in classroom discourse. In Mary, EH & William, R (Eds.). *On TESOL*. Washington, DC: Teachers of English to Speakers of Other Languages.

Schwartz, S. H. (1994a). Beyond individualism/collectivism: New cultural dimensions of values. In U Kim, HC Triandis, C Kagitcibasi, S-C Choi, & G Yoon (Eds.), *Individualism and collectivism: Theory, method and applications*, pp. 85-119. Newbury Park, CA: Sage.

Schwartz, SH (1994b). Are there universal aspects in the content and structure of values? *Journal of Social Issues*, 50, 19-45.

Schwartz, SH and M Ros, M. (1995) Values in the West: A theoretical and empirical challenge to the Individualism–Collectivism cultural dimension. *World Psychology, 1*, 99–122.

Schwartz, SH. (1992). Universals in the content and structure of values: Theory and empirical tests in 20 countries. In M Zanna (Ed.), *Advances in experimental social psychology* (Vol. 25), pp. 1-65. New York: Academic Press.

Selmer, J and RF Littrell (2004). Work value change during economic decline: A longitudinal study of Hong Kong managers. Working Paper, Institute for Enterprise Development and Management Research, School of Business, Hong Kong Baptist University, http://net2.hkbu.edu.hk/~brc/HRSWP200405.PDF [accessed 28 September 2004].

Smith, PB and MH Bond (1998). *Social Psychology Across Cultures: Analysis and Perspectives, 2nd edition*. Allyn & Bacon.

Smotherman, R and S Kooros (2001). Assessing cultural differences: Comparing Hofstede's and Trompenaars' dimensions, Proceedings, 2001 Conference of the Academy of Business Disciplines.

Song, B (1995). What does reading mean for East Asian students? *College ESL*, 5(2), 35-48.

Sue, DW and BA Kirk (1972). Psychological characteristics of Chinese-American students. *Journal of Counseling Psychology*, 19, 471-478.

Sundqvist, S, L Frank, and K Puumalainen, Kaisu (2001). Cross-cultural adoption of wireless communications: Effects of cultural distance and country characteristics. http://marketing.byu.edu/htmlpages/ccrs/proceedings01/papers/Sundqvist-Frank-Puumalainen.doc. [31 July 2003].

Tang, J (1998). The Four Golden Project in China: the pathway to electronic commerce. Information Development, Vol. 14 No 3, pp. 133-5.

Tang, J (2000). Recent Internet Developments in the People's Republic of China: an overview. *Online Information Review*, 24(4): 316-321.

Taylor, OL (1990) *Cross-cultural communication: An essential dimension of effective education, revised edition*. Washington, D.C.: The Mid-Atlantic Equity Center.

Trompenaars, F. (1993). *Riding the waves of culture: Understanding diversity in global business*. Irwin. New York.

Wallace, B., and RL Oxford (1992). Disparity in learning styles and teaching styles in the ESL classroom: Does this mean war?" *AMTESOL (Alabama-Mississippi Teachers of English to Speakers of Other Languages) Journal*, 1, 45-68. http://www.ce.msstate.edu/eslc/amtesol/, [accessed 1 October 2004].

Worthey, KM (1987). Learning style factors of field dependence/independence and problem-solving strategies of Hmong refugee students. Unpublished master's thesis. University of Wisconsin,

Stout, WI. Discussed and referenced in numerous articles, esp. in Rao, Z (2001) Matching Teaching Styles with Learning Styles in East Asian Contexts. *The Internet TESL Journal*, VII(7), http://iteslj.org/Techniques/Zhenhui-TeachingStyles.html [18 September 2004].

Yu, L (1999). *The Analects of Confucius (English-Chinese)*, translated into English by Arthur Waley, translated into Modern Chinese by Yang Bojun. Beijing: Foreign Languages Press.

Zhang, N (2004). PR China university graduate, private communication.

Zittrain J and B Edelman (2003). Internet filtering in China, *IEEE Internet Computing Online*, 7(2), 70-77.

Chapter 7

Teaching in China:
Culture-based Challenges

Herman Aguinis
University of Colorado at Denver

Heidi A. Roth
University of Colorado at Denver

1. Introduction

Management education has become increasingly popular in China since the formal introduction of the first MBA program in 1990 (Guo, 2000). China's Ministry of Education reported that applications for Master's in Business Administration (MBA) degrees rose 18% from the year 2000 to the year 2001 (Cui, 2001). Currently, China hosts dozens of Western-based higher education institutions offering management and business undergraduate degrees, graduate degrees, several types of certificates, as well as shorter non-degree programs. Some examples include China Rutgers University, China European International Business School, California State University, and The International College at Beijing (Heytens, 2001). The presence of Western-based education programs in China is likely to continue to increase given China's "desperate need for high-quality business leaders" (Guo, 2000). Furthermore, this trend is likely to be accentuated because many companies are starting to follow the Western model and sponsor business and management programs as a tool to retain and attract top talent (Heytens, 2001). Our main goal in this chapter is to describe how cultural differences between the United States (U.S.) and China pose unique challenges to U.S. instructors teaching in China, and to relate these cultural differences to instructor-student dynamics in the classroom, student expectations and behaviors, and the learning process in general. An additional goal is to provide suggestions regarding pedagogical strategies and techniques for U.S. instructors teaching in China to address challenges posed by cultural differences.

141

We make two clarifications. First, we frame our analysis from the perspective of educational dynamics inherent in Western and, specifically, U.S.-style business instruction in China. Our manuscript addresses the fact that numerous Chinese institutions are embracing the U.S. approach, including an emphasis on English instruction, because this makes graduates more attractive to potential employers. We emphasize that we are not advocating the adoption of U.S. culture and business style education in China; we are addressing a situation that is already in place. And, although some of our propositions could be considered pejoratively, they are based on careful derivation from literature. Thus, we adopt a normative framework that may be perceived as "resolutely American" because this is the framework adopted by an increasing number of higher-education institutions in China.

Second, our manuscript does not include a consideration of the typical U.S. management curriculum and its applicability to the Chinese political and business environment. There is substantial evidence challenging the transportability of U.S. management theories and practices to China (Berrell, Wrathall, & Wright, 2001; Fan, 1998; Newell, 1999). This topic goes beyond the scope of the present chapter and deserves in-depth treatment elsewhere; therefore, we focus on pedagogical as opposed to curricular issues.

The chapter is structured as follows. The first section reviews general cultural differences between the U.S. and China, as well as some unique features of Chinese culture, and links these differences to specific instructional challenges. This section also offers 9 testable propositions based on theory considerations to help direct future empirical research. The second section provides a discussion of pedagogical approaches and techniques that may prove useful for non-Chinese instructors teaching in China.

2. U.S.-China Cultural Differences and Their Consequences for Instruction

In spite of hundreds of cross-cultural articles published every year in management and the social sciences in general, the definition of culture continues to remain elusive. In fact, a common criticism of cross-cultural research is that investigators fail to provide a definition of culture as their focal construct of interest (House, Wright, & Aditya, 1997).

We view culture as a construct that results from *shared experiences,* applies to a *collective,* and is *multi-faceted* (Aguinis & Henle, 2003). First, culture results from shared experiences such as a common history and geography. However, these common experiences are antecedents that create a culture, and are not culture per se. Second, culture is a collective construct because it applies to groups of individuals. Third, culture is multi-faceted.This means that to describe a group's culture we need to examine more than one dimension (e.g., individualism-collectivism, power distance, Confucianism, and so forth). The examination of a group's relative position on simply one dimension does not suffice to describe a group's culture. And, we must keep in mind that when we describe a group's relative position regarding a specific cultural dimension (e.g., individualism-collectivism), we are necessarily making a generalization. Because there is variation within each cultural group (Bond, 1997), the fact that person A belongs to a more collectivistic society than person B does not make person A automatically more collectivistic than person B. When we discuss cultural dimensions, we are referring to group-level generalizations that may not apply to the individual level of analysis. Numerous articles and books have been published about Chinese culture. The majority of these sources originate from scholars in academic institutions in Hong Kong. However, authors from Mainland China have had an increasing presence in English language publications since the 1980s. Because the history, geography, and other common experiences are different for the Mainland and Hong Kong Chinese (e.g., Communism vs. English rule), some cultural aspects also differ. Most of the studies of Chinese culture are based on extrapolations of studies conducted in Hong Kong, Taiwan, and Singapore. Nevertheless, there are some cultural features that seem to be common to all, or most, of China, particularly if we contrast these features to the U.S. and the West in general.

Next, we provide a brief review of three salient cultural dimensions together with a discussion of how these cultural dimensions are linked to instructional challenges for U.S. instructors teaching in

China. We focus our discussion around the following three salient cultural dimensions: Individualism-collectivism, power distance, and Confucianism.[2] By necessity, we must describe each of these dimensions separately. But, these dimensions are artificially separated for the sake of clarity. In truth, they form an interrelated pattern of cultural dimensions that, together, serve as good indicators of the underlying Chinese culture.

2.1 *Individualism-collectivism*

China has been identified as a collectivistic society (Triandis, 1995). A collectivistic society is one in which the individuals define themselves as part of one or more collectives such as family, tribe, nation, and are primarily motivated by the norms and duties imposed on them from these collectives.

Individuals in collectivistic societies are willing to give priority to the goals of the collective over their own personal goals, and emphasize their connection to the members of these collectives. In contrast, the U.S. is considered an individualistic society (Hofstede, 1980). An individualistic society is one in which the members see themselves as independent of collectives and are motivated by their own preferences, needs, and contracts established with others (Triandis, 1995). In the Chinese cultural context, individualism is seen as a pejorative term (Triandis, 1995). According to the Chinese, individualism connotes selfishness, a lack of concern for others, and an aversion to group discipline, whereas collectivism is understood to affirm the solidarity of the group (Ho & Chiu, 1994). Cultural groups like the Chinese, who espouse collectivistic values, focus their trust and solidarity toward the norms of the members of their collectives, also called ingroups, and are often distrustful of outgroups. In other words, the Chinese society, by virtue of being collectivistic, shows more dissociation from outgroups and more subordination to ingroups than members of individualistic cultures (Triandis, 1995).

Triandis (1995) refined the concepts of individualism and collectivism further by identifying their vertical and horizontal facets. This distinction allows for the following four possible cultural preferences regarding the individualism-collectivism dimension: vertical individualism, horizontal individualism, vertical collectivism, and horizontal collectivism. For collectivistic societies, the vertical preference includes a sense of serving the ingroups and sacrificing and doing one's duty for the ingroups' benefit. Inequality and rank are an integral part of a vertical collectivistic group, as well as ethnocentrism and prejudiced views that are used as a means of distinguishing themselves from outgroups (Triandis, 1995). Alternatively, a horizontal collectivism preference includes a sense of social cohesion and of oneness with the members of the ingroup (Triandis, 1995).

Although both facets of collectivism seem to be present in Chinese society, several independent studies suggest that, overall, the Chinese lean towards vertical collectivism (Chen, Meindl, & Hunt, 1997). For instance, although their study did not include a sample from Mainland China, results reported by the Chinese Culture Connection (1987) indicate that both Taiwan and Hong Kong are low on integration, a value that emphasizes tolerance of others, harmony, non-competitiveness, and solidarity. Therefore, these two Chinese cultural groups could be classified as low on the horizontal collectivism facet. In addition, vertical collectivism is manifested by the Chinese preference for an orderly and hierarchical society based on rank and obedience (Triandis, 1995).

In short, the Chinese society is collectivistic and, specifically, displays characteristics of vertical collectivistic societies.

2.1.1 Relationship between collectivism-vertical collectivism and instructional challenges

How do the general collectivistic and more specific vertical collectivistic societal orientations affect specific educational practices in China? First, collective cultures display a preference for a high-context as opposed to a low-context approach to communication. A high-context form of communication emphasizes indirectness, implicitness, and nonverbal expressions over a low-context approach that utilizes directness, explicitness, and expressiveness (Gao, Ting-Toomey, & Gudykunst, 1996).

In China, confrontation and directness are strongly avoided. For example, Chua and Gudykunst (1987) found that Taiwanese students are more likely to gloss over differences and conceal ill feelings as compared to U.S. students. Stated differently, the concept of *hanxu* (i.e., implicitness) is preferred. This implicitness applies to the use of both verbal and non-verbal communication. As a result, not only are emotions not expressed verbally, but also they are often difficult to determine through a person's nonverbal behaviors. Contrary to the U.S., non-verbal behaviors are more subtle and, to a Western eye, do not seem to convey social influence and emotional expression (cf. Aguinis, Simonsen, & Pierce, 1998).

Moreover, the expression of emotion is seen as embarrassing and shameful (Kleinman, 1980). For example, we have observed that in the classroom it is rare for instructors to receive positive or negative feedback from students, either verbally or nonverbally, regarding their level of satisfaction with the material being taught. Thus, we offer the following proposition:

> Proposition 1: *Because of a vertical collectivistic orientation, students in China are more likely to use a high context approach to communication including a preference for indirectness and implicitness, and they are not likely to express their opinions, beliefs, and feelings as openly and directly as compared to students in the U.S.*

Second, another putative consequence of vertical collectivism is the indigenous (i.e., emic) concept of *lian* (i.e., "face"). Face refers to "the confidence of society in the integrity of ego's moral character, the loss of which makes it impossible for him [or her] to function properly within the community" (Gao *et al.*, 1996, p. 289). Saving face is of great concern to most Chinese and face management is essential to maintaining harmonious relationships (Gao *et al.*, 1996). Overall, the Chinese attempt to protect the face of both parties involved in a communication process. Direct confrontation or questioning can be seen as a potential threat to the face of either party and could invite chaos or imbalance. Consequently, in the classroom, rarely do students ask questions or challenge the instructor for fear of shaming themselves or the teacher (if s/he does not know the answer to a question), which would disturb the structure and balance of the roles. What in the U.S. is seen as assertiveness, a positive trait (Aguinis & Adams, 1998), in China is interpreted as bad character and perceived as threatening (Gao et al., 1996). Based on the preceding discussion, we offer the following proposition:

> Proposition 2: *Because of the fear of losing face or making the instructor lose face, students in China are less likely to ask questions and participate in class as compared to students in the U.S.*

An additional issue related to face management is a course's syllabus. In the U.S., a syllabus represents a formal agreement between the instructor and the students. Collectivistic societies including China have a preference for informal and private agreements as opposed to formal and public agreements. An informal agreement is less likely to be scrutinized and the chance of losing face is minimized (Leung, 1997). Thus, "informal agreements are preferred because an agreement that unexpectedly causes one side to lose face can then be easily revised to restore that party's face" (Leung, 1997, p. 650). Congruent with this argument, we have observed that very few Chinese instructors distribute a syllabus at the beginning of their course. Additionally, Chinese students in our classes did not view our syllabi as formal and fairly final documents. Instead, students treated the class syllabi as "informal documents in progress" which could be revised at any time regarding reading assignments, examination dates, nature and goals of outside projects, and so forth. Thus, we offer the following proposition:

> Proposition 3: *Because of the fear of losing face, students in China are more likely to view a course syllabus as an informal "in progress" document as opposed to a formal agreement between an instructor and the students as compared to students in the U.S.*

2.2 Power distance

Hofstede's (1980, 2001) seminal study identified power distance as one of four values that differentiate cultural groups. Power distance refers to the degree to which inequalities in the distribution of power are tolerated and accepted (Hofstede, 1980, 2001). Hofstede's study did not include a sample from Mainland China, but it included ethnic Chinese groups from Taiwan, Hong Kong, and Singapore. Based on Hofstede's results regarding these samples, Chinese culture can be classified as high on power distance. Cultural groups that score high on power distance have a tendency to prefer to obey without question those who are in authority positions and have clearly defined role differentiation of a hierarchical nature. In the Chinese cultural context, these preferences can be understood through the indigenous concept of *filial piety*.

Filial piety is a cultural value indigenous to China that serves as a guiding principle for socialization and intergenerational conduct for the length of one's lifespan (Ho, 1996). Filial piety refers to a hierarchical relationship of social roles such as father to son, husband to wife, and older son to younger son, whereby the senior in age has authority over the younger person. The younger person is to bring honor to his or her elders and eventually be responsible for providing for these elders. While it traditionally refers to behavior toward one's parents and ancestors, Yeh and Yang (1989, cited in Ho, 1996) showed that filial piety can be generalized to all authority relationships.

Based on the indigenous concept of filial piety, Ho (1996) argued that "authoritarian moralism" is a central characteristic of Chinese socialization processes. Ho identified the following two components of authoritarian moralism: (a) hierarchical ranking of authority in family members, the educational system, and socio-political situations, and (b) a pervasive application of moral principles as a primary standard from which people are judged.

2.3 Relationship between power distance and instructional challenges

How does high power distance, and the related emic concepts of filial piety and authoritarian moralism, affect specific educational practices in China?

First, instructors in China have absolute authority and are treated with high deference. In fact, the word teacher in Chinese can be literally translated as "born early," implying that teachers (because they were born earlier) deserve respect and deference. In exchange, instructors are expected to demonstrate wisdom and to form the moral character of their students. Thus, filial piety teaches Chinese students to fear authority figures, to adopt silence, negativism, and passive resistance when dealing with authority demands (Ho, 1996). Instructors, in return, focus on the demonstration of proper behavior, impulse control, and the fulfillment of obligations (Ho, 1996). Thus, we offer the following proposition:

> Proposition 4: *Because of the indigenous filial piety and authoritarianism moralism values, students in China are more likely to accept a professor's instructions and rules without question and give instructors more deference as compared to students in the U.S.*

Students' filial piety and authoritarian moralism results in levels of respect, obedience, and submission that are unusually high for Western standards. Moreover, there is evidence that compared to U.S. students, Chinese students are more willing to accept insulting remarks from a high-status individual (Bond, Wan, Leung, & Giacalone, 1985). Teachers are respected as authority figures second only to their parents and Chinese students do not challenge teachers' authority (Siu, 1992). Detrimental effects for students may result from Western instructors' lack of understanding of these issues and violation of social codes of which they are not aware.

Chinese students may risk losing face and being socially embarrassed when Western instructors make atypical role demands, which students feel they cannot refuse from an authority figure. One example of this kind of violation that we saw frequently was the practice of Western instructors to use Chinese students to show them the city and help with non-educational activities including shopping or sightseeing. Some Western instructors had little awareness of the stress this may put on the extremely busy students or the inappropriateness of making such requests. When a Chinese student is asked such an inappropriate favor by a professor, she or he may not be feel it is appropriate to decline the request. Moreover, as noted above in the discussion regarding the Chinese preference for a high-context (i.e., implicit and indirect) style of communication, a Western instructor may miss an indirect effort of refusal. Missing an indirect refusal from a student can become a very serious issue and Western instructors may violate serious norms such as maintaining a professional relationship with students inside and outside of the classroom. In short, we offer the following proposition:

> Proposition 5: *Because of a combination of filial piety and authoritarian moralism with a preference for an implicit and indirect communication style, U.S. instructors are more likely to not understand when Chinese students wish to refuse an instructor's inappropriate request as compared to a refusal by U.S. students.*

As discussed above, instructors are expected to reciprocate students' deference and respect for authority by demonstrating proper behavior, impulse control, and the fulfillment of obligations (Ho, 1996). This may lead Chinese instructors to display a rigid and structured teaching style. Thus, it is not infrequent for a Chinese instructor to enter the classroom, read from notes for the entire period while writing on the board, and leave at the end of the period without deviating from the pre-arranged "script." In turn, this shapes students' expectations regarding classroom interactions in that Chinese instructors, in fulfilling their role and obligation, are expected to disseminate large amounts of information, which does not allow much time left for dialogue and instructor-student interactions. Thus, we offer the following proposition:

> Proposition 6: *Because of authoritarian moralism values, classroom interactions including Chinese instructors are more likely to be more rigid, structured, and include a teaching style featuring one-way communication and less student participation as compared to classroom interactions including U.S. instructors.*

2.4 *Confucianism*

In the previous two sections, we discussed cultural dimensions created by Western researchers (i.e., individualism-collectivism and power distance) and their relationship with indigenous Chinese values. In describing the cultural dimensions of individualism-collectivism and power distance, we also touched on some aspects of Chinese Confucian philosophy (e.g., filial piety, saving face). Confucianism is a multi-layered philosophy that has been part of Chinese culture for more than two thousand years and deserves to be discussed on its own. Also, there are aspects of Confucianism that are purely emic and cannot be directly related to more universal values. For example, the Chinese Culture Connection (1987) found that a value survey including indigenous Chinese themes yielded a "Confucian work dynamism" factor that was not related to any of the four cultural dimensions identified by Hofstede (1980) (i.e., individualism-collectivism, power distance, masculinity-femininity, and uncertainty avoidance).

It can be argued that the Communist system has attempted to erode the Confucian tradition. However, the Confucian tradition is still very much present in Mainland China, particularly if we compare Mainland China with the U.S. Many Confucian concepts (e.g., respect for authority figures) are present, but have been modified and adapted to fit a Communist system of government. For instance, our students could not say the name "Mao" without noting his title of "Chairman" before his name. And, roles within the Communist party structure have clearly-defined obligations and perks. This clear definition of roles and one's place in society is, as described below, one of four core Confucian values. In writing essays for class assignments, our students provided illustrative statements regarding the prevalence of Confucian values. Randomly selected quotes include the following: "All these huge piles of thought (Confucianism) are melted in Chinese people's mind and blood through its effective education system," "Confucianism influences much of Chinese politics, economics, and social value," "Confucianism is the main system of thought in China, from the past to the present," and "Confucianism has influenced the Chinese attitude toward life, set the standards of social value."

Confucianism can be summarized in four points. First, Confucianism includes a belief that the stability of society is based on unequal relations between people. In spite of the inequality, however, these relationships are based on a sense of mutual and complementary obligation. In the words of Confucius, "jun jun chen chen fu fu zi zi," which in its context means "let the ruler rule as he should and the minister be a minister as he should; let the father act as a father should and the son act as a son should" (Fairbanks & Goldman, 1998, p. 52). Second, the family is the prototype of all social organizations. The dynamic that helps to maintain a sense of balance in the family is saving face. Third, each person must demonstrate virtuous behavior, which means developing self-control and finding one's proper place within society. Lastly, each person is expected to acquire skills and education, work hard, and have patience and perseverance (Hofstede, 1991; Triandis, 1995).

In the Confucian tradition, individuals strive to accomplish a number of achievements. These achievements are (in order of importance) (a) attaining virtue, (b) providing meritorious service, and (c) contributing scholarship (Yu, 1996). However, empirical examinations of Chinese popular culture concluded that the relative importance of achievements is different for the majority of Chinese and that the original Confucian ordering of achievements seems to apply to a small minority only. Several studies have shown that the desired popular achievements are (in order of importance) (a) economics, (b) reputation, (c) health, and (d) morality (e.g., Johnson, Nathan, & Rawski, 1985; Yu, 1994, 1996). This more "popular" hierarchy of desired achievements seems to reflect more accurately the actual practices of Confucians since pre-Qin times (i.e., 221-207 B.C.E.), who aimed toward achieving successful official careers, fame, and reputation over self-cultivation (Yu, 1996). The traditional way to achieve economic and reputational success, and simultaneously provide meritorious service, has been through the passing of the civil service examinations and entry into the official bureaucracy. An official career was a way of achieving wealth, fame, and honoring one's family (Yu, 1996). Passing these exams became a teleological goal of such importance to the society that if a person failed the exams and had to resort to trade, they would attempt to earn enough wealth to provide their children with the best education so that their children could then pass the exams.

At present, it seems that things have not changed significantly in China in this regard. Multiple studies have shown that Chinese students aim toward dutiful service to their family and community (Kornadt, Eckensberger, & Emminghaus, 1980; Wilson & Pusey, 1982), and succeeding in examinations is a way of accomplishing this goal (Cui, 2001). More generally, there is a stress on duties rather than rights (Fairbanks & Goldman, 1998), which Yu (1996) referred to as a "social orientation achievement motivation" (SOAM). SOAM is the motivation to achieve goals set by significant others such as family, community, or society, instead of the more individualistic U.S. approach to achieve goals set by and for oneself.

2.4.1 *Relationship between Confucianism and instructional challenges*

How does Confucianism affect specific educational practices in China? First, dutiful SOAM tends to be in the direction of educational and career-based accomplishments demonstrated through succeeding in examinations. Education is highly valued in China and is seen as a ladder to social hierarchy and even as a means for the development of the person (Gow, Balla, Kember, & Hau, 1996). Through this service, students demonstrate their obedience and love for their families (Gow *et al.*, 1996). The need to fulfill the obligations to family and community refers back to the vertical collectivistic nature of the Chinese society. Instructors, parents, and other family members judge the students based on their demonstration of academic performance and often place high and strict demands on them regardless of their actual abilities.

The one-child policy of the Chinese government may have accentuated and contributed to the fierce competition that exists in China and the strong need to succeed and "get an A" that all students demonstrate. The one-child policy means that each student will eventually be responsible for supporting 2 parents and 4 grandparents. So, while growing up, a child receives the love and support of 6 adults. Together with this love and support come very high expectations and the heavy burden of having to support one's elders without the help of other siblings.

In short, succeeding in examinations is seen as a status change or a rite of passage, a key means of assessing achievement (Gow *et al.*, 1996), and failing examinations is seen not only as a personal failure, but a failure that reflects negatively on one's entire family. In Hong Kong, for instance, "the pressure for success in examinations is so great that some educators are concerned about the detrimental effects of examination on students' social development" (Gow *et al.*, 1996, p.116). In sum, we offer the following proposition:

Proposition 7: *Because of a Confucian orientation emphasizing success regarding examinations, and the sense of collective shame associated with failure, examinations are likely to generate higher levels of anxiety and students are more likely to focus on the examinations in China as compared to the U.S.*

Gow *et al.* (1996) noted that Chinese students use rote memorization to further their chances of success on examinations. However, Gow *et al.* argued that this does not mean Chinese students lack a deeper understanding of the material taught (see also S. Chan, 1999). Chinese students' deeper knowledge of the material often takes place in their own language, be it Mandarin or Cantonese, but the use of rote memorization aids students in the ability to learn complex concepts in English.

On a related note, multiple studies conducted in Hong Kong (Luke & Richards, 1981; Richards, Tung, & Ng, 1992), revealed that the use of English tends to be limited to educational settings, whereas Cantonese is used for all other areas of life. Also, some Chinese instructors resort to Cantonese in the classroom to explain complex material. These factors result in severe English language difficulties for a large number of students. [3]

The emphasis on rote memorization can be problematic because the concept of plagiarism has a different meaning in China. Traditionally, Confucian scholarship consisted of compiling the works of the classics (e.g., K'ung-fu-tzu a.k.a. Confucius, Mencius), rather than creating original texts (Fairbanks & Goldman, 1998). Scholars would memorize vast portions of the classics and then construct their own works by cutting and pasting phrases and passages from older sources. The Chinese scholars did not see this as plagiarism, but as a way for them to be the "preservers of the record more than its creators" (Fairbanks & Goldman, 1998, p.101). The combination of needing to memorize textbooks, cases, and other course materials word for word because of a lack of English proficiency with a Confucian tradition of scholarship leads to misunderstanding and confusion regarding the meaning of plagiarism. Thus, we offer the following proposition:

> Proposition 8: *Because of a Confucian orientation defining scholarship as compilation rather than creation and emphasizing the need to succeed, and a lack of proficiency with the English language, students in China are more likely to (a) resort to rote memorization of course materials and (b) engage in behaviors defined as plagiarism (in the U.S.) as compared to students in the U.S.*

The Confucian definition of scholarship as compilation rather than creation is also the putative cause of why higher educational systems in Hong Kong have not succeeded in promoting a deeper approach to learning that incorporates independent and critical thinking (Gow & Kember, 1990; Gow, Kember, & Cooper, 1994). Critical thinking does not seem to be required of students from Chinese instructors as much as it is from U.S. instructors. For example, we have gathered illustrative statements from students who noted that one of the differences between Chinese and U.S. instructors is that "Chinese instructors demand silence in class; no questions; U.S. instructors encourage opinion and critical thinking." Although students state they value the freedom of a U.S. instructor, they feel that "U.S. instructors demand critical thinking, and this is hard" and "U.S. instructors should provide more guidelines about what's expected from students." In short, we offer the following proposition:

> Proposition 9: *Because of a Confucian orientation defining scholarship as compilation rather than creation, students in*

China are more likely to be unfamiliar and feel uncomfortable with examinations and in-class exercises involving critical thinking as compared to students in the U.S.

3. The Chinese Cultural Challenge: Suggested Pedagogical Approaches and Techniques

As described in the 9 propositions above, U.S. instructors teaching in China are likely to face numerous culture-based challenges. Below we offer some suggestions regarding how to address these challenges. We include suggestions originating from (a) our own teaching experiences in Beijing and Hong Kong, (b) U.S., Canadian, and European faculty teaching in Beijing, and (c) a qualitative study including two samples of Chinese students ($n_1 = 48$ and $n_2 = 88$) enrolled in a joint U.S.-Chinese university in Beijing.

Suggestion # 1: Use Chinese, as well as U.S., examples and stories. Results of the student study showed that the most frequent suggestion regarding how to teach more effectively is that instructors include not only U.S. examples and stories, but also examples and stories directly applicable to the Chinese business environment. Thirty percent of students noted that many of the illustrations and "war stories" told by faculty apply to the U.S., but not necessarily to China. Thus, many students cannot relate to these examples. For instance, one student wrote that "because cultural background or language problems, we feel it is difficult to understand some materials about the U.S."

Suggestion # 2: Distribute copies of lecture notes and overheads. Results of the student study showed that the second most frequent suggestion on how to teach more effectively is that faculty make their lecture notes available to students. Because of language difficulties, and the one-way traditional Chinese instructional model, students feel they would benefit from having access to the lecture notes. This includes sharing overheads with students. Overheads can be particularly useful because they help students focus on the key concepts.

Note, however, that allowing students to have "advance organizers" could potentially bring up the unintended effect that students may not pay as much attention in class or choose to not attend class altogether. In our experience, we found that the benefits of sharing lecture notes and overheads outweighed the risks.

Suggestion # 3: Learn and learn to appreciate Chinese history and culture. Results of the student study showed that the most frequent suggestion (21%) on how to solve culture-related problems is that U.S. instructors learn more about Chinese history and culture. For example, one student noted that "everyone [U.S. instructors] has an ethnocentric thinking," another one wrote that "[U.S. instructors] speak with a sense of pride for being an American; there is a national superiority complex," and a third wrote that "instructors should know more things about Chinese culture and language."

Suggestion # 4: Speak slowly and emphasize and repeat key points and concepts. Results of the student study showed that the most common difficulty which students face when taking a class from a U.S. instructor is the language. Obviously, Chinese students are not native English speakers. And, in spite of many years of English instruction, learning management and business concepts in a foreign language is a big challenge. Consequently, students suggested that instructors speak slowly and emphasize key points. Students also suggested that it would be helpful to write key words and concepts, with their definitions, on the board.

Suggestion # 5: Allow student participation in a culture-sensitive manner. Results of the student study showed that the second most frequently mentioned difficulty of learning from a U.S. instructor was students' fear of asking questions in class. The educational system in China does not encourage students to ask questions. On the contrary, as noted above, Chinese instructors require complete silence while they lecture. As one student put it, "I don't like to participate in class because my Chinese teachers don't like it; I don't have that habit." Thus, U.S. instructors are appalled when they teach in China, ask a question to a class of 60, and receive no answers.

First, a method that we and other colleagues have used effectively to allow student participation in a way that is culture-sensitive is to distribute pieces of paper at the beginning of the class and allow students to write anonymous questions and pass them to the instructor. In this way, students can write questions anytime during the class period, and the instructor can read the questions and choose to answer those that are most relevant. Thus, because the instructor has a choice regarding which questions to answer and which to ignore, students feel that the risk of the instructor's losing face is minimized.

Second, another method that we have found to be effective is to have students develop questions or responses in groups. This shifts the focus from individuals to the group. In our experience, Chinese students find collaborative group work to be more comfortable than working alone and are more willing to participate in class when speaking for a group.

Third, another technique that seems to be effective is to allow for one-on-one interactions outside of the classroom. Thus, it is helpful to schedule office hours because students feel that they can ask questions and interact with the instructor without losing face and, perhaps more importantly, one-on-one interactions minimize the chances that the instructor may lose face. A word of caution is in order, however. We suggest that office hours have a clear beginning and a clear end. Some of our colleagues noted that students are extremely eager to interact with faculty individually. It is not unusual for students to call an instructor's home telephone number, and even stop by an instructor's residence without advanced notice. Thus, one Canadian colleague advised that instructors "set limits so you don't wear out too quickly; a lot of students want a lot of your time."

Suggestion # 6: Define plagiarism clearly. Results of the student study showed that the third most frequent difficulty in taking a class from a U.S. instructor is understanding the concept of plagiarism. Students are surprised that U.S. instructors believe this is such an important problem. For instance, one student wrote that "U.S. and Chinese have two quite different cultures; the biggest conflict is on plagiarism; non-Chinese think it's very serious." Another student wrote that "we have different cultures, so there are some problems; for example, cheating in a paper; Chinese don't pay much attention to that, but non-Chinese instructors are very sensitive on it." Consequently, we suggest that U.S. instructors define the different forms of plagiarism at the beginning of the class, and it is important that examples of various forms of plagiarism be offered.

Suggestion #7: Define and treat the course syllabus as a formal contract. As noted above, Chinese students are not likely to view a course syllabus as a formal agreement with the instructor. Instead, they are likely to view the syllabus as ongoing "work in progress." Thus, based on our experience and that of other Western faculty, we suggest that U.S. instructors emphasize, from the beginning of the class, that the syllabus is a *formal contract* to which both students and the instructor are bound. Unless instructors make very clear and forceful statements regarding the importance of following this "formal contract," students are likely to not take deadlines and commitments (e.g., projects, reading list) seriously, and are likely to attempt (most likely in indirect ways) to constantly revise and make changes to the class structure.

Suggestion #8: Maintain clear boundaries with students. In China there are clearly defined roles for instructors and students. When these roles are altered, the boundaries become fuzzy for both instructors and students. Contrary to U.S. students, Chinese students do not feel comfortable setting boundaries with professors or voicing discomfort about inappropriate requests. Thus, our own experiences and that of other colleagues strongly suggest that instructors set clear and appropriate boundaries to protect the students.

Suggestion #9: Have an "email coach-buddy" back home. Teaching in China is a big challenge and instructors may not know how to handle certain situations. Thus, it would be very useful to be able to stay in touch (e.g., via email) with a "coach" back home. This person is someone who has taught in China before and is likely to have faced similarly challenging situations in the past. Having this email coach back home can be instrumental regarding teaching outcomes, but also useful as a source of personal support.

Suggestion #10: Have a plan B, a plan C, and a plan D. The instructional setting in China includes many surprises for U.S. instructors. For example, textbooks are regularly inspected by government officials and, on occasion, some of the material is censored. Thus, because this process can be lengthy, it is likely that the books may not be ready by the beginning of the course. Thus, it is advisable to have back-up materials for the first few classes. Similarly, because of the high cost of transparencies and other instructional materials, it is advisable to bring all necessary office supplies from home. And, of course, bringing one's laptop computer is a must. In short, it is advisable to have back-up plans regarding instructional materials and to not count on the availability of reliable local instructional technology.

4. Concluding Comments

We have had a highly enjoyable and rewarding experience teaching in China. In spite of facing some adverse conditions in Beijing including noisy classrooms and hygienic standards much lower than those in the U.S., Chinese students are eager to learn and work very hard towards the attainment of their educational goals. Because of the increased proliferation of Western-sponsored management and business programs in China, it is important that U.S. and other Western educators understand cultural differences and how these cultural differences may affect student behavior, classroom interactions, and the learning process in general.

We hope the present chapter will serve as a catalyst for empirical research on the link between cultural dimensions, the teaching process, and teaching effectiveness of non-Chinese instructors in China. Also, we hope our suggested pedagogical approaches and techniques will be useful for Western instructors who are preparing for the challenging assignment of teaching in China.

Endnotes

[1]A previous version of this manuscript was presented at the 2002 Academy of Management meetings in Denver and nominated by the Management, Education, & Development Division for the Academy of Management Carolyn Dexter Award. Both authors contributed equally to this research. The research reported herein was supported, in part, by grants from the Institute for International Business and The Business School at the University of Colorado at Denver to Herman Aguinis. This research was conducted while Herman Aguinis was on sabbatical leave from the University of Colorado at Denver and holding visiting appointments at The International College at Beijing-China Agricultural University (Beijing, People's Republic of China), City University of Hong Kong (People's Republic of China), and Universidad de Santiago de Compostela (Spain). We thank Mark Evers, Kang Rae Cho, Chen Ji, and Charles A. Pierce for helpful comments on previous drafts.

[2] We chose to focus on these three dimensions after a careful and thorough review of over 40 cultural dimensions and values (cf. Hofstede, 1980, 2001; Lytle, Brett, Barsness, Tinsley, & Janssens, 1995; Schwartz & Sagie, 2000). Based on this review, we concluded that a discussion around individualism-collectivism, power distance, and Confucianism provides a high degree of predictive power as well as parsimony and unnecessary repetition.

[3] Given the difficulties with English, one may argue that instruction should take place in the local language (e.g., Mandarin). However, students choose to enroll in Western-style business programs precisely because instruction is in English and they are expected to learn "the Western way" of doing business. Historically, the interest in learning English can be traced to a suggestion made to emperor Tong Zhi by his Regents in 1862, who said they "had seen foreigners in China learn the language from native Chinese; why, they argued, should foreigners not teach their native language to Chinese?" (Porter, 1990, p. 10). The contemporary relevance of this story is now evident even at the elementary and secondary school levels. For instance, the government of Guangdong province recently announced a pilot program under which 200 of its primary and secondary schools will teach some of their subjects in English. The goal is to "prepare the next generation of business managers to be fluent in English and, if successful, the program will be expanded to all 20,000 schools in the region" (M. Chan, 2002).

References

Aguinis, H., & Adams, K. R. (1998). Social role versus structural models of gender and influence use in organizations: A strong inference approach. *Group and Organization Management, 23,* 414-446.

Aguinis, H., & Henle, C.A. (2003). The search for universals in cross-cultural organizational behavior. In J. Greenberg (Ed.), *Organizational Behavior: The State of the Science* (2nd ed.) (pp. 373-411). Mahwah, NJ: Lawrence Erlbaum Associates.

Aguinis, H., Simonsen, M. M., & Pierce, C. A. (1998). Effects of nonverbal behavior on perceptions of power bases. *Journal of Social Psychology, 138,* 455-469.

Berrell, M., Wrathall, J., & Wright, P. (2001). A model for Chinese management education: Adapting the case study method to transfer management knowledge. *Cross Cultural Management, 8,* 28-44

Bond, M. H. (1997). Adding value to the cross-cultural study of organizational behavior. In P. C. Earley & M. Erez (Eds.), *New perspectives on international industrial/organizational psychology* (pp. 256-275). San Francisco, CA: The New Lexington Press.

Bond, M. H., Wan, K. C., Leung, K., & Giacalone, R. C. (1985). How are responses to verbal insult related to cultural collectivism and power distance? *Journal of Cross-Cultural Psychology, 16,* 111-127.

Chan, M. (2002, January 24). Hong Kong losing its language edge. *The Guardian*. Available on-line: http://education.guardian.co.uk/Print/0,3858,4342582,00.html.

Chan, S. (1999). The Chinese learner: A question of style. *Education + Training*, 6/7, 294-304.

Chen, C. C., Meindl, J. R., & Hunt, R. G. (1997). Testing the effects of vertical and horizontal collectivism: A study of reward allocation preferences in China. *Journal of Cross-Cultural Psychology*, 28, 44-70.

Chinese Culture Connection. (1987). Chinese values and the search for culture-free dimensions of culture. *Journal of Cross-Cultural Psychology*, 18, 143-64.

Chua, F., & Gudykunst, W. B. (1987). Conflict resolution styles in low- and high-context cultures. *Communication Research Reports*, 4, 32-37.

Cui, Y. (2001, January 16). Postgraduates turn to business, law, high-tech degrees. *China Daily*. Available on-line:
http://www.chinadaily.com.cn/cndydb/2001/01/d3-2exam.116.html

Fairbanks, J. K, & Goldman, M. (1998). *China: A new history*. Cambridge, MA: The Belknap Press of Harvard University Press.

Fan, Y. (1998). The transfer of Western management to China. *Management Learning*, 29, 201-221.

Gao, G., Ting-Toomey, S., & Gudykunst, W. B. (1996). Chinese communication processes. In M. H. Bond (Ed.), *The handbook of Chinese psychology* (pp. 280-293). New York, NY: Oxford University Press.

Gow, L., Balla, J., Kember, D., & Hau, K. T. (1996). The learning approaches of Chinese people: A function of socialization processes and the context of learning? In M. H. Bond (Ed.), *The handbook of Chinese psychology* (pp. 109-123). New York, NY: Oxford University Press.

Gow, L., & Kember, D. (1990). Does higher education promote independent learning? *Higher Education*, 19, 307-22.

Gow, L., Kember, D., & Cooper, B. (1994). The teaching context and approaches to study of accountancy students. *Issues in Accounting Education*, 9(1), 56-74.

Guo, N. (2002, August 14). Degrees promote economic expansion. *China Daily*. Available on-line:
http://search.chinadaily.com.cn/isearch/i_textinfo.exe?dbname=cndy_printedition &listid=14278&selectword=NEI%20GUO [note: can spacing be improved for this citation?]

Heytens, A. (2001, June 5). Profiting from education. *China Daily*. Available on-line: *http://www1.chinadaily.com.cn/bw/2001-06-05/11720.html*

Ho, D. Y. F. (1996). Filial piety and its psychological consequences. In M. H. Bond (Ed.), *The handbook of Chinese psychology* (pp. 155-165). New York, NY: Oxford University Press.

Ho, D. Y. F., & Chiu, C. Y. (1994). Component ideas of individualism, collectivism, and social organization: An application in the study of Chinese culture. In U. Kim, H. C. Triandis, C. Kagitcibasi, S. C. Choi, & G. Yoon (Eds.), *Individualism and collectivism: Theory, method, and application* (pp. 137-156). Newbury Park, CA: Sage.

Hofstede, G. (1980). *Culture's consequences.* Beverly Hills, CA: Sage.

Hofstede, G. (1991). *Cultures and organizations: Software of the mind.* London, U.K: McGraw-Hill.

Hofstede, G. (2001). *Culture's consequences: Comparing values, behaviors, institutions, and organizations across nations* (2nd edition). Thousand Oaks, CA: Sage.

House, R. J., Wright, N. S., & Aditya, R. N. (1997). Cross-cultural research on organizational leadership: A critical analysis and a proposed theory. In P. C. Earley, & M. Erez (Eds.), *New perspectives on international industrial/organizational psychology* (pp. 535-625). San Francisco, CA: The New Lexington Press.

Johnson, D., Nathan, A. J., & Rawski, E. S. (1985). *Popular culture in late imperial China.* Berkeley, CA: University of California Press.

Kleinman, A. (1980). *Patients and healers in the context of culture.* Berkeley, CA: University of California Press.

Kornadt, H. J., Eckensberger, L. H. & Emminghaus, W. B. (1980). Cross-cultural research on motivation and its contribution to general theory of motivation. In H. C. Triandis & W. Lonner (Eds.), *Handbook of cross-cultural psychology*, vol. 3 (pp. 223-321). Boston, MA: Allyn and Bacon.

Leung, K. (1997). Negotiation and reward allocations across cultures. In P. C. Earley, & M. Erez (Eds.), *New perspectives on international industrial/organizational psychology* (pp. 640-675). San Francisco, CA: The New Lexington Press.

Luke, K. K., & Richards, J. C. (1981). English use in Hong Kong: Function and status. *English Worldwide,* 3(1), 46-64.

Lytle, A. L., Brett, J. M., Barsness, Z. I., Tinsley, C. H., & Janssens, M. (1995). A paradigm for confirmatory cross-cultural research in organizational behavior. *Research in Organizational Behavior,* 17, 167-214.

Newell, S. (1999). The transfer of management knowledge to China: Building learning communities rather than translating Western textbooks? *Education + Training,* 41, 286-293.

Porter, E. A. (1990). *Foreign teachers in China: Old problems for a new generation, 1979–1989.* Westport, CT: Greenwood Press.

Richards, J. C., Tung, P. & Ng, P. (1992). The culture of the English language teacher: A Hong Kong example. *RELC,* 23(1), 81-102.

Schwartz, S. H., & Sagie, G. (2000). Value consensus and importance: A cross-national study. *Journal of Cross Cultural Psychology,* 31, 465-497.

Siu, S. F. (1992). *Toward an understanding of Chinese-American educational achievement: A literature review.* Boston, MA: Center for Families, Communities, Schools, and Children's Learning.

Triandis, H. C. (1995). *Individualism and collectivism.* San Francisco, CA: Westview Press.

Wilson, R.W. & Pusey, A. W. (1982). Achievement motivation and small-business relationship patterns in Chinese society. In S.L. Greenblatt, R.W. Wilson, & A.A. Wilson (Eds.), *Social interactions in Chinese society* (pp. 195-208). New York, NY: Praeger Publishers.

Yeh, K. H., & Yang, K. S. (1989). Cognitive structure and development of filial piety: Concepts and measurement [in Chinese]. *Bulletin of the Institute of Ethnology,* 56, 131-69.

Yu, A. B. (1994). The self and life goals of traditional Chinese: A philosophical and psychological analysis. In A. M. Bouvy, F. J. R. Van de Vijver, P. Boski & P. Schmitz (Eds.) *Journeys into cross-cultural psychology* (pp. 50-67). Lisse, the Netherlands: Swets and Zeitlinger.

Yu, A.B. (1996). Ultimate life concerns, self, and Chinese achievement motivation. In M. H. Bond (Ed.), *The handbook of Chinese psychology* (pp. 227-246). New York, NY: Oxford University Press.

Chapter 8

East Meets West:
The Dilemma of Management Pedagogy
in China

Xiaoyun Wang
University of Manitoba

Wei He
Boston College

Kaicheng Yu
Dalian University of Technology

1. Introduction

Due to the unique nature of managerial practice, managerial development should be differentiated from other professional development such as medicine and law. The nature of the knowledge in management education is relativism (pragmatic truth, subjectivity, and contextual relativity) contrasting to objectivism (universal truth, generic laws). Accordingly, the pedagogy of management education should also be different in order to develop effective and pragmatic managers to meet society's needs and foster desirable attitudes (Holman, 2000; Raelin, 1995). Therefore, the action learning model, the critical reflection learning model, the experiential learning model and service learning projects should be considered and promoted in management education systems against the traditional "academic liberalism" and "professional" models (Holman, 2000; Kolenko, Porter, Wheatley, & Colby, 1996; Raelin, 1995; Reynolds, 1998). In other words, management education pedagogy should focus on experiential and participative learning, instead of traditional one-direction (from teachers to students) lecturing.

These Western thoughts of management education have been introduced to China, thanks to the aggressive search for international assistance in management education by the Chinese government (Boisot & Fiol, 1987; Bu & Mitchell, 1992). Several major developed countries such as United States, Canada, Japan, and Germany have been involved in assisting the development of management education in China since 1978 (see Boisot 1986 for review). However, despite the fact that hundreds of Western professors have come to China to help train Chinese managers and faculty over the past two decades, the pedagogy in Chinese management education institutions has not changed much. Problems listed by Bu & Mitchell (1992), such as lack of student participation and inefficiency of trainees' group discussions, still exist in Chinese management education. Why was it so hard for the Western management pedagogy to be accepted by the Chinese management institutions? We argue here that the reason for the slow acceptance of the above mentioned Western management education pedagogy is that it contradicts with Chinese values in terms of effective education. The purpose of this paper is to explore the dilemma between the Western management education pedagogy and Chinese cultural values.

In the Chinese management education literature, there are some studies focused on Chinese management education development (e.g., Chan, 1996; Warner, 1991). However, there are very few articles analyzing Chinese management education pedagogy and how it is influenced by cultural values, with an exception that Boiso & Fiol's (1987) described the pedagogical differences between Chinese and Western management education. This paper tries to analyze the main reasons for the difficulties from a cultural value perspective. To achieve this objective, this paper will first review the evolution of China's management education, along which the Chinese traditional pedagogy will be introduced. Then, the cultural and historical roots of this traditional pedagogy will be presented. Thirdly, suggestions will be given to Western professors teaching in China. Finally, the future of China's management education will be discussed.

2. The Transformation of Management Education in Contemporary China

2.1 *China's economy evolution: a brief review*

Management education is a function of economic development (He, Wang, & Yu, 2002). Its prosperity closely follows the rise and fall of the national economy. Moreover, in a transition economy like China's, management education has experienced a roller-coaster cycle of rise, fall, and rise again, following the dramatic transformation of its economic system.

Since the People's Republic of China was founded in 1949, the conspicuous economic achievements under the new government have been widely acknowledged, especially when considering the dreadful conditions that New China inherited from the old regime. The path it has passed, however, is far from being straight as a ramrod. The process can be roughly divided into three stages.

During the first stage (1949-1957), the newly established government was strongly supported by the people and cleared up the shambles quickly. The economy has been restored and re-built efficiently by following the former USSR's economic model and with financial and technical aids from the "Big Brother", China achieved much higher economic growth than several past decades.

With the gradually vicious expansion of the extremely "Leftist" ideology, however, China ran counter to the objective economic laws during the following two decades (1957-1978). The failure of the so-called "Great Leap Forward" policy followed by the even more disastrous "Cultural Revolution" once again led the country to the fringe of economic collapse.

Fortunately, since 1979 when Deng Xiao-ping regained the paramount power in the government, he and his pragmatic colleagues initiated the "Reform and Opening to the World" policy. It saved the country's economy from bankruptcy and turned it on a right and promising track. The economic miracle that China has then created is a noticeable and undeniable fact during the past two decades.

2.2 A three-stage transformation of management education

In accordance with the economic transition, the transformation of China's management education can also be roughly separated into three stages.

Stage I: 1949 - 1957. Before the People's Republic of China was established in 1949, there already existed a handful of economic and business administration departments or schools in some colleges and universities in the country, such as Peking University, Shanghai Jiaotong University, Nankai University, Tsinghua University, and Fudan University. A number of these universities even had granted graduate degrees, although their programs were generally weak and of very small scale. When the new government was first established, it soon began a policy called "Total Acceptance" of the practice and personnel of the old management education.

After keeping the old education system basically untouched for three years, the new government implemented a strategic measure called "the Readjustment of Schools and Departments" in 1952. On one side, almost all the established management education institutions were either disbanded or re-structured. On the other side, two new institutions were set up to serve as prototypes in the new education system by copying mainly two corresponding institutions in the then USSR.

The first was the People's University in Beijing, a Chinese version of the Moscow National Economy College that trained officials of various ranks in the economy planning and control system of a highly central planned economy. The other one was the Department of Management of the Harbin Polytechnic Institute, copying the model of Leningrad Engineering Economy College that developed mainly economic engineers, a job somewhat similar to industrial engineers in the west. The former focused on the studies of Marxist-Leninist political economic concepts, using mainly qualitative methods. The latter mainly concentrated on applying a highly engineering-oriented curriculum with intensively quantitative methods. Russian professors were invited to either teach directly or act as senior advisors in these two institutions. Hundreds of Chinese students and scholars were sent to study there. None of these two institutions, however, was designed to develop general managers of independent organizations in a market economy. Both of them regarded management knowledge as objective subjects, which could be learned through lecturing and passive learning.

The two institutions then acted as "seeds" spread throughout the whole country. Dozens of colleges and universities set up their own management programs based on the two models. Thousands of managers were developed through these schools, forming the core force of China's enterprise management system in the 1950's and even early into the 1960's.

During this period, the then government strongly believed in the former soviet pattern of economy and the rigidly central planning system. All market factors in economy were rejected and eliminated because those were exclusive components of capitalism and thus were absolutely harmful to socialism. The government also denied the fact that management itself is a sophisticated and separated body of knowledge which needs training and practice to master. Consequently, the training of general managers of enterprises as a relatively independent decision-maker was completely a nuisance. The government believed that Marxism-Leninism principles were the key for management. Any one who had been exposed to some basic concepts of Marxism-Leninism principles in general were supposed to be automatically and naturally an effective manager of any kind of institution or organization. Specific expertise or skills of management were of no need. All these oversimplified and lopsided biases originated from naive and dogmatic understanding of Marxism and more importantly from the ideology cultivated in an underdeveloped economy of rural society like China dominated the society at that time. Therefore, management education in this period was basically the passive learning of Marxism principles.

Stage II: 1958 – 1978. During this two decades, the ever-expanding extremely "Leftist" ideology in the government censured management education programs as "Bourgeoisie and Revisionist Hotbeds". The lopsided and dogmatic understanding ideas about management education went to the extreme during the Cultural Revolution (1966-1978). All universities and colleges were closed down and the People's University was even completely disbanded under the accusation of "acting as the incubator of revisionists". When many engineering and science education programs were partly restored in the later period of Cultural Revolution, those management development programs based on the two USSR models were still excluded from the government plan. By end of 1970s, management education in China was near to none.

Stage III: 1979 - present. Under Denng Xiao-ping's leadership, the reform and opening policy has caused profound and broad changes in every aspect of China's social and economic life since 1979. Due to the dismissal of management education programs in the previous stage, China was in serious shortfall of highly educated management personnel (Bu & Mitchell, 1992; Child, 1994; Warner, 1992). Therefore, education was one of the very first areas in which Deng Xiao-ping initiated his reform policy. He included management education in those areas that China should learn from the Western developed countries.

During Deng Xiao-ping's visit to U.S.A. in 1979, he asked President Jimmy Carter for assistance and cooperation with China in setting up a joint senior management development project. This project resulted in the establishment of the first China-West joint management training project in 1980 -- the National Center for Industrial Science & Technology Management Development (at Dalian), Dalian, Liaoning Province. Meanwhile, the Chinese government decided to strive for training a big team of ambitious managers to equip them with modern management concepts and techniques. In 1982, it proposed a guideline statement for management development in China, popularly known as the 16-Character Principle, i.e. "Taking our own practice and national situations as the main body, extracting and adopting the strengths of various countries extensively, combining them all together through refining to form our own unique management system eventually."

Being aware of the great demand for competent managers, the government invested a great amount of funds and efforts into improving and expanding its management education and training system. Since 1982, management education and training have been mushrooming throughout the country. Thousands of economic officials, managers, scholars, and students have been sent abroad to learn Western management theories and practices. Meanwhile, hundreds of Western management scholars and executives were invited to visit China and to train Chinese managers and faculties. By the early 1990's, under the State Education Commission, various management programs and departments had been restored or established in around 400 universities and colleges. Among these 400, at least 40 universities had their own management/ business schools by late 1980's. Under the State Economy and Trade Commission System, one the other hand, more then 90 economic managerial cadre colleges and nearly 30 national centers for management development had also been set up. Some of them were cooperative projects with Western developed countries, such as centers in Dalian (with the United States as mentioned above), Beijing (with European Community), Xian (with the United Kingdom), Shanghai (with Germany), Tianjin (with Japan), and Chengdu (with Canada).

In 1990, the State Education Commission authorized 9 universities to run China's MBA programs on an experimental basis. These MBA programs were highly engineering or management science oriented (Child, 1994). By 1994, 26 universities had been authorized to grant MBA degrees. In 1996, the government established a National MBA Education Guiding Committee under the State Education Commission to unify MBA admission exam and to guarantee the quality of MBA students. In 1998, an additional batch of 30 schools joined the 26 universities to run MBA programs.

3. The Dilemma of Management Pedagogy and Their Roots

Boisot & Fiol (1987) developed a model (learning cubes) to describe the differences between traditional Chinese management education pedagogy and Western management education pedagogy. In their paper, they identified two extreme vertexes A and H to represent Chinese and Western learning styles respectively. Vertex A means directed/abstract/passive learning, in which a learner learns from textbook exercises under the guidance of a teacher passively. Vertex H is autonomous/concrete/interactive learning style, with which a student learns by world problem solving with his/her team members. Boisot & Fiol (1987) pointed out that Western professors brought in Vertex H teaching and learning styles, while Chinese managers used Vertex A teaching and learning styles. Both sides felt frustrated with the difficulties to merge these two sides synergistically (Bu & Mitchell, 1992).

In Western business schools, more and more management education programs adopted action learning, critical reflection learning, experiential learning and service learning projects that represent the Boisot & Fiol's (1987) Vertex H learning model (Holman, 2000; Kolenko, Porter, Wheatley, & Colby, 1996; Raelin, 1995; Reynolds, 1998). Boisot & Fiol (1987) suggested that Chinese management education should also move toward Vertex H in order to train practical managers to meet the demands of the market economy. However, twenty years have passed. The Chinese traditional education model — pursuing objective knowledge through passive one-direction lecturing — is still the dominant force in China's management education. As Bu & Mitchell (1992) found, the preference of Vertex A (Boisot & Fiol, 1987) learning style caused many problems that could be identified in many areas, such as suspicious of pedagogy used by Western professors, lack of student participation, and inefficient group discussions in classroom. The main reasons for these problems in China's management education come from the cultural, political, and historical roots.

We argue that the Western management pedagogy clashes with Chinese traditional cultural values, which makes it hard for Chinese trainees to comfortably adapt Vertex H learning style. Although Chinese scholars realize the importance of the autonomous/concrete/interactive management learning style (e.g. Deng & Wang, 1992; Warner, 1987; 1992; Wo & Pounder, 2000), there are difficulties at both trainers' and trainees' sides to implement an autonomous, concrete and interactive management learning model. The following will analyze these dilemmas faced by Chinese management education scholars and practitioners.

3.1 Nature of management knowledge: objective or subjective?

The Chinese government tended to think that natural sciences and engineering were the major forces that could help China in her modernization course. This belief could be traced back to the late Qing Dynasty (1644-1911), and it has naturally led to an emphasis on engineering education over management training in the Chinese education system. Managerial knowledge, if any worth at all, was also believed to be as objective as to other engineering subjects.

Under this type of mentality, in the 1980's, bachelor and master degrees in management departments or schools were offered only in the area of Managerial Engineering. More than 80 percent of management programs were based in engineering schools, which prefer objective and quantitative-based disciplines to subjective and qualitative-based disciplines. The preference was reinforced by the "fear" of involvement in social science studies, which were perceived as politically sensitive and apt to cause troubles. Added by the bias that the central planning system was the only optimal economic pattern for a socialist country, there was strong doubt against and resistance to the introduction of Western management education models. Although a few schools have eventually established comprehensive and multi-functional management programs, the primitive understanding of management being merely a physical, rational, "hard," and precise science has not been much changed yet. The opinion that all management problems should mainly be approached by and solved with quantitative analysis still exists. There is still a long way to go for taking management as more subjective, pragmatic, experiential, and critical subjects of knowledge in China.

3.2 Objective of management training: specialists or generalists?

In the former central planning economy of China, the government expected managers of State –owned Enterprises (SOEs, the dominant economic cells then) to do operation management only. Other management functions, such as finance and marketing, were none of the SOE managers' responsibilities. These managers used to be taken care of by governmental agencies at different levels. Therefore, a good manager in the Chinese sense was traditionally supposed to be a specialist in a specific engineering field, such as mining, steel making, or ship building. In fact, most present managers in China have been promoted from experienced engineers.

Based on this belief, the curriculum designed for developing managers was highly engineering-oriented. Courses about fund raising, marketing, human resources, laws, economics were excluded, as well as those "soft" courses such as organizational behaviors, communication, leadership, etc. This was related to the mentality of avoiding political risk and the bias of these courses being too subjective to master. Instead, political and ideological courses such as Marxism and Socialism Economics were included to guarantee the political correctness of Chinese managers.

As we all know, in a market economy, an executive should be, as a final decision maker, responsible for all the aspects of the business of his or her firm in a broader context, and hence should have a much broader, pragmatic and flexible understanding of management knowledge. However, it is not necessary and may even be impossible for him or her to be an expert in every functional field. They should be generalists or general managers instead of specialists in a specific function.

When Western thoughts of management education were gradually introduced into China and the transition of the planned economy toward market economy occurred, government officials gradually accepted "westernized curriculum". However, the basic ideology of the manager's role as an independent decision-maker has not been totally accepted by the Chinese education participants. In addition, the government still takes a significant role in intervening in corporate decision making. All these barriers hinder the implementation of western management education pedagogy in China.

3.3   Teaching methodology: lecturing or experiential?

Traditionally, the only favorite teaching/learning style in China was highly structured lecturing given by a knowledgeable and respected instructor. Instructors who strictly followed a well-conceived and detailed syllabus were regarded as a Master of Classroom Teaching. These masters were well prepared to cover every detail in a class, even watching out which sentence should be spoken at which minute and which word should be written on which part of the board.

According to the Learning Cubic Model (Boisot & Fiol, 1987), which depicts teaching styles with three dimensions (conceptual versus practical, individual versus collective, and under instruction versus via self-study), the typical Chinese teaching/learning pattern fits the conceptual-individual-under instruction style. This means that Chinese students are accustomed to and prefer the way of studying as separate individuals under the detailed instruction of their teachers focusing mainly on theoretical topics. They expect and are expected simply to listen to, to take notes of, and to copy down what their instructors say and write. In contrast, Western teaching methodology is typically presented as practical-collective-self-study. It involves students actively participating in classes with experiential methods such as case study, role-play, and simulation.

Therefore, it was not surprising at all how shocked Chinese managers and faculties were when first exposed to case teaching method by American professors in the early 1980's at the Dalian Center. Both Chinese managers and faculty were skeptical about the effectiveness of the case teaching method. The Chinese faculties, mostly with an engineering background, felt especially confused when they found that many cases even had not had an optimal and clear-cut answer with which they could judge whether the participants' analysis was correct or wrong. The Chinese managers were particularly upset that many US professors, well known for their expertise in their own fields, let the participants discuss amongst each other and therefore gave few lectures. These participants even questioned: "As instructors, if they don't lecture, why should we pay them with such a high price?"

Generally speaking, the "instructor centralism" in Chinese management pedagogy is derived from two major sources: the traditional Confucianism culture, and the former Soviet pedagogy.

3.3.1 Confucianism

Teacher was ranked with Heaven, Earth, Emperor, and Parents as the Five Tops in ancient China. Han Yu, a top scholar of Confucianism in the eighth century, once defined the role of teacher as imparting doctrines of the sages, teaching a trade, and solving puzzles. Thus, a teacher should always be regarded as an authority that is more knowledgeable and more skillful than students, acting as the center or boss in the classroom. Teachers were supposed to be dominating and initiative lecturers and senders of knowledge, while students were passive listeners and receivers. In addition, the Confucian value of "saving face" also discouraged students from expressing their own opinions and from confronting or debating with their classmates, let alone from challenging their teachers. They usually intended to avoid losing their own faces or those of their peers or teachers.

3.3.2 Soviet pedagogy

The core of the Soviet Pedagogy was represented by the "Five Basic Pedagogic Principles" and the "Six Links in Classroom Teaching" developed by the then most authoritative Russian pedagogist Kalov. These principles and rules, however, did not mention anything about students' participation in teaching process. Instead, teachers were viewed as the dominating factor in classes and students were recipients of knowledge. These guidelines were very popular in China in 1950s and early 1960s, as they well matched the Chinese traditional teaching philosophy.

Over the past two decades, particularly since 1990, case teaching as well as other experiential methods has gradually been accepted in Chinese management education institutions. More and more instructors and students have participated in the process and experienced the advantages of them. Nevertheless, there is still a long way to go to make these methods more effective and relevant to the Chinese context. In fact, Chinese scholars did make efforts to develop their own cases and simulations more relevant to Chinese management circumstances. For example, a series of case-teaching workshops for management instructors have been organized since the Management Case Study Association (MCSA) was formed in 1986. Many Western sources also have contributed to the dissemination of the methods in China. For example, the World Bank has sponsored several case teaching workshops in China; and the University of Western Ontario supported the publication of the Chinese edition of its two key textbooks regarding case teaching method in the early 1990's.

3.4 Sources of trainees: prospective or incumbent managers?

When considering the reform of China's management education and training system, the Chinese government was facing two knotty problems: Should the emphasis be placed on the training of millions of incumbent managers or on the development of prospective managers? Furthermore, in terms of developing prospective managers, should the undergraduate or graduate programs be highlighted?

In addition to the training of incumbent managers in those national centers and managerial cadre institutes, China's management-degree-education started with undergraduate programs under the State Education Commission in the early 1980's. One A The government's key argument for this decision was a comparison to the training of military officers: Since the Chinese armed forces have been very happy with the qualified military officers provided by undergraduate programs in various military schools, why don't we similarly run undergraduate programs in management schools to provide qualified managers to our companies? Consequently, for quite a while, most of the management programs in universities focused mainly on the development of young undergraduates with little working experience. On the other hand, believing that the managerial job is a profession and getting a bachelor degree in management would result in a promising executive career, thousands of top students enrolled in management programs.

However, unlike most of their counterparts in the West, these Chinese undergraduate students had no working experience at all when entering universities right after high schools. The pedagogical problem of passive learning in Chinese management education as described above reinforced the disadvantages of undergraduate students. They often complained that they were trained to be neither fish nor fowl and their prospects were far away from brilliant as they originally expected. In fact, these undergraduate students of management were not welcome by enterprises after their graduation, as they were neither qualified managers nor engineers. If assigned an ordinary staff job at entry level, these graduated students tended to feel that it was a waste of their talents. Therefore, when management tried to select candidates for managerial jobs, they often rather preferred engineers with good work performance to those management majors despite the latter's management education background.

In 1986, there appeared some criticism claiming that the overemphasis on developing undergraduate management education was a strategic mistake, as it had not produced enough quality managers to meet the urgent demand of the economy as expected. Instead, it caused some "double wastes of talents' by producing less qualified managers while spoiling those management majors with falsely promising executive career. The defenders' argument was that China's education system was embedded in its economy. It was not the undergraduate management programs but the economic system that did not provide suitable opportunities for those management majors to use the managerial knowledge they have learned. By now, the defender's ideas have lost their market. China has come to highly emphasize MBA programs, which take incumbent managers and professionals.

4. Implications and Conclusion

China's management education has stepped on the right track and has made a great progress as a result of efforts contributed from various circles of the country. The government has been aware of the importance of a large pool of qualified managers to its economic growth. It has started to implement a plan to develop and to upgrade thousands of competent managers to meet the demand of Chinese enterprises in the new century.

This is obviously a tough task given the twisty route that China has passed most of the time over the past half century. The conflicting pedagogical values and social institutions between modern management education in the West and China's own circumstances further reinforce the difficulty. A lot of efforts still need to be put into management education to improve it not only quantitatively but qualitatively as well. Summarizing experiences and drawing lessons from the past 20-year practice in management education, and receiving the increasing influence from more and more frequent interactions with the West, the Chinese government has continued to set up its own MBA education system. The Program's design has imbibed a lot of useful elements from the MBA system of the West. At the same time, it should also keep some features that are unique to China. For example, the content of management education should be more China-related. The pedagogy of management education should also consider the above mentioned historical and cultural beliefs to make a unique Chinese management education model by combining western merits and Chinese values.

The above analyses reveals that although China's management education is moving toward adopting autonomous, concrete and interactive learning styles, there are still traditional value and cultural roots that hinder this progress. This suggests that Chinese scholars and Western scholars teaching in China should realize these difficulties and adopt a compromising pedagogy, such as a learning style that combines the features of Vertex A and H. For example, case studies could be arranged in team discussion as Western business schools do, but teamwork reflections and after-discussion summaries should be followed to make sure students understand what they learned in a directed way. Vivid real world examples will also be welcomed by students in class-room learning and Chinese-specific cases and examples will be considered more appropriate than Western cases. We would suggest that while adopting Western management education pedagogy, Chinese circumstances should also be considered and after-activity reflection and summary should be emphasized to make Chinese trainees feel that they did learn something from those concrete and interactive activities.

References

Boisot, M., & Fiol, M. (1987). Chinese boxes and Learning Cubes: Action Learing in a Cross-Cultural Context. *Journal of Management Development, 6*, 8-18.

Bu, N., & Mitchell, V. (1992). Developing the PRC's Managers: How Can Western Experts Become More Helpful? *Journal of Management Development, 11*, 42-53.

Chan, M. (1996). D. Brown & R. Poffer (Eds.), *Management Issues in China: Volume I: I. Management Education in the People's Republic of China*. London & New York: Routledge.

Child, J. (1994). *Management in China During the Age of Reform*. London: Cambridge University PRess.

Cova, B., Kassis, J., & Lanoux, V. (1993). Back to Pedagogy: The EAP's 20 Years of European Experience. *Management Education & Development, 24*, 33-47.

Deng, S., & Wang, Y. (1992). Management Education in China: Past, Present and Future. *World Development, 20*(6), 873-880.

He, W. (1996). *Strategic Inertia and Organizational Decline: A Case Study* [Working Paper, Boston College].

He, W., Wang, X., & Yu, K. (2001). *A Visible Hand: Government as the Change Agent in the Transformation of Management Education in China.* Paper presented at the meeting of the Academy of Management, Washington D.C.

Holman, D. (2000). Contemporary Models of Management Education in the UK. *Management Learning, 31*, 197-217.

Kolenko, T., Porter, G., Wheatley, W., & Colby, M. (1996). A Critique of Service Learning Projects in Management Education: Pedagogical Foundations, Barriers, and Guidelines. *Journal of Business Ethics, 15*, 133-142.

Raelin, J. (1995). Reformulating Management Education: Professional Education, Action Learning and Beyond. *Selections*, 20-30.

Reynolds, M. (1998). Reflection and Critical Reflection in Management Learning. *Management Learning, 29*, 183-200.

Ring, P., & Perry, J. (1985). Strategic Management in Public and Private Organizations: Implications of Distinctive Contexts and Constraints. *Academy of Management Review, 10*, 276-286.

Warner, M. (1987). Industrialization, Management Education and Training Systems: A Comparative Analysis. *Journal of Management Studies, 24*(1), 91-112.

Warner, M. (1991). How Chinese Managers Learn. *Journal of General Management, 16*(4), 66-84.

Warner, M. (1992). *How Chinese Managers Learn: Management and Industrial Training in China.* London: Macmillan.

Wo, C., & Pounder, J. (2000). Post-Experience Management Education and Training in China. *Journal of General Management, 26*(2), 52-71.

Yu, K., Wang, X., & He, W. (1994). *Teaching Values as a Critical Determinant of Business Education: The Evolution of Business Education in the P.R.C.: Vol. . Proceedings of the Inaugural Conference of the Center for the Study of Business Values.* Hong Kong: Hong Kong University.

Chapter 9

Optimizing Expertise: A Case Study of Team Teaching on an International MBA Program Conducted in China

Catherine Sutton-Brady
The University of Sydney

Glenn Pearce
University of Western Sydney

1. Introduction

This paper, in providing a documented case study of team teaching in southern China, highlights how an understanding of the challenges of engaging adult learners, coupled with teamwork in teaching can result in a program that not only satisfies the learning and professional needs of postgraduate students but enhances the reputation of the institution offering the qualification. The case study showcases: the success of the team teaching approach and co-operation between the subject teaching team, their depth of understanding of each others' teaching approach, pace and desired results, engagement of students in enjoyable yet challenging experiential learning activities and subject content specialization in order to expose students to each team member's areas of expertise. In addition it provides insights into teaching in China and recommends ways of overcoming problems and differences which may arise. It also helps to dispel many of the myths which exist about teaching in China.

2. Location Southern China

To set the scene for this case study it is important to understand the context of the team teaching experience. The team consisted of two experienced academics from an Australian university teaching International Marketing on the University's overseas Masters in Business

Administration (MBA) program. The MBA program was offered in partnership with an educational authority in Guangzhou, Southern China. The Australian university provided the lecturers for the program and the partner in Guangzhou provided the administrative staff and interpreters.

The program was taught over intensive weekend blocks with tutorials mid-week in the evenings. Each unit ran over two weekends from Friday evening to Sunday evening with tutorials on the intervening Tuesday and Wednesday evenings. The Australian academics were accommodated on campus for a two week period. The program was split between two groups of students, those who only spoke Cantonese or Mandarin and the bi-lingual class consisting of students who also spoke English. An interpreter was provided for the class that did not speak English and all material was translated for them.

It was open to each academic team to decide how they approached teaching the same unit to both classes. Many teams just split the content and swapped-over as appropriate; others used the approach of one academic per class and therefore did not work as a team but two separate individuals. The team from this particular case study spent an inordinate amount of time arriving at the decision to team teach their unit based on each individual's area of expertise. The following section outlines how the decision to team teach was made in consideration of extant literature.

3. Team Teaching

What is team teaching? As pointed out by Brudnak (1999) team teaching can mean different things to different people. For the purpose of this case study, team teaching involves two academics planning and developing a unit of study together, dividing up the subject content in terms of the academics' expertise and then teaching that unit to two classes simultaneously by rotating between classes.

In deciding to design their unit around a team teaching approach, the academics in this case study referred to the relevant literature and found benefits not only for the students, but also for the academic team. In particular, as posited by Hollister and Nelson (2000), team teaching allows academics to improve their teaching practice and in a spirit of trust forge a relationship that enables teachers to undertake problem solving, take risks and further develop overall teaching strategy.

To date, much has been written about the advantages and disadvantages of team teaching and how it can enrich and enhance student learning (Anderson, 1989; Bondi, 1999; Doebler & Smith, 1996; Saccoman, 1996; Schamber, 1999; Ulveland, 2003). Advantages of team teaching can include: concentration on areas of expertise - allowing team members to fully develop their expertise by researching in the area and keeping up-to-date with changes and trends in that area; exposure of students to different and often diverse teaching styles; use of creative techniques whereby team members are more prone to take risks; and opportunity for team members to collaboratively develop and plan the subject. Disadvantages of team teaching can include: overlap of content (minimized by communication between members); compartmentalization of topics rather than bringing the whole subject together; and conflicting teaching philosophies (Anderson, 1989; Doebler & Smith, 1996; Hollister & Nelson, 2000).

While some teachers may resist the idea of team-teaching, others see it as a way to thrive professionally (Anderson, 1989). Those who have seen it work to their benefit point out that when you work in teams you become more aware of problems and you can be inspired by watching the work of others (Anderson, 1989; Bondi, 1999). It is by no means the easy option, as it requires much more preparation and ongoing communication to be successful. Some tips given for effective team teaching are offered by Folly and Baxter (2001) who state that team members must be given time to talk and common planning time must be carefully scheduled. These authors reiterate that the success of teams depends on the members' willingness to work together and the adequate provision of time for planning and communication.

4. Organization and Logistics

Three months before the unit was scheduled for teaching, the two lecturers were chosen by the Graduate School in Australia administering the overseas MBA. It was fortuitous that the lecturers were located in the same School and University. This convenience in location allowed them to work closely together to initially develop the unit. The lecturers concerned had very similar teaching philosophies which made it easy for them to harmoniously develop a unit that they would both be comfortable teaching. The unit was developed in line with Bloom's taxonomy of cognitive learning (Bloom, 1956).

A wide range of approaches were used to capture and keep students' interest in what they were learning, but always maintaining the focus on achieving the desired educational objectives. These activities were in line with Bloom's six taxonomic levels: Level 1, knowledge-remembering facts, terms, principles, definitions and so on; Level 2, comprehension-translating ideas from one context to another, interpreting, extrapolating and so on; Level 3, application-using rules and principles in certain situations; Level 4, analysis- breaking down and making clear the nature of components and the relationship between them; Level 5, synthesis-arranging and assembling elements to arrive at a new statement, plan or conclusion; Level 6, evaluation-assessing the value of materials or methods regarding internal accuracy and consistency or though comparisons with external criteria.

Once the unit was developed, the next task was to determine the unit structure and teaching arrangements. It was agreed that there would be a common introduction and conclusion and that the unit content would be divided based on areas of international marketing knowledge and expertise. (See Table 1) The common introduction and conclusion avoided any perception of compartmentalization of the topics (Doebler & Smith, 1996) and clearly tied together the overall unit. The introduction in particular highlighted the teaching styles and gave students an opportunity to see how the unit would flow. The division of topic areas allowed for switching between the two classes at preordained intervals. At various stages in the program there were common activities taking place in each classroom at others times the activities differed since some were content dependant as opposed to subject specific.

Prior to overseas departure, the team worked closely together fine-tuning delivery of the unit. To ensure greater cohesion, the team traveled together, constantly discussing teaching process, scheduling and logistics. On the first Friday morning in Guangzhou, the team met for one last briefing session with subject interpreters to ensure interpreters were aware of the program timing.

Table 1. Unit Plan

Session	Chinese Language Class	English Language Class	Activities and Case Studies
	Lecturer 1	Lecturer 2	
Friday	Introduction	Introduction	
	Marketing Mistakes	Marketing Mistakes	Activity 1
	Domestic v International	Domestic v International	
Sat. A.M.	Marketing Research	Political/Legal/Economic Environments	
	Lecturer 2	Lecturer 1	Activity 2
Reading	Chapter 8	Chapters 6, 7 & 9	
Sat. P.M.	Political/Legal/Economic Environments	Marketing Research	Activity 3
	Lecturer 1	Lecturer 2	Case Study 1-3
Reading	Chapters 6, 7 & 9	Chapter 8	
Sun. A.M.	Cultural Environment	Product and Service Strategies	
	Lecturer 1	Lecturer 2	Activity 4
Reading	Chapters 3, 4 & 5	Chapters 12 & 13	
Sun P.M.	Product and Service Strategies	Cultural Environment	
	Lecturer 2	Lecturer 1	Activity 5
Reading	Chapters 12 & 13	Chapters 3, 4 & 5	Case 2-1
Tues. Evening	Tutorial	Tutorial	
	Lecturer 1	Lecturer 2	
Friday Evening	Negotiation and Globalization	Pricing and Counter trade	
	Lecturer 2	Lecturer 1	
Sat. A.M.	Pricing and Counter trade	Negotiation and Globalization	Student Case Study Presentations
	Lecturer 1	Lecturer 2	
Reading	Chapter 18	Chapter 19	
Sat. P.M.	Market Entry Strategies	International Marketing	Student Case Study Presentations
	Distribution & Logistics	Communications	
	Lecturer 1	Lecturer 2	
Reading	Chapters 11,14 & 15	Chapters 16 & 17	
Sun. A.M.	International Marketing	Market Entry Strategies	Student Case Study Presentations
	Communications	Distribution & Logistics	
	Lecturer 2	Lecturer 1	
Reading	Chapters 16 & 17	Chapters 11, 14 & 15	
Sun. P.M.	Review	Review	Student Case Study Presentations
	Lecturer 2	Lecturer 1	

At scheduled breaks during teaching time, the team met to discuss progress and class developments. In addition to these meetings, the team had all their meals together and as a result of this high level of interaction became totally immersed in the educational experience. The sessions were all videotaped and the team used these videos to discuss how they could change or improve the program. This technique is in line with the idea of incorporating change into practice as you practice (Hawkins, 1994). The team also changed the program where necessary to suit the differing learning styles of the students (Fatt, 2000).

The key element of the organization and logistics of this unit was the ongoing communication and interaction between the team. This organization, which led to the seamless presentation of the unit, ensured that the students had the security of knowing that the expectations and standards of the two lecturers were the same (Hollister & Nelson, 2000).

5. Lessons and Implications

The feedback the team received from interpreters and students was extremely positive. The students, who were exposed to twelve teaching teams over their twelve-month block-course MBA, rated this team as the best team by far. This rating was empiricized in student evaluations of the unit and its lecturers. Students in their open-ended responses referred to the outstanding organization of the unit, which they believed allowed the individual lecturer's unique style and expertise to be exhibited. One student even commented that there was a "perfect match between the two lecturers". Students also commented on such things as: good time management; logical; easy to follow; and systematic approach. In terms of student learning their responses included: stimulating student thinking; interesting classroom atmosphere; made difficult subject easy to learn; lively, energetic; and enhances student learning and thinking.

This positive student feedback was echoed by the Chinese MBA director, based in China, who in a letter of commendation wrote: "definitely the best pair among the 12 teaching teams for the program. Their careful team preparation and deep understanding of each other's teaching approach, pace and desired results, as well as materials used, have produced a seamless cooperation in their delivery of the unit. Both students and our teaching assistants were impressed by their perfect team teaching".

Reflecting on praxis, the key to the team's educational success was the organization of the unit and the continuing improvement brought about by ongoing communication between team members. Optimizing expertise allowed students to be exposed to the most up-to-date research in the specialist areas. This specialization by topic has been shown in other studies to provide students with a richer presentation of that topic than otherwise might have been the case (Doebler & Smith, 1996).

Working in teams also exposes students to different styles of teaching and learning as was the situation with this case (Hollister & Nelson, 2000). While educational outcomes were achieved for this team, it is clear that there is one overriding implication: the teaching philosophies of individual team members should be compatible. In addition to compatibility of teaching philosophy, the key to good team teaching would seem to be ongoing communication and a desire for continuous improvement.

It is clear that the overriding issue found in the feedback from both students and staff was clearly the team teaching aspect however there are other lessons which can be taken from this case and generalized to teaching in China. There is a traditional perception of what is expected when teaching in China, this perception is based on Confucian culture of the Chinese and the strong power distance rating of the Chinese culture (Hofstede, 1980). The idea being that the teacher is right and in a sense must not be questioned. Therefore, education has been traditionally based on the lecture format where all the information is given to the students. In this case the lecturers were conscious of this fact especially since their teaching style clearly reflects an experiential approach. They were careful to illicit information from academics who had previously worked in China to see if the traditional view still held. They were told that they may need to change their approach slightly and make sure that as much information as possible was available for students. However the lecturers felt that given results from research in the area of education in China things were changing. This change has since been highlighted by various authors, for example Thompson (2001) found that MBA students considered the use of case studies in class highly important in their learning experience. This finding clearly goes against the traditional view.

Alon and Lu (2004) have also highlighted the problem of integrating western style experiential-based and participatory teaching methods to students unaccustomed to that style of teaching. It is however clear from this case study that it can work if the lecturers are prepared and well organized and ready to change to suit the students. Ongoing monitoring of activity in the class room gave the lecturers the opportunity to change and suit the pace and expectations of the students. The students in this case enjoyed the engagement, were happy to participate in role plays and other drama based exercises. Overall, this activity challenged the traditional view of education in China. It has been pointed out by other authors (Hollister & Nelson, 2000) that team teaching increases the individuals' willingness to take risks and it is evident in this case that the lecturers were more willing to take risks and go against what was considered the norm in China. The result of this risk taking led to a more participatory style of teaching and inclusion of students in the learning process through experiential based learning techniques.

6. Recommendations for Enhanced Team Teaching

This case has, as previously pointed out, highlighted various issues in regard to team teaching. Based on the lessons learned, we first make the following recommendations to any academic given the opportunity to team teach. (See Table 2)

Table 2. Recommendations for Enhanced Team Teaching

Issue	Recommendation
Utilizing Expertise	Capitalize on the strengths of individual team members
Teaching Philosophy	Take time to get to know other team members particularly with regard to teaching philosophies and style
Planning	Spend time up front planning the subject content and delivery
Communication	Build relationships through regular communication and meetings (if location permits)
Equity of teaching load	Ensure equity in division of duties

The success of team teaching is clearly dependent on the amount of quality time spent planning the subject. While this time may seem onerous to many the resultant success out weights the effort needed to achieve it. There are a number of things which should be taken into account in planning; the overriding issue is one of location. In this case it was convenient for the academics to meet and plan the subject content and delivery as they were in the same location.

If academics are separated by distance then planning could be more of a challenge. Meeting this challenge may need some creative solutions. Technology and especially use of email will make things easier, it is further recommended that setting up a web page or having each academic access a system like WebCT or Blackboard where all teaching materials can be progressively developed, will enhance the experience of the team. This system of planning could even be expanded and utilized where the teams are teaching in different locations.

The other key success factor to team teaching is to take advantage of the relative strengths of each team member. As was evidenced in this case designing the course to make the most of each individuals expertise area leads to students being provided with a greater depth of knowledge. Team members may also have other skills which can be exploited for the benefit of the overall team. These skills may include designing interesting classroom activities, developing assignments or utilizing their technical abilities to enhance the overall learning experience of the students.

To fully capitalize on the strengths of each team member it is recommended that prior to developing the unit the team meet and discuss issues relating to teaching. In these sessions the academics will be able to get to know each other particularly with regard to teaching philosophies and teaching style. Furthermore areas of subject expertise and other expertise can be investigated to ensure that the optimum solution is found for the smooth running of the team. These sessions will also allow for a clear division of labor to ensure equity in teaching load.

One of the issues known to case problems in team teaching is the load attributed to each academic in the team. A clear up front and open discussion, of what each academic is required to do, helps to alleviate any misunderstandings and misconceptions of equity. It is also our experience that building a good relationship in the team means that equity never becomes an issue, because the discussions are open and frank and tasks are split equally no team member tends to feel they are doing more. There may of course be times when one is doing more than the other, but good team work means that at another time it equals out.

7. Recommendations for Teaching in China

From the lessons we learned while teaching in China, we would like to put forward some recommendations for academics lucky enough to get the opportunity to teach in this dynamic environment (See Table 3). We would also like to attempt to dispel many of the myths which exist about education and teaching in China.

Table 3. Recommendations for Teaching in China

Issue	Recommendation
Planning and Logistics	Have all material translated and sent to students and interpreters well ahead of arrival in China
Student Questions	Unlike in Western classrooms, students like to independently try to work things out before asking. Be prepared to wait for questions and don't be too pushy early on in the course.
Language Difficulties	Liaise closely with interpreters before classes start and ensure ongoing communication throughout the course.
Experiential Learning	Be prepared to take risks, the results will surprise you, our experience shows they do like activity, but be careful to debrief them so they see the value of the activity.
Socialization	Be ready for numerous banquets with various groups of students.

The first lesson we learned was the importance of planning and logistics. While this is the case in all teaching, its' importance gathers momentum when faced with the challenge of teaching in a different country and different language. The best recommendation we make is to make sure that all material is translated well ahead of undertaking the teaching. Back translation, if affordable, is also advisable, especially if you have subject specific terms whose meanings may be lost. And ensure that the material gets to students before class starts as it is our experience that Chinese students like to prepare ahead of time. This aspect of Chinese education ties in with our second point concerning student questions.

One of the overwhelming myths we encountered when discussing Chinese students with colleagues was the misconception that students do not like to ask questions in class. We were curious about this and on investigating the issue found that previous research has shown that it is not a fear of asking questions as many academics thought, but a cultural issue where it is expected that questions are based on knowledge (Watkins 2000). Hence our recommendation that information be sent ahead of time so students can prepare and work things out independently and then ask questions when you get there. If you have not been able to send the information ahead of time our warning is not to expect too many questions early on in the course and do not be pushy in asking for questions as the students will not want to appear ignorant, unlike many western students who will ask questions out of ignorance quite happily.

While language difficulties are unavoidable if you are not fluent in the language of instruction, we have recommendations to make the experience easier. As mentioned, get the material translated ahead of time and ensure that the interpreters have access to all material that you will present in class. Doing this will make the translation process a lot smoother since you will then be unlikely to throw in any technical or subject specific terms with which they will be unfamiliar.

It is also recommended that the interpreter have a background in your teaching area as that ensures more accurate translation and transfer of knowledge. For example, in our case we were lucky enough to have an interpreter with an MBA who had excellent subject knowledge. We realize this is not always possible and consequently our overriding recommendation is getting the information to them early so they can prepare. We should stress here that it is not necessary to have a script or definitive lecture notes, a good interpreter once they have the overview will be able to follow as you go.

The first time you carry out a lecture in another language can be quite daunting. The trick is to keep sentences short and try not to say too much at any one time. We found that a discussion of one point on PowerPoint and then a stop was the best compromise. It is not necessary to stop after each sentence; for one thing the class timing would probably be disastrous. It should however be noted that using an interpreter will slow down your delivery and this should be worked into the course content planning.

The final recommendation here is ongoing and regular communication with your interpreter as this will allow you to change pace as necessary. In our case interpreters meet with us for an hour each evening after class to assess how we all performed, these meetings we found invaluable in fine-tuning our delivery.

As we have previously pointed out experiential learning can be very successful in China, even though there is a mistaken belief that Chinese students from a cultural stance are not happy with experiential learning. We recommend that you ignore this fallacy and be prepared to take risks. Our experience verifies that Chinese students enjoy classroom activity. Our only caution is to ensure that students are debriefed on the activity and that its' value in their learning is highlighted. Many students in our case specifically commented on the value of our debriefing sessions.

The major difference we actually found between Chinese students and other MBA students we have taught is their friendliness and delight in socializing with academic staff. While in western cultures this socialization would be frowned upon to some extent it is seen within China as a necessary part of the teaching experience. It relates very much to the relationship with the teacher from a cultural point of view. Watkins (2000) found that Chinese students considered their relationship with the teacher would be a "friendly warm one well beyond the classroom".

As a result be prepared to socialize, in our case students had arranged a roster to make certain that all students got to meet with us socially over the two week period. The assigned group of students would then take us for dinner and deliver us back to the campus afterwards. While this can be trying having taught all day, especially since many use the opportunity to ask more questions, we found to refuse was insulting and culturally insensitive. Our final caveat therefore, is depending on the groups you teach be prepared for many large banquets and some wonderful eating experiences.

8. Conclusions

In conclusion, this paper has highlighted the success of this team over all others in a demanding overseas postgraduate program. It also confirms that optimizing expertise by working in teams not only enhances the learning experience of students, but clearly develops teaching excellence. Furthermore it shows that a willingness to take risks and go against what are considered the norms in a certain environment is easier to do when working in a team.

This paper has provided some recommendations based on our experience for others faced with the challenge of team teaching or teaching in China. Overall, in the context of teaching in China it is clear that things are changing especially in business education and lecturers must be prepared to move with these changes to achieve success in their teaching and most importantly the student's learning experience.

References

Alon, I., & Lu, L. (2004). The state of marketing and business education in China. *Marketing Education Review, 14*(1(Spring))).

Anderson, R. H. (1989). A second wave of interest in team teaching. *The Education Digest, 54*(6), 18-21.

Bloom, B. (1956). *Taxonomy of educational objectives: cognitive domain.* New York: McKay.

Bondi, R. (1999). A true teacher. *The Christian Century, 116*(33), 1176.

Brudnak, K. (1999). Keeping current. *Mailbox Teacher, 27*(4), 26-29.

Doebler, L., & Smith, C. (1996). Enriching a survey course in educational psychology through a team teaching format. *Education, 117*(1), 85-88.

Fatt, P. (2000). Understanding the Learning Styles of Students: Implications for Educators. *International Journal of Sociology and Social Policy, 20*(11/12), 31-45.

Folly, L., & Baxter, K. (2001). Forming general education and special education teams. *Principal Leadership (High School ed.), 2*(3), 73-74.

Hawkins, J. (1994). Designing technology for professional development. *Electronic Learning in Your Classroom, 13*(4), 10-11.

Hofstede, G. (1980). *Cultures Consequences: International differences in work related values.* Beverly Hills, CA: Sage.

Hollister, W., & Nelson, S. (2000). Teaming for learning success. *Primary Voices K - 6, 8*(4), 20-28.

Schamber, S. (1999). Surviving team teaching's good intentions. *The Education digest, 64*(8), 18-23.

Thompson, E. (2001). Are teaching cases appropriate in a mainland Chinese context? Evidence from Beijing MBA students. *Journal Education for Business, 76*(2), 108-113.

Ulveland, R. (2003). Team teaching and the question of philosophy. *Education, 123*(4), 659-662.

Watkins, D. (2000). Learning and teaching: a cross-cultural perspective. *School Leadership & Management, 20*(2), 161-173.

Chapter 10

Meeting China's Need for Case-Based Teaching Material: The Ivey Business School Experience

Paul W. Beamish
University of Western Ontario

Gigi Wong
University of Western Ontario

Joanne Shoveller
University of Guelph

1. Introduction

MBA education in China has a relatively short history. In 1991, the People's Republic of China started the first MBA degree programs at nine selected business schools, all at top-tier national universities. Recognizing the rapidly escalating need for Chinese managers with international business skills and knowledge, the National MBA Education Supervisory Committee quickly increased its MBA programs from the 9 test sites in 1991, to 26 in 1994, and to 56 in 1998. By 2001, at the anniversary of China's ten years of MBA education, 62 universities nationwide offer MBA programs to 32,393 candidates for the Masters of Business Education degree. Here we provide a brief historical overview of the Richard Ivey Business School and its China involvement in order to set the institutional context.

In 1922, the first undergraduate business department in Canada was established at The University of Western Ontario (UWO). In 1948, the first MBA program in Canada was established at UWO and in the same year, Canada's first executive development program. From the beginning, faculty members were required, as part of their responsibilities, to produce case material for the new programs being designed. In 1975, Ivey opened its own case and publications office. Ivey Publishing now holds an inventory of more than 2,000 current cases (5,500 in total) and is the Canadian clearing house for Harvard cases. In 2004, Ivey cases were being distributed to more than 500 teaching institutions and 700 corporations in over 50 countries. Ivey is the second largest producer of management case studies in the world, with over 1,000,000 copies studied each year by people outside the university.

In 1997, a *Journal of International Management* article named Ivey the world's leading contributor to the international strategic management literature in the previous decade, a point reaffirmed by them in 2003. The Asian Management Institute (AMI) was established in 1997 to focus Ivey's efforts in research and learning material development with Asian relevance. In 1998, the Cheng Yu Tung Management Institute was officially opened in Hong Kong offering the HK Executive MBA. Ivey's Asia campus was the first overseas campus to be established by a North American business school in Asia.

2. China Activities – Before the MBA Era

1984 marked the beginning of a continuing linkage between Ivey and Tsinghua University in Beijing. The School made a commitment to prepare Chinese MBA and Ph.D. students for studies at Ivey, work with visiting scholars, provide some short-term instruction in China, and to assist Tsinghua University's School of Economics and Management in the development of its management faculty. Another goal of the project was to help Ivey become more familiar with China and the conduct of business in that country. This project was funded by the Canada-China Management Education Program, an initiative of the Canadian International Development Agency.

During Phase I of the project: 35 articles, cases, and notes were written; nine Ivey faculty participated in short teaching visits to China; twelve visiting scholars spent one year each at Ivey; there were eight graduates of the MBA program; all visiting Chinese attended the annual Case Writing Workshop.

An expanded Phase II of this program took place until 1994. A five-year endeavor, the project was a joint venture with the University of

Waterloo, and in China, with Tsinghua, Dalian University of Technology, and Southeast University. Ivey's commitment was to continue to assist in the development of Chinese institutional capacity for management education. A major element was the design, development and delivery in August 1992 of a program on teaching Joint Ventures, Technology Transfer, and International Trade via The Case Method. This train-the-trainers program was offered to academics from across China, through interpreters. All of the teaching material was translated into Chinese.

A large scale joint publishing effort was undertaken. In April 1992, the first volume of five international business casebooks was published in Chinese by Tsinghua University Press. This series was a joint undertaking of Ivey and Tsinghua. This series constituted a comprehensive collection of international business cases for Chinese managers and students. In 1992-93, six international texts were published in Chinese by presses arranged through our partner schools at Dalian and Southeast.

3.   A Total Solution (Model)

Ivey's off shore projects have typically involved the establishment of local management training capability. Our emphasis is on building human capacity in a sustainable fashion. Together with Tsinghua University's School of Economics and Management, and the China Machine Press (Huazhang Graphics), the three partners embarked on the project: *"A Total Solution for Management Education Material in China"*.

Dr. Sun Lizhe, President of Multi-Lingua Publishing International Inc., a joint venture partner with China Machine Press, recognized that the Chinese universities had an urgent demand for high quality teaching materials, and that Ivey was the school to provide such material. True to the significance of "guanxi", Dr. Sun was a close friend of a Tsinghua professor who was part of the first group of visiting scholars to Ivey in 1984, and a supporter of Ivey's initiatives in China ever since.

Three components of the model were devised.

(1) Customization of case books based on the curriculum needs of the China MBA program;
(2) Recommendation of best text books for the MBA curriculum; and
(3) Introduction of Case Method Workshops for all MBA instructors across China.

3.1 *Books of cases*

In 1998, 32 volumes of case books (16 in English and 16 in Chinese translations) were prepared for the China market. Cases selected for each volume were based on the core curriculum of the MBA program in China. The series was supplemented by subsequent titles based on electives and new topics as the curriculum continued to be revised. (Exhibit 1) Here a case study refers to a comprehensive, field-based, decision-oriented description of an administrative situation. It does not include descriptive case histories (which require students to make no decision); mini-cases or vignettes (which are anecdotal, and not suitable as a stand-alone basis for an 80-90 minute class); or library-based cases (such secondary sources produce far fewer insights than actually interviewing managers for the cases).

Several elements of this project were considered ground-breaking at Ivey. First, 17 of Ivey's 70 faculty members served as editors. They volunteered their time to select cases from Ivey's collection and from other leading providers of cases. They consulted with their colleagues in China on the curriculum needs, and they provided an introduction for each case book speaking specifically to the content and its use in classrooms. Second, as copyright holder to its intellectual capital, Ivey Publishing waived all of its normal permission fees to translate and use the cases. More than 300 Ivey cases were translated into simplified Chinese characters. Third, corporate sponsorships were secured to subsidize the project to ensure affordable price for broad distribution. Each case book typically had 10-15 cases and was priced in the range of 15-30 RMB (less than US$4). Last, any royalty collected from the sale of case books which were owing to Ivey was donated to charities in China. To date, more than 100,000 copies of the case books have been sold.

3.2 Text books

We also organized 18 Ivey professors, experts in their respective fields of teaching, to work closely with faculty from Tsinghua University and consulting professors from other Chinese universities in selecting 18 of the most highly regarded textbooks from around the world for reprinting (Exhibit 2). Dr. Sun had the reprinting rights in China from a number of major US and European publishers. These main stream recommended text books represented the state-of-the-art of business education and corresponded to the core courses of the Chinese MBA curriculum. These textbooks were available in major bookstores in China priced at 1500 RMB (US$180) for the set of 18.

3.3 Case workshops

The case method approach represented a new way of thinking for Chinese educators. Students learn through lively discussions and debate. Traditionally, Chinese students would not confront professors or provide opinion due to the sense of hierarchy and cultural deference to people in positions of authority. We found that the instructors and students were ready for this "Western" approach in their MBA experience. To people unfamiliar with this method, sharing the "dos" and "don'ts" with experts, and understanding the opportunities and risks in teaching and learning with cases are critical in building up the confidence to help improve the overall experience for both students and instructors.

Tsinghua University in Beijing and Fudan University in Shanghai provided the venue and on-the-ground support for the pan-China Case Teaching Workshop in 1998. Organized by the MBA Education Supervisory Committee, a two-week workshop, repeated in both locales was delivered by Ivey Professors James Erskine, Michiel Leenders, Paul Beamish and Ivey PhD graduate Kent Neupert. 57 MBA instructors from universities across China attended the 1998 workshop. Since then, the annual "Train-the-Trainer" workshop has trained more than 250 Chinese educators. There are more than 2800 professionals involved in MBA education in China.

4. Lessons Learned

The total solution model worked. The reaction to the case books and text books was tremendous. As one associate dean at a Shanghai business school commented in 1998 on receiving the set of 16 case books and 18 recommended text books, compliments of the publisher, "We need these cases desperately, and there are no other collections like these. There is no choice but to purchase them for our classes. I am happy Ivey has produced these for China." We were assured that the model provided the framework and expertise to enhance the resources and capability of management educators in China.

The experience of working with foreign colleagues in sourcing the material and in translating our cases into Chinese was invaluable. It has improved the quality of the original English-language versions by forcing us to recognize and remove colloquialisms, clarify ambiguous words or phrases, and eliminate any ethnocentric biases which may have unconsciously crept in. It reinforced the fact that many of the case needs are "culture bound". In certain instances, we recognized the "inappropriateness" of the Western style cases and acknowledged the practical needs of the local teachers. Such collaboration has provided opportunities for our faculty to engage in joint case writing with colleagues in China.

Some would view Ivey's publishing initiative in China as a loss leader – foregoing permission fee, pricing low, collecting no royalties, risking copyright infringement. We viewed it as an opportunity, one that is in accordance with the School's strategy in Asia – building a strong brand. It is also in accordance with the School's mission to develop business leaders who think globally, act strategically and contribute to the societies within which they operate.

5. Next Steps

MBA education in China has come a long way in its short history. The rapid growth of the number of "case centres" at management schools designated by the National MBA Education Supervisory Committee is a firm signal that this is a policy area China's leadership is paying a lot of attention. Management development in China has been, and continues to be, a pressing concern of multinational and local companies. Human resources executives are competing for creative, solution-oriented managers.

By early 2005, there were already 90 management schools across China offering MBA degrees plus hundreds offering undergraduate programs. It seems certain that we will continue to witness the demand for new and relevant case material. Furthermore, we all recognize that the environment in which the cases are set changes rapidly, particularly in developing countries such as China. One challenge to academics is how to become aware of new materials in order to keep a course current, to use cases which the students will consider as relevant. Our colleagues in China are quickly grasping the solutions: searchable database and catalogs (Ivey, COLIS, HBSP), casebooks in local markets, word of mouth, or write their own.

There are numerous case centres actively pursuing case writing and developing a significant collection of cases written in Chinese; Dalian University of Technology, Peking University and Tsinghua University to name a few. Dalian alone has a collection of more than 900 cases and was the pioneer in China in case writing/publishing. At the institutional level, we work towards partnering with reputable case centres: to help the Chinese faculty enhance the quality of their cases by streamlining the teaching focus; to write about companies and issues where a non-local case writer will normally not get access to; to make available more case material (translations from Chinese to English) for the rest of the world.

6. Conclusion

Management development is a key concern for the People's Republic of China as the country continues in the direction of a market-driven economy. The cultivation of talented people is a critical component of the success of the country's transition. As business educators, we believe in human capacity and intellectual capital building. We believe that

China presents a vast market for learning material providers. We believe that we should capitalize on the local needs in its fullest potential to explore new case leads. We believe that new cases written on doing business in China will benefit students around the world in understanding the market dynamics in China.

Exhibit 1. China Case Book Titles

English Casebook Titles	Chinese Casebook Titles
Business Ethics	商业伦理学
Corporate Finance	公司财务
Finance and Money Market	金融与货币市场
Financial Accounting	财务会计
Human Resource Development and Management	人力资源管理
International Business	国际商务
International Trade and International Finance	国际贸易与国际金融
Management	管理学
Management Communications	管理沟通
Management Information Systems	管理信息系统
Management Science	管理科学
Managerial Accounting	管理会计
Managerial Statistics	管理统计
Marketing Management	市场营销管理
Production and Operations Management	生产与运作管理
Strategic Management	战略管理學
E-Commerce	电子商务
International Entrepreneurship	国际企业家
Organizational Behavior	组织行为学

Exhibit 2. Recommended Text Books

1. Financial Accounting: An Introduction to Concepts, Methods, and Uses, 8th Edition – Stickney/Weil
2. Essentials of Investments, 3rd Edition – Bodie/Kane/Marcus
3. Managerial Accounting, 3rd Edition – Hilton
4. Management, 4th Edition – Daft
5. An Introduction to Management Science: Quantitative Approaches to Decision Making, 8th Edition – Anderson/Sweeney/Williams
6. Principles of Corporate Finance, 5th Edition – Brealey/Myers
7. Basic Marketing: A Global-Managerial Approach, 12th Edition – Perreault/McCarthy
8. Production and Operations Management: Manufacturing and Services, 8th Edition – Chase/Aquilano/Jacobs
9. Management Information Systems for the Information Age – Haag/Cummings/Dawkins
10. Strategic Management: Concepts and Cases, 10th Edition – Thompson/Strickland
11. Business Law & the Regulatory: Environment: Principles & Cases, 13th Edition – Anderson/Fox/Twomey/Jennings
12. Statistics for Business and Economics, 6th Edition – Anderson/Sweeney/Williams
13. Human Resource Management: A Tool for Competitive Advantage – Kleiman
14. International Management: Text and Cases, 3rd Edition – Beamish/Morrison/Rosenzweig
15. Business Ethics: A Global and Managerial Perspective – Fritzsche
16. Management Communication: Principles and Practice – Hattersley/McJannet
17. Communication for Managers, 6th Edition – Sigband/Bell
18. Principles of Economics – Mankiw

Endnotes

Tong Yunchun et al. editors. (2001) China's MBA Education, China Machine Press, Beijing, China. ISBN 7-111-09558-8F

Chapter 11

Pedagogical Implications of Studies of Soft Technology Transfers to Chinese Firms

Peter H. Antoniou
Pomegranate International

Kern Kwong
California State University

Catherine E. Levitt
California State University

1. Introduction

The 1997 study examined enterprises' perceived need for management skills transfer across the various stages of organization. Analyzed was the degree of success of transfer, acquisition, and assimilation of management skills especially focusing on the relationship of the Chinese firm and the accomplishment of a successful transfer agent.

In an effort to examine what has transpired in the intervening six years and building from the base established in 1997, the Chinese firms which participated in the original study were re-contacted in 2003. Of the original 93 firms, 77 participated fully in the study. Six firms had gone out of business completely. Four firms had been absorbed by other entities and were no longer able to participate. Five firms did not respond at all. One firm replied to the survey but not to the request for interview. The number of firms self-identifying as State-owned or as entrepreneurial went down substantially while the number of self-identified transitional firms increased.

Changes in the structure of firms and their relationships with government, other business entities and the agents of transfer were observed. The types of the skills sought by Chinese firms are different in priority and scope than those sought in 1997. The choice of transfer agent and method of transfer had changed, as had the expectations of the firms. These changes hold implications for management education. This paper analyzes the results of the 1997 and 2003 studies toward an understanding of these pedagological implications and offers suggestions toward integration into curricula for management courses.

2. Background of the Problem

With the collapse of the Soviet Union and the Eastern Bloc, the reunification of Germany and the move toward Market Socialism in China, nearly half the population of the world is participating in the transition from a command economy toward free market practice at the close of the Twentieth Century (World Bank, 1997.) At the same time, western nations are increasingly seeking both markets and suppliers on a world wide basis as the global village becomes a reality (Cao, I 995; Chau, 1995; Drucker, 1992 and 1994; Hax, Klenner, Kraus, Matsuda and Nakamura, 1995; and Naisbitt, 1995). Western firms are eager to include these transitional economies in their strategic vision (Culpan, 1995; "Lessons...," I996; Ricardo, 1817).

Transitional economies afford a strategic window and an opportunity to earn supra-normal returns both to domestic and to foreign firms resulting from significant market imperfections. These market discontinuities and disorganizations allow those with knowledge or special conditions, circumstances, people and relationships to experience major, non-scientific breakthroughs. This strategic window, however, requires an approach that takes into consideration the needs and expectations of the very special markets which are beginning to recognize the need for free market skills (Naisbitt, 1996; Tung, I982; 1995). In the planned economic structure originally defined by Karl Marx in 1889, the emphasis was not to sell but to produce. In contrast, the market economy requires a focus on consumers and marketing activities (Chen and Babcock, 1996).

After the death of Mao Tse Tung and the trial of the "Gang of Four", Deng Xiaoping announced, in 1978, China's "opening to the West", with the introduction of the "Four Modernizations" (Deng, 1997). The Chinese transition, however, is quite unique in the length of time afforded to the transition. Unlike the former Communist nations of such as the Soviet Union and Eastern bloc countries or socialist, controlled economies such as India which have shorter time horizons, the Chinese transition has been "typically Chinese". It has not abruptly shifted gears but, already nineteen years in process, the Chinese transition is far from complete. Like the Chinese proverb about 'moving an island in a stream a grain of sand at a time so it is eventually moved downstream, the Chinese transition is slow and steady (de Mente, I995; A lessons..,1996). Despite recent dramatic efforts on the part of Zhu Rhongi to substantially reduce the dysfunctional state-owned enterprises (SOEs), the command economy is not completely gone (Barnathan, et. al., 1993; Baugn and Bixby, 1996.) The market economy is the aspiration and the expectation of many stakeholders, both domestic and foreign, but the definitions of the Chinese market economy differ substantially (Dekeijzer, 1994; Wong, 1995). Many players within the Chinese economy see their advantage in preserving an incomplete market economy system in which the right connections and the possibility of pleading ignorance are frequently the keys to success (She, I 996; Campbell, 1989). Since June 1991, China has increased its free market efforts substantially, identifying four steps to free market participation: privatization, restructuring, liberalization and stabilization. To be able to affect any of these without a necessary joint-venture arrangement the mechanism for private ownership, enterprise zones or village enterprises, were created (Deng, 1991; Gao, 1995). Domestic firms increasingly realized the need to acquire free market management skills. Ministerial institutes of technology were enjoined to include Western style management and economics courses in their curriculum beginning in 1992.

2.1 *Strategic importance of soft technology transfer*

Recent studies in transitional economies indicated that the commonly held definition of success for a newly privatized firm is the acquisition and adaptation of technology rather than bottom line profit (Baird, Lyles, and Wharton, 1996; Culpan and Kumar, I 995; and An and Gray, 1994). This "soft technology" sought was explained as the skill required to build and sustain indigenous management competency, and capability and capacity in the free market. The transition economy requires more than the simple redistribution of ownership to the private sector to be successful. It must also be able to develop a culture that sustains and nurtures innovation. Generally, this element requires acquisition and development of skills and vision not commonly found in organization driven by quotas rather than by market needs (Kao, 1995; Kirby and Pay, 1995; and Selmer, 1992). Subsequently, the acquisition and assimilation of soft technology often mandates substantial changes in the structure and the strategy of organizations (Prahalad and Hamel, 1990; Bartlett and Ghoshal, 1987, 1992, 1997; and, Ansoff, 1979; 1988).

While the definition of the role of transfer agent was drawn from the literature in technology transfer and strategic management (Ansoff, 1985), the cultural go-betweens operating to facilitate cross-cultural learning, both indigenous and foreign, have had a particularly long history in China. The Chronicle of the Yellow Emperor written 213, B.C., and the Art of War (Sun Tze, 220, B.C.) both mentioned the importance of acquiring skills through the offices of brokers and go-betweens. The writings of Marco Polo in the Thirteenth Century (Latham, 1969,) and later, in the early Seventeenth Century, Francis Xavier and Matteo Ricci both explained their role in the court of China in much the same way as the transfer agent is described in East meets West, 1934. Sir Victor Sasoon and the Noble Houses of Hong Kong and Shanghai all employed "compradores" in order to interface with Chinese businesses and the government offices (Redding, 1993). Since the 1949 Liberation of China, the State Party Congress has employed foreign experts who are recruited and employed through the Foreign Experts Bureau in Beijing. The "web" of overseas Chinese business as described by Kirby, (1996), Kao (1993), and by Kraar (1994) is another example of transfer agency. In the context of management skills transferred to Chinese firms, five types of transfer agents are identified in the literature and are listed in Table 1.

In addition to five types of transfer agents, there are three levels of transition to free market participation in which the firm may exist. The literature commonly describes three stages of loosening control: command, transition and free enterprise (World Bank, 1994). The length of time since the initial redistribution of ownership, the percentage of ownership retained by the State and the independence of the firm in resource allocation are the criteria by which stage of control is determined. The domain of this research centered on the relationship of the receiver to the transfer agent and on the implications that the relationship had on the performance variable, success of the transfer. Organizational behavior studies and cultural management research have long described Asian culture as relationship based (Bond, 1988; Harris and Moran, 1991; Hofstede, 1991; and Hofstede and Bond, 1988). Such descriptions find their roots in Confucian teachings which defined society and very specifically ordered the relationships of man. *Guanxi* is a primary principle that developed out of these teachings (Tung, 1996; Kirby, 1994). The principle dynamics of *guanxi* are trust, care, commitment, and the perception of similarities that outweigh differences. There is a need for mutual dependencies such that in Chinese society, guanxi has greater force than the rule of law Redding (1993), Shi (1996), Tung (1990), Child and Lu (1996). An and Gray (1994), Stedlmeier (1991), DeMente (1995), like Khong (1994), found that the use of brokers, agents, and go-betweens was not predicated on need but on a desire to strengthen relationships. There are a number of studies of joint venture failings which indicate that such failures occur when *guanxi* is not developed (Worm I 996; Zhan Su, 1996).

3. Research Design

This study attempted to combine both qualitative and quantitative approaches in an effort to avoid the shortcomings inherent in each method, as well as to facilitate the cross-cultural exchange and maximize the nature of Chinese data collection. The primary data instrument was a structured, undisguised questionnaire that contained both scaled Likert-type data and multichotomous data which was used to test the research hypothesis. The instrument was administered in small focus groups of managers within each of the ninety-three enterprises. Open-ended questions were used to draw qualitative data from group discussions after the group had been presented the structured portion of the instrument.

The focus group context and the group discussions were important in bridging some of the language and cultural barriers (Wong,

I 995). Focus groups have been used extensively in marketing research (Kotler, 1994) and in psychological interviews. According to An (1995), focus groups are traditionally used when group discussion tends to focus on the issue rather than on the interviewer or the interviewee. This method of data collection was far from perfect. However, since data collection for Chinese management respondents is so culturally sensitive and is controlled by the Chinese government, it was a method that was determined to be effective by all parties involved. Evidence of the control of Ministry of Light Industry was the 100% response rate.

The primary researcher was assisted by a team of two bilingual, indigenous Chinese assistants in the facilitation of group discussion and the recording of answers. Written minutes and tape recordings of each discussion were taken. Following the discussions, each of the researchers assigned numerical values for the variables based on their perception of the group responses to the questions. An average score was then calculated for the researchers and recorded as the numerical value of that variable for that focus group. Every effort was made to reduce personal and cultural bias via the averaging technique and by testing inter-rater reliability tests. A total of 2,508 separate judgments were made, and then classified into three levels of judicial agreements:

Level 1: Complete Agreement: All three judges agreed unanimously, 73.3 percent of all judgments.

Level 2: Substantial Agreement: Two judges agreed and the other differed in evaluation by Less than or equal to one scale point. 23.6 percent of all judgments.

Level 3: Judicial Disagreement: Any outcome amounting to greater departure from agreement than a one point scale, 3.1 percent of all judgments.

One focus group consisting of three to five upper Level managers was held at each of ninety-three Chinese firms. The firms were all directly linked to the Ministry of Light Industry, subsequently renamed the Council of Light Industry during the study. None of the participating firms were at the time of this study, involved in foreign joint ventures. Between four and thirteen firms were studied in each of ninth provinces and in two autonomous cities. Thirty-four of these firms had 500 or fewer employees and are identified by the ministry as small. Thirty-one firms were considered medium-sized having 501-2,000 employees. The remaining twenty-eight firms employed 2,000 or more, with the largest firm having 31,132 employees.

Changes in the socio-economic environment in China are so rapid sod so frequent that the time frame of the studies must be identified. It was conducted over a two month period extending from February 1, 1997 through April 1, 1997. An historic event occurred during the course of the data collection period which had substantial impact on the research. The February 22, 1997, death of Deng Xiaoping, who was credited the development of the market economy in China. This event was coupled with the rededication of the country to the principles of economic progress expressed by both the President and Premier, Jiang Zemin and Li Peng, who seemed to have profoundly affected most of the Chinese people at diverse levels. This was reflected to such an extent in the qualitative answers to research questions that the researcher recorded data as pre- and post-February 22, 1997.

In 2003, all the 93 original participated companies were re-contacted. Out of them 15 went out of business or were sold to other entities. 78 of them were still in business and all responded. Those enterprises still in existences and willing were surveyed using the same questionnaire and the same approach as described above. The primary researcher was the same but the assistants were different. Due to time constraints, the interviews and focus groups were conducted during two 3-week periods one in March of 2003 and the other in late August of 2003. It should be noted that the Ministry of Light Industry does not exist any more. It has been replaced by the Bureau of Light Industry which has a different, less all encompassing role.

4. Research Results

Type of Transfer Agent, The definitions and descriptions of the five types of transfer agents were derived from the literature. Within the ninety-three firms surveyed, all five types of transfer agents were found but they were not evenly distributed as shown below. In every firm studied, a transfer agent had been identified. Transfer agents were seen by most Chinese firms as the first step and key activity toward modernization and the successful transfer of soft technology. The frequency of each of the five types of transfer agents is listed below in Table 1.

Table 1. Types of Transfer Agents Employed

Type	Relationship	#Firms 1997 2003		Author
1	External to both sender and receiver, professional consultants participating in the culture of the sender	22	12	Steidlmeier, 1995
2	External to both sender and receiver, professional consultants participating in the culture of the receiver	22	27	J. Kao, 1992; Wong, 1996
3	Internal to the sender, acting as expatriate management for the receiver	9	6	Selmar, 1992b
4	Internal to the receiver, acting as liaison with the sender	22	24	Selmar,1990; Wong, 1996
5	External to both sender and receiver acting as expatriate Management for the receiver	19	9	R. Kao, 1995

The qualitative input from the focus groups indicated that accessibility and availability of foreign, professional consultants exists to a much greater degree in coastal provinces and the Special Enterprise Zones of autonomous cities. Respondents also indicated that Overseas Chinese and other Asian consultants are categorized as culturally unlike the Chinese, i.e., Type 1, unless they have considerable life experience in a socialist environment. In contrast, professional consultants from Germany with previous experience in the reunification of East and West Germany were categorized as culturally similar, Type 2 because of their transitional experience. This represents a connotative difference from the literature which suggested that cultural similarity is predicated on language and ethnicity rather than on political experience. Most frequently (eleven instances in 1997 and 19 in 2003), Type 2 transfer agents were described as Peoples' Republic of China nationals, either university professors or municipal government officials, with some experience in joint venture operations and participation in overseas training programs. Chinese executives viewed municipal government officials and Chinese technical experts as professionals, while the literature tended to equate professionalism with external or foreignness. These differences in definition have distinct implications for the definitions of Length of In-Country Presence, the Intensity of In-Country Presence, and for the subsequent results of the study.

Length of In-Country Presence. In-Country Presence ranged from one to twenty-two years. However, when presence exceeded ten years, the transfer agent was generally a native of the PRC and the number of years measured industry experience rather than Chinese residency. This was substantially different than the instances of a few years in which the transfer agent was foreign and the number of years represented active consultancy in China.

Intensity of In-Country Presence. Intensity ranged from low to high on a five-point scale with the highest levels of intensity attributed to native Chinese working internally to the firm. The focus group discussions implied that intensity was a function of accessibility and connectedness to the goals of the social unit, the firm. The majority of transfer agents were described as exhibiting moderate to moderately high intensity. Generally, the higher the level of success reported by the group, the more intense the involvement of the transfer agent.

Scope of Technology Being Transferred. All of the firms studied actively sought to acquire and assimilate more than free market skills. Recent changes in commercial law, the 1995 establishment of accounting standards, changes in the welfare/benefit system, and desire to develop private sources of finance for growth were cited by respondents as the reasons these new skills were sought. In twenty-three instances it was described specifically that increasingly more skills were sought in the long term but that acquisition of new skills had to be done gradually and in stages. The planning horizon for this acquisition and assimilation was stated as over twenty years with a completion date of 2020 cited in sixty-seven instances. Prior to the death of Deng Xiaoping-ping, the specific phrase "if the heavens do not change course" was mentioned in relation to the plans to acquire skills in eighteen of the twenty-three focus groups who volunteered a long-term perspective.

5. Research Hypothesis: Transfer Success and In-Country Presence and Intensity, Commitment to the Transfer, Trust, Scope of the Transfer, and Stage of Privatization

It was hypothesized there would be a direct relationship between the success of the transfer and six variables that characterize the transfer; two aspects of In-country presence, the commitment to the transfer, scope of the transfer, type of transfer, trust, and stage of privatization. Each of the variables tested either employed Pearson's correlation or Analysis of Variance, ANOVA, as was appropriate. Results of each of the six sub-hypotheses are listed below in Table 2.

     <u>In-Country Presence and Its Intensity</u>. It was expected the transfer agent's in-country presence and especially the intensity of that presence, such as the daily involvement of the transfer agent in the firm's operations, would be positively correlated with the success of the transfer, The highest levels of intensity were attributed to the native Chinese working actively in daily operations of the firm. Focus group comments suggested intensity was a function of accessibility and responsiveness. In more than twenty-two interviews, the transfer agent was described specifically as *ging,* translated as passion. Beepers, E-mail, and personal visits were specifically and repeatedly mentioned as mechanisms by which intensity relationships was developed. Further, interviews conducted after Deng's death, gave even greater attention to the value of intensity.

     <u>Level of Commitment</u>. The level of commitment to the transfer and the vesting of similar objectives was significantly correlated to the degree of success the technology transfer experienced by the firm. Comments from interviews, conducted after the death of Deng Xiaoping indicated that uniform commitment from all parties involved was very important to the transfer of soft technology.

Trust. Closely related to the level of commitment was the level of trust in soft technology transfer success. Both of these variables are integral parts of the Chinese *guanxi* dynamics. In firm interviewed as number forty-one, the comment was made that, 'for Chinese, trust is a harmonic value'. It is personal, between people. Foreigners talk about trust in the organization such as a company or government. Chinese do not trust that which has no blood, no eyes, no soul." Consequently, it was not surprising that the most strongly correlated variable with transfer success was trust evidencing an "*r*" value of .79670. The degree of trust the firm had in its transfer agent was an extremely strong predictor of the degree of success in the transfer of management skills.

Table 2. Success of' Transfer and Directly Related Characteristics of the Transfer

Variable Related to Transfer Success	Test Used	Statistical Significance 1997	2003	Implications
In-Country Presence	Pearson	.009	.009	The longer the transfer manager's tenure in China, the more successful the transfer
Intensity of In-Country Presence	Pearson	.050	.041	The more the transfer agent was involved in the daily activities of time firm, the greater the transfer success, This relationship was even greater when the post-Deng firms were analyzed.
Commitment to the Transfer	Pearson	.005	.011	Commitment to the transfer process fairly well correlated with the success of the transfer.
Trust	Pearson	.0005	.001	Trust was identified as single most significant variable correlated with the success of the technology transfer.
Scope of the Transfer	ANOVA Chi-Square	NS .013	NS .011	Scope of the skills to be transferred was not related significantly to transfer success. Differences associated with stage of privatization.
Stage of Privatization	ANOVA Kendall Tau	.007 NS	.008	Statistically significant differences in the success of the transfer depending whether the firm was state-owned, transitional, or entrepreneurial; substantially higher rate of success among transitional firms.

Scope of the Transfer The scope of the transfer, one of the two related variables tested through ANOVA, was not able to support the alternative hypothesis. Because there was a large variety of skills to be transferred in management technology transfers, it was discerned upon further review of results that differences existed across the three stages in which the firms existed. In each focus group, respondents were presented in advance of the interview with a World Bank list of soft technology requirements for transfer to firms in developing nations. These eighteen skills are quite different which may have contributed to the nearly random responses to the priority of the skills respondents required. Essentially, across all ninety-three firms, in all three stages, the responses canceled out each other.

To better identify what the scope of the technology transfer was, the priority of management skills desired was tested by stage of privatization. A Chi-Square goodness of fit test evidenced there was a statistically significant difference across stages. Skills important in command economies were somewhat different from transition economies and transition economies desired substantially different management skills from entrepreneurial firms. See Table 3 for full ranking of preferences both for 1997 and 2003.

Generally in the 1997 responses, command economies were told what to do and were given resources so they preferred skills that had more priority in "political activities" such as knowing how to get resources, financial and human, and how to negotiate in a more tactical, or short-term environment. On the other hand, entrepreneurial firms reported they need strategic management skills such as being able to see the whole framework for decision-making especially in the long-term perspective. Financial skills indicated by the entrepreneurial firms were more likely to be financial management not political acquisition of resources as was viewed as important in SOEs. While SOEs also reported Longer-term perspectives and stressed clearly reported the importance of a gradual transfer of new skills, entrepreneurial firms voiced a greater expediency in acquiring skills.

There are some interesting changes in the priority listing in the 2003 responses. In all categories the first choices remained the same. However, in the Command category finance and marketing were the only

Table 3

Skills Most Sought by Stage of Privatization 1997

PRIORITY	COMMAND	TRANSITION	ENTREPRENEURIAL
1.	Finance	Marketing	Strategy
2.	Training	Human Resources	Finance
3.	Marketing	Finance	Marketing
4.	Human Resources	Decision Making	Decision Making
5.	Economics	Information Tech.	Competing
6.	Negotiation	Organizational Design	Human Resources
7.	Information Tech.	Training	Accounting
8.	Travel	Advertising	Org.Design
9.	Planning	Competing	Culture
10.	Strategy	Strategy	Negotiation
11.	Accounting	Leadership	Sales
12.	Org, Design	Travel	Advertising
13.	Advertising	Sales	Training
14.	Leadership	Planning	Information Tech.
15.	Sales	Negotiation	Travel
16.	Decision Making	Accounting	Leadership
17.	Competing	Economics	Planning
18.	Culture	Culture	Economics

Skills Most Sought by Stage of Privatization 2003

PRIORITY	COMMAND	TRANSITION	ENTREPRENEURIAL
1.	Finance	Marketing	Strategy
2.	Accounting	Finance	Marketing
3.	Marketing	Accounting	Finance
4.	Information Tech	Information Tech	Decision Making
5.	Training	Decision Making	Competing
6.	Negotiation	Org. Design	Advertising
7.	Human Resources	Training	Accounting
8.	Law	Advertising	Org. Design
9.	Planning	Competing	Culture
10.	Strategy	Strategy	Negotiation
11.	Economics	Leadership	Information Tech
12.	Org. Design	Travel	Sales
13.	Advertising	Sales	Training
14.	Leadership	Planning	Leadership
15.	Sales	Negotiation	Human Resources
16.	Decision Making	Law	Travel
17.	Competing	Economics	Planning
18.	Culture	Culture	Economics

attributes which remained the same and in the same ranking for the top 5 choices. In the Transitional category all top five choices remained the same except the second one which was replaced in 2003 from human resources to finance. In the Entrepreneurial category the top remained the same. The only difference was an interchange between the finance (2d choice) in 1997 and marketing (2d choice in 2003).

It is also need to be noted that marketing and finance were the only choices which appeared in the top five ranking for all three categories. Strategy appeared only in Entrepreneurial. It is indicative of the Command category that training, human resources and economy held such a high position while the same did not appear at all in the Entrepreneurial and only human resources appeared in Transitional.

Stage of Privatization. Finally, the stage of privatization was tested as a measure of the success of the soft technology transfer. ANOVA results indicated differences across the three levels and the transfer success with transition economies reported the greatest degree of transfer success. The degree of success however, was not a linear relationship between stage of privatization and transfer success when tested employing a Kendall tau test of rank order correlation. The interpretation of transfer success may have been fairly imprecise for the Chinese sample. Focus group discussions revealed that it is a Western managerial assumption that firms seek success, increased profits, and growth through increasing the freedom of their operation or by becoming increasingly entrepreneurial.

This model was clearly not appropriate for many other responding firms. Repeatedly researchers found firms, which had begun in an entrepreneurial stage, but with limitations on size and resources of the entrepreneurial firm as well as a lack of political leverage needed for adequate growth, frequently sole proprietors sold stock in their firms directly to municipal governments or ministries, essentially, by Western standards, a regressive move. Comments from respondents indicated the power of this relationship was very favorable in developing the political guanxi the firm needed. One manager related that:

"Freedom has different faces. Including the government in strategy and ownership of the firm opens doors and windows to profitable opportunities that are closed to the man who acts alone. The transitional firm is more in keeping with the Chinese character."

Especially in light of the death of the Chinese leader in the early part of the interviewing, it is not surprising respondents would rally behind Deng's goal for the PRC. Transitional firms support the socialist value system while enabling the firm to approach Western style and size profits.

6. Discussion and Implications

It was hypothesized by researchers that several characteristics of the transfer agent and the setting would have an effect on the success of the transfer. The level of trust, which evidenced high degrees of colinearity with most other variables tested, emerged as the single most significant variable in identifying the success of the transfer. There were several elements in the definition of the transfer agent found to differ within the sample of ninety-three Chinese firms from the parameters identified in the literature. Because familiarity is so important to develop trust and networking with the transfer agent, she Chinese managers, in the firms interviewed, did not generally consider overseas Chinese managers as adequate transfer agents to ensure success. Instead. Chinese nationals who were technical experts, academics, or even municipal government officials were seen as valid, trustworthy agents preferred to "foreign", non-mainland Chinese agents. This definition of transfer agents is an Eastern definition which supports the role of guanxi in successfully operating within the Chinese culture. Respondents' comments indicated trust and commitment were developed through personal relationships and in good conscience could not be attached to groups or inanimate categories. Respondents specifically related that the workers and managers needed to feel personally entrusted by and to the transfer agent in order for the firm to successfully adopt more Western management techniques.

7. Predictors of Soft Technology Transfer Success

Six variables were measured to identify their contribution to the prediction of success in the technology transfer. Six variables: in-country presence, intensity of in-country presence, commitment, trust, and stage of privatization, were all found to influence the extent to which the transfer was successful. Only scope of the transfer of technology was not statistically significant. Because quite varied free market management skills were needed by a firm depending on whether it was a command, transitional, or free market firm, it was assumed the scope of the transfer, in each of the three categories, canceled each other out and none emerged as uniformly significant. Command firms evidenced a high priority for financial skills, especially in the direction of seeking funding. Those command firms expressed little need for traditional Western management skills; strategy, leadership, and decision-making, in command firms, with virtually no internal leadership, the managers are told what to do and only need to be able to execute the orders.

As the firm moved out of a command status and into transition status, the type of management skills required a shift from political and execution oriented to more operational. Transitional firms need to be able to operate in the short-term and make tactical decisions. However, entrepreneurial firms have very different skills required to effectively manage with their greatest need being strategy. As Western Firms and agencies are seeking to offer management technology transfer to Chinese Firms, their requirements are quite varied (Chen, I 996.)

The remaining four variables were all found to positively contribute to the prediction of the success of the soft technology transfer. It was important to the Chinese firm looking to adopt Western management skills that the transfer agents have great standing within the country. Chinese nationals with Western management experience were the ideal. If that type of agent was not possible, then the longer the agent's Chinese experience, the better he was accepted. Perhaps of greatest meaning was the finding that a large cultural gap was perceived when the transfer agent was not a Chinese national and did not have substantial presence in country. There may be no advantage to having an Overseas Chinese manager over a Western manager as a transfer agent. There may actually be a preference for the managing transfer agent to be Western not Overseas Chinese. Overseas Chinese may not be the best at successfully developing the necessary guanxi to affect the transfer of

Western management skills as they are not automatically trusted by managers and employees who perceive a substantial cultural gap between them.

There is an inherent contradiction in the Chinese firm's requirement for extensive Chinese in-country experience. In order for trust to develop to a point that enables a successful technology transfer, the agent must have many years experience in China. However, in order to be really knowledgeable in Western management practices, which are to be transferred to the Chinese firm, the transfer agent would, historically, have spent adequate time outside the country learning Western management techniques. This desire on the part of Chinese firms to "have it both ways" is evidence of increasing indications that Chinese industries and firms want Western management practices but want to adopt the portions that are most effective for their operation. One responding managers suggested,

> "Chinese don't need Western ways. For 5,000 years we have gotten by without them. Now, we want these skills-having help makes it faster- but, we could get there with out help."

In 1996, Chinese telephone surpassed AT&T as the world's largest telephone company (Bracchius, 1997). This was accomplished with virtually no outside help in technology, production, or management. A more recent replication of this has occurred with cellar telephone service and with the provision of broadband. There is an increasingly apparent desire for self-reliance within the Chinese industrial sectors suggesting very different parameters for the Chinese firm's need for and requirements of a transfer agent. It should be understood that Chinese firms seek Western management and marketing skills to allow them to successfully compete in the global economy. However, they do not expect to simply mirror Western firms.

8.   The Role of Trust in the Success of the Transfer

The most unquestionable result of the study was the power of trust between players in the Chinese firm in effecting a successful transfer of

Western management skills. Commitment surfaced as an integral element to the transfer of soft technology and was clearly identified in discussions of the ninety-three firms interviewed as a critical part of developing guanxi and trust. While Chinese firms are pragmatic about seeking Western management skills to be competitive globally, they are not abandoning the Confucian dynamism that has guided the culture and all social networks for the past 2200 years (Confucius, 220 BCE; Tung, 1995). That sense of trust in a network of social obligations, responsibilities, and privileges supersedes the Western definitions and extends beyond legal codes to act as a powerful glue that bonds people together. The identification and selection of a transfer agent in many cases defines the success of the transfer even before the agent enters the firm. He must ha a trusted, respected part of the Chinese social network who understands that guanxi is not the same as the Western definition of an "Old Boy Network". The Chinese social network is an integral part of all of Chinese life. Members of the firm must be able to trust the transfer agent implicitly and, reciprocally, he must be able to trust the employees of the firm in order to make the transfer of Western management skills a success. Perhaps, a comment from respondents at one firm best captures the pragmatism of the Chinese perspective:

> "If there is to be success in business, it will be born of the relationship of people who will trust each other to work for the same interest. Western people emphasize competition, this is overrated and of no virtue. Maybe they should think about cooperation and trust. The greater their success together, the more they will trust each other."

9. Pedagological Implications

There is a realization that there is a need to increase the transfer agents' skills so that there is convergence of thought and approach between the parties involved. There are clearly some areas need to be addressed to enhance the learning of the transfer agents. These are: trust, selection of transfer agent, skills needed, learning expectations and commitment.

1. Trust as the single best predictor of success of the transfer implies instructor credibility, i.e., demonstrable academic and applied experience, capable of discussing applications of theory in real-life practice.

   a. Increasingly important is the need for the instructor to validate the experience of the professional student.
   b. Demonstrative applications at to what others have done in similar situations.
   c. Illustrate course of actions of successful benchmarked companies instilling confidence of method and approach.

2. Changes in the choice of transfer agent from international professional to Chinese domestic government official imply an increasing requirement to teach not only the subject but the methods used to communicate that information to a third party end-user…train the trainer.

   a. There are two sets of tools necessary; one pertaining to content and the other on the methodology approach.
   b. Both assume that there are measurable timely results. However, each contain different types of measurements.

3. Changes in the ranking of skills needed imply a move away from theory toward practical applications and hands-on formatting for classroom instruction; from observational site-visits to internships or shadowing.

4. The Chinese academic expectation is that there is a one best way to achieve success which can be communicated as a prioritized list of action items through lecture: that there is one right answer to every question on a quiz and that there is a successful solution to every case study. This expectation carries the implication that course curricula need to include explanations of teaching methodology and instructor expectations of student participation. Positive reinforcement of participative efforts is of great importance.

a. The case study approach could be utilized, however, the emphasis is increasingly needed not so much on the actual solution of the case itself but on the thought process of analysis and substantiation of the approached solution.

b. The emphasis is increasingly shifting to instill learning in "teaching how to do it" versus "following the best approach".

5. The significance of commitment of the transfer agent implies the need for the instructor to connect with students as individuals with whom a long-term relationship is expected. The interpersonal relationship allows for a lot more open communication and flow of information between the parties allowing imbedded knowledge to be transferred in a non-threatening way.

References

Ansoff. H. Igor. 1979. Strategic Management, New York: Macmillan Publishing.

Ansoff, H. Igor 1998. The New Corporate Strategy, New York: John Wiley and Sons.

Baird, I. S., Lyles, M.A. and Wharton, R. 1990. "Attitudinal Differences between American and Chinese Managers Regarding Joint Venture Management". New York: Colombia University Press,

Barmathan, J, Pete Engardio, Lynne Curry, and Bruce Einhorn, 1993. "China: The Economic Powerhouse of the Twenty-First Century," Business Week May 17, p. 54-61.

Bartlett, C, and Ghoshal, S. 1988. "Organizing for Worldwide Effectiveness: The Transnational Solution," California Management Review, Fall, pp. 54-74.

Bartlett, C, and Ghoshal, S. 1992. 'What is a Global Manager"? Harvard Business Review. Sept-Oct, Vol 70(5). Pp. 124-132.

Bartlett, C, and Ghoshal, S 1997. "Rebuilding Behavioral Context," Sloan ManagementReview. Vol 37(I). Fall. pp. 11-23.

Baughn, C, Christopher and Bixby, Michael. 1996, International Technology to China. Hong Kong: Asia House.

Bond, M. Ed 1986, The Psychology of the Chinese People, Hong Kong: Oxford University Press.

Bracchius, M. 1997. "Chinese Telecom Surpasses Any." Wall Street Journal. September, 12, 1997, A-12. Campbell. Nigel, et al. Eds- 1989- 1994. Advances in Chinese Industrial Studies, 4 vols., Connecticut: JAI Press.

Cao F.Q, (December, 1995), "Entrepreneurial Managements in China's Enterprise Reform", China Business Review, pp. 81-90. Shanghai: Fudan University.

Chau, S. 1995. "The Development of China's Private Entrepreneurship". Journal of Enterprising Culture. Vol. 3 (3), September. pp 261-276, Singapore! Nanyang University.

Chen, R and Babcock, R. 1996. 'Bridging Chinese and Western Business: An Analysis of Intermediary Firms". Proceedings of the Cross Cultural Management Conference, Hong Kong, August 1996. pp 66-72.

Child, J.. and Lu , Yan (1996), Management Issue for China in the 1990's, London: Routledge. Chronicle of the Yellow Emperor. 213 BCE, Reprinted 1990. Upper Saddle River, NJ: Prentice-Hall.

Culpan, R, and Kumar, B. 1995, Transformation Management in Post-Communist Countries. New York: Greenwood.

De Keijzer, A. 1995. China Business Strategies for the '90s, Berkeley, CA: Pacific View Press.

De Mente, B.L.. 1995. Chinese Etiquette and Ethics In Business. Lincolnwood, IL: NTC Books.

Deng X. June, 1991. Address to the Fourteenth Party Congress.

Deng X. 1997. Selected Works of Deng Xiaoping: Commemorative Edition, 4 vols. Beijing.

Drucker, P.F. 1992. "The New Society of organizations". Harvard Business Review, Vol. 70 (5). September-October. Pp. 95~104.

Drucker, P.F. 1994, "The New Super Power: The Overseas Chinese", The Wall Street Journal. Nov. 20, A20, East Meets West: The Jesuits in China. 1582-1773. 1934. Jesuit House, Chicago: Loyola University.

Gao, S. and Chi, Fulin. 1995. Theory and Reality of Transition to a Market Economy, Beijing:Foreign Language Press.

Harris, P.R. and Moran, RT, 1991, Managing Cultural Differences, Houston: Gulf Press.

Hax, H., Klenner, W., Kraus, W., Matsuda, T., and Nakamura, T. 1995, Economic Transformation in Eastern Europe and Asia. Oxford: Oxford University Press.

Hofstede, Geert. 1991. Software of the Mind: Cultures and Organizations, London: McGraw-Hill.

Hofstede, Geert and Bond, Michael H. 1988. "The Confucius Connection". Organizational Dynamics, Vol. 16, pp. 4-21.

Kao, J. 1993, "The Worldwide Web of Chinese Business". Harvard Business Review. Vol. 71 (2) March-April1993. pp. 24-36.

Kao, R. W.Y. 1995, Entrepreneurship: A Wealth Creation and Value Adding Process, Singapore: Prentice Hall.

Khong, E. and Virginia Trigo. 1994. "Training Policies of Joint Ventures in China" EnroAsia Journal of Management, no. 7, pp. 5-21.

Kirby, D.A. and Pan, Y. 1995, "Chinese Cultural Values and Entrepreneurship: A Preliminary Consideration", Journal of Enterprising Culture, Vol. 3 (3). September. Singapore: Nanyang University.

Kirby, D. 1996, "The Chinese Enterprise". Presentation at the Western Regional Conference of Academy of Management. Academy of International Business, Southwest Conference, Rancho Santa Fe, California.

Kraar, L., 1994. "The Bamboo Network." Fortune. April 4, p. 46-5 I.

Latham, R.. Trans. 1969. The Travels of Marco Polo, London: The Folio Society.

Legge, J. Ed, 1934. The Four Books: Confucian Classic Text. Oxford: Oxford University Press, "Lessons of Transition," 1996, The Economist. June 29, 1996, p. 81.

Marx, K. 1889. The Communist Manifesto, New York: W, W. Norton, Co.

Naisbitt. J. 1995, Global Paradox, New York: Avon, 1996. Megatrends Asia. Hong Kong: Morrow.

Prahalad, C.K. and Hamel, Gary. 1990, "The Core Competence of the Corporation". Harvard Business Review, May-June. pp 79-91.

Redding. S. Gordon. 1993, The Spirits of Chinese Capitalism, New York: de Gruyter.

Ricardo, David. 1817. The Principles of Political Economy and Taxation, London.

Selmar. J. 1990, Expatriate Business Manager in the People's Republic of China. Department of Business Administration, Stockholm University, Sweden.

Selmar, J. 1992. "Cultural Preparation of Expatriate Top Managers". BRC Working Paper. Hong Kong.

Selmar, J. 1997. Western Expatriate Business Manager in the People's Republic of China, Hong Kong: Arrow.

Shi, Yuwei. 1995, "Selecting Strategic Windows When There Are Too Many: Strategic Management in Emerging Markets", China Business Review, pp. 91-108. Shanghai: Fudan University.

Steidlmeier, Paul, 1995. Strategic Management of Chinese Venture. New York: Greenwood.

Tung, R. L. 1982, "U.S.- China Trade Negotiations". Journal of International Business Studies. Fall, 25-37.

Tung, R. 1990. "Business Negotiations with Chinese: A Longitudinal Study". Proceedings of the International Management Conference, Xian, China.

Tung, R. March 18, 1995, 'A Survey of China", The Economist. pp 7-9.

Wong, Tom, December, 1995, "Exploring Human Resource Management in China". China Business Review, pp. 1-9, shanghai: Fudan University.

World Bank. 1994, China: Issue and Prospects. Washington, D.C.

Yan, A. and Barbara Gray, 1994, "Bargaining Power, Management Control and Performance in United States- China Joint Ventures". Academy of Management Journal, 37 (6), pp. 1478-1517.

Yan, A. December, 1995. 'The formation Dynamics of U.S.- China Joint Ventures", China Business Review, pp. 31-49, Shanghai: Fudan University.

III. Professional Business Training in China

Chapter 12

Trends and Practices in Management Development in China

Nandani Lynton
Thunderbird, The Garvin School of International Management

Fabienne Bressot
Metizo, The Personal Development Company

1. Introduction: The Need for Management Development in China

Corporations in China are in great need of good managers, yet the press is rampant with stories of students with MBAs from Chinese and overseas institutions who cannot find jobs. This apparent contradiction reflects both demographic and historical factors in China. The generation that should represent the senior managers of today was denied a formal education during the Cultural Revolution. While there are some CEOs and numerous entrepreneurs from this group, the bulk are not trained managers and few speak foreign languages. On the other hand, the young MBAs of today tend to lack lengthy work experience but have high position and salary expectations. This divergence leaves a gap that must be filled if corporations are to grow and function well.

A new Economist Intelligence Unit White Paper survey demonstrates that, while multinational companies in China expect the availability of skilled managers and support staff to improve by 2009, currently 44% experience the shortage of staff as detrimental to their business success in China (2004:126). The second McKinsey Global Survey of Business Executives reports that companies in China and India are planning to do much of the hiring globally in the next year (July 2004: Exhibit 4). However the head of the Education Committee and previous President of the American Chamber of Commerce in Beijing, Michael Furst (2004), states that "At present, a large proportion of American enterprises in China face a shortfall of personnel, especially skilled professionals. This shortage of personnel has led to recruiting and retention problems and is in some cases chilling investment enthusiasm and slowing growth."

This shortage of professionals, especially of managers who can work in international settings, impacts all industries and operations. Foreign invested companies in China, Chinese companies with international operations, or purchasing, sourcing, or sales functions with suppliers and customers of different national origins all need the same people with both functional and soft skills.

Given the talent shortage, companies in China must retain their current managers, develop high potentials into management positions, and maintain a sound work environment with overall employee satisfaction and healthy interpersonal relations (Illustration 1). This chapter focuses on management development, which takes place alongside other types of training and education in the quadrant "Career Development".

The next section of this chapter examines two particularly Chinese cultural traits: the special role of the group and the traditional expectations of leaders. We presume that these local cultural traditions can provide a strong basis for developing and retaining managers, and therefore have influenced new trends in management development. This is truly a case of a global system adapting locally.

Section three outlines the conditions and challenges for management development in China and examines pedagogical methods in use in the past decade. We identify three major current trends: high-potential programs, the varied preference for degree or non-degree education, and the separation of learning centers from human resources functions.

Section four discusses six future trends in management development: a focus on mentoring and succession planning, the accompanying disappearance of fast-tracking, a move toward preparing managers for cross-functional responsibilities and roles, a demand for specific action learning, increased coaching, and precise planning of international experience. Each of these trends can be found elsewhere, but the way they are implemented on the mainland is specific to the conditions and culture of the Chinese environment.

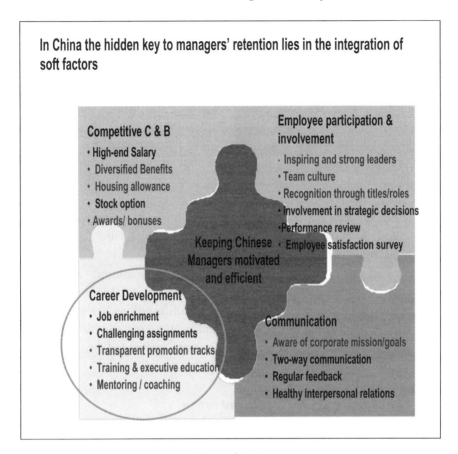

In China the hidden key to managers' retention lies in the integration of soft factors

Competitive C & B
• High-end Salary
• Diversified Benefits
• Housing allowance
• Stock option
• Awards/ bonuses

Employee participation & involvement
• Inspiring and strong leaders
• Team culture
• Recognition through titles/roles
• Involvement in strategic decisions
• Performance review
• Employee satisfaction survey

Keeping Chinese Managers motivated and efficient

Career Development
• Job enrichment
• Challenging assignments
• Transparent promotion tracks
• Training & executive education
• Mentoring / coaching

Communication
• Aware of corporate mission/goals
• Two-way communication
• Regular feedback
• Healthy interpersonal relations

Illustration 1

2. Management Development with Chinese Characteristics

"Professionally, China has always attracted me because it is culturally different and somehow mysterious" said a French businessman, discussing his experiences managing a major site in Nanjing. For decades, the Western world has been flooded with business literature by Overseas Chinese and Western writers emphasizing the complexity of working in China and with the Chinese. They attribute difficulties to ignorance of Chinese cultural patterns and concepts such as "face" and "guanxi" and provide guidelines for foreigners in China (examples of such literature include Hoon-Halbauer 1994, Pye 1992, Seligman1999, Tang and Reisch 1995, Yang 1994).

Since the mid-nineties, the Chinese business community has increasingly lived the opposite message: "doing business in China is not fundamentally different from doing business in any other part of the world". Chinese firms like Lenovo (ex-Legend) or Haier and multinational companies have supported the message by massively integrating global systems into their China operations. Chinese MBA graduates add proof by operating global systems successfully in their companies. Whiteley describes this as "the emerging paradigm based on the notion of complex adaptive systems in business presented as being harmonious to valued Chinese practices such as *guanxi* and face-work as well as acceptable to Western business" (2001:17).

The next sections examine two major cultural and social elements that impact the way Chinese employees are being developed into future leaders: the clan, its rules and manifestations in the corporate life, and the traditional image of the leader. We conclude by explaining how these cultural patterns can be efficiently embedded into a modern strategy of management development in China.

2.1 The clan: the key to identity and action

One cannot discuss Chinese characteristics in Management Development without knowing the importance of the clan, the group, the community. Chinese society is built on the principle that individuals belong to various circles representing the rules one should respect. Respecting the rules allows an individual to accomplish their duties and receive recognition in exchange. Although in recent years the younger generation of Chinese managers is increasingly individualistic in its goals and attitudes, even for them the clan remains the common reference when it comes to building trust and success in the corporate world. As Warner explains it, in "Confucianism and later the Chinese version of Marxist-Leninism ... The individual was subordinated to the group or larger collectivity. His or her role was of course relatively defined. Clan, family and work-groups governed allegiances." (1995:147).

Members of the clan create a close-knitted, protected and codified circle where all the individuals know the rules, share values, support each other and are supported in return. Where Westerners often perceive duties towards a group as a necessary sacrifice and focus on the visible and usually short-term outcome of such an effort, Chinese usually see such sacrifices as a natural part of life and wait for the long-term results.

Chinese reciprocate favors in a paradoxical way, granting favors without expecting an immediate return, thereby increasing their chances of obtaining unconditional support from others in the group. Because this environment is built on trust, when an individual breaks the code of values, the clan immediately evicts him from the circle to prevent further harm or disharmony. Faure explains: "in a clan society there is no concept of *I think therefore I am*. (The concept) is in fact *If I do not belong to a circle I do not exist.*" (2003:96). Outside of a circle, the individual has no identity.

Chinese import and reproduce the logic of circles of dependence in the corporate world. When entering a new work environment, they seek out circles that provide them with enough support (information, guidance, resources etc.) to function well. If they do not find such circles, they start to create their own circle from the most personal (the smallest circle on the illustration) to the more formal (the second circle) and finally to the most outward connections.

Entering a new department or company, the individual creates a comfort zone of shared values as she builds systematic relationships with her superiors and with subordinates, constituting a solid corporate circle. These are "high-maintenance circles" as opposed to the outer circle of potential members who are low-maintenance. The outer circle guarantees that the circles can evolve and attract fresh resources into the network to make it more effective and powerful. Typically, a Chinese manager belongs to several circles within and outside the organization. This is his way to identify others and build an identity, to receive and transfer information, in a word to be effective and constantly adaptable to a moving environment where he has to position himself, communicate with the right people and ensure optimal performance.

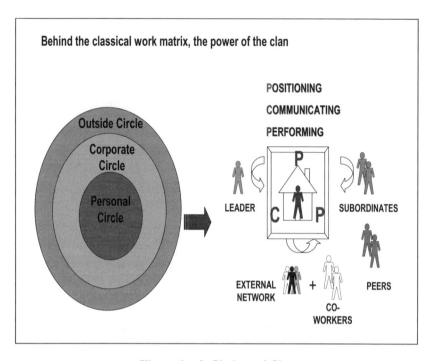

Illustration 2. Circles and Clan

Most Western managers build and channel relationships and information through formal streams reflecting the "architecture" of the organization, Chinese managers use both personal and formal circles to build trust and efficiency in their work. Illustration 3 contrasts the formal structures with the networks Chinese individuals build to support each other. Chinese managers have learned to navigate between these circles efficiently as the context requires.

A few years ago, foreign firms were skeptical, even a little paranoid about informal communication channels. In the mid-nineties, for example, Ericsson, Nokia and Motorola all had Joint Venture operations with the same state-owned partner. In some cases the ventures were neighbors, and each Western General Manager complained that his Chinese colleagues literally lived with their competitors. The idea that technical details and strategies might be discussed over mah-jong tables with old friends was difficult to bear. Some foreign managers tried to prohibit these relationships, but to little effect.

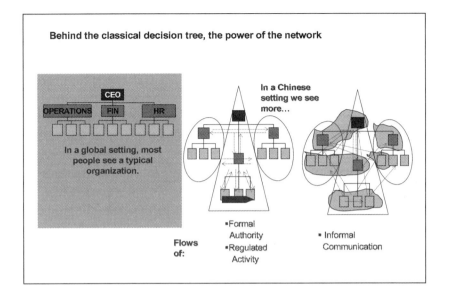

Behind the classical decision tree, the power of the network

In a global setting, most people see a typical organization.

In a Chinese setting we see more...

Flows of:
- Formal Authority
- Regulated Activity

- Informal Communication

Illustration 3. Clan and Networks

Informal networks can be very effective and are thus preserved and encouraged by management in foreign-invested firms. One must reflect that, although 'teambuilding' and 'peer networks' were announced as new Western concepts, they are pale reflections of an eon-old Chinese method of managing people and systems. Today, management development strategies in China build on this method to create efficient learning environments for future Chinese managers.

2.2 Paternalistic leadership

"Authoritarian and benevolent" is how Chinese culture describes the perfect leader (Li, Tsui, and Weldon 2000:94). Those qualities allow the leader to keep a certain distance from his/her subordinates in order to maintain control while providing the members of the group with protection and guidance. Once again directly inherited from the Confucian code of relationship, the Chinese leader carries the double role of an absolute controller and of a caring and inspiring father. Ideally, group members do not have to ask for help, the leader has the duty to provide them with the necessary support automatically. Conversely, members of the group are not asked to abide by the rules, they naturally live by them and only contest them if they harm the group and therefore negatively impact its performance.

In the new management matrix in China as shown in Illustration 4, developing Chinese leaders today results in merging two complementary rather than opposite models, creating a flat organization where functions are not seen as vertical silos but as flexible horizontal entities that communicate and cooperate through a powerful support network.

The image of the manager has changed in China in the sense that seniority is no longer the absolute criteria for being a good leader. The shortage of talent has naturally contributed to the lack of "grey hair" mentors as ultimate models for tomorrow's leadership pools. However what remains is that the leader, although younger than his timeless "heroes", has the responsibility to carry the group and lead it to success before thinking of his own interest. In fact, placing the group as the first priority guarantees the leader's personal success. This is a fundamental difference in the way management development is carried out in a Chinese context.

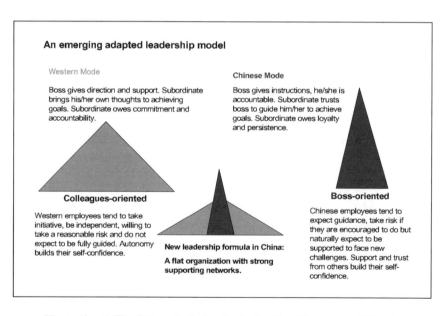

Illustration 4. The Paternalistic Leader in the New Management Matrix

3. Current Management Development Practices in China: "A Global Purpose Built in the Local Culture"

Integrating Chinese characteristics into today's management requirements means leveraging soft factors (clan, network, leadership) to enhance existing systems in the company. The secret of efficient management development in China does not lie in the replacement of existing processes and tools by "culturally correct substitutes" but rather in identifying and building on the transferable habits and skills among those processes and tools Chinese managers already have.

Management development tools can be roughly divided into short and longer-term training, job rotation and planned promotion as shown in Illustration 5. Corporations generally use a variety of these tools, with some purely internal and others in cooperation with a variety of providers. The difference in China is the emerging trend away from

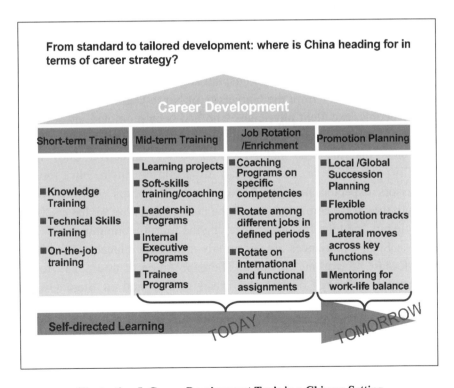

Illustration 5. Career Development Tools in a Chinese Setting

standardized development programs towards tailored solutions to grow individuals and teams through job enrichment and rotation within the organization. In a clan culture, team coaching, local and international peer and alumni networks, and quality circles become powerful tools for building the backbone of management development.

3.1 *Pedagogical methods for management development*

Until the mid-nineties, training of all kinds consisted primarily of frontal instruction, often with a focus on technical and functional skills. Many operations established technical training centers; one example of this is the Beijing Tianwei Fuel Injections Joint Venture between ASIMCO and Beijing Automotive Group that worked with the German government to build a German-style technical training school on the factory site for staff and customers. Structured management development began similarly, with multinational companies such as IBM and Ericsson using training programs and trainers from overseas, often with disappointing results.

The methods used in management development programs have changed dramatically in the past decade. "From 1995-98 I participated in a multi-phased program to train hospital administrators in management," reported a professor from the University of North Carolina. "These were senior people, excellent physicians who had been promoted into leading hospitals but never given management training. With their experience, it was clear that the case method would be very effective. They were initially perturbed because instead of lecturing them, the foreign professors expected them to discuss in small groups. After a week, though, they were comfortable with the method and now we have several participants from the first group teaching the fourth group this way."

Such experiences are commonly shared by educators who have the pleasure of working in China. The expectation of traditional frontal instruction is higher outside the urban centers and in State Owned Enterprises. Yet even in conservative areas this is changing, as illustrated by the following experience in 2002. At a half-day strategy workshop conducted by a brilliant Chinese consultant for executives from State Owned Enterprises in northern China, the consultant used charts and gave examples but otherwise lectured the audience in traditional style.

During the tea break, three managers in their fifties stood together and commented. "He is so smart, he really knows his stuff," said one, "but his teaching is really old-fashioned." Nodding their heads they shuffled off. Even old China has new expectations.

Some things remain fairly constant. A survey done in 1997 showed that Chinese excel at hard skills and need to learn soft business skills (Motorola conference presentation 1997). They have the advantage of an overall strength at face-to-face relationship building, however, which many Western engineers lack. Eight years later the story is similar, managers still need to focus on soft skills: communication and presentation skills, assertiveness, the ability to build teams over distance and time zones. Preparing managers to move up in the organization as executives, means developing an understanding of the head office culture and politics, and the ability to integrate international and local constraints into a coherent management style.

This provokes difficult questions about the need to adapt methods and content for management education in China. The trend seems to be towards using international methodology but with content that reflects Chinese business experience. Delivery language varies, with multi-national companies using English-medium programs for their corporate managers and operations heads, but Chinese training for the operations staff. Chinese companies naturally expect most programs in Chinese, but the larger firms that deal with international customers, suppliers, and international markets often want foreign providers of executive education and therefore accept or even encourage English-based programs.

3.2 Job rotation and succession planning

"The thing that wakes me up in the middle of the night is not what may happen to the economy or what our competitor may do next. What wakes me up is worrying about whether we have the leadership capability and talent ..." said one CEO talking about his company's development strategy in China (Lynton 2002[1]). Despite the shortage of good managers, few companies commit the resources for detailed career development. BASF, the German chemical firm, is an exception. Having invested about 3 billion US-dollars in China, the corporation prioritizes development of their Chinese managers. Working from a 15-year business plan, tied to a parallel HR plan, the regional executive team meets annually to discuss key individuals in Asia, tracking their development and outlining their next move.

Job rotation between operations within a country and internationally has been key in the paths of their top Chinese managers. The goal is to build a high powered Asian team for Asia; and the number of Asian managers heading operations in Asia and local managers heading operations in country is tracked closely. Division heads' own targets include letting their best people move on within the company. The result: BASF currently has 4 German, 2 Asian and 8 Chinese General Managers in China with most other top managers Chinese. These highly visible localization success stories are important proof that Chinese have real opportunities.

Novozymes, the Danish world leader in biotech for enzymes and microorganisms, is another example of successful development. With an R&D center in Beijing and 3 production sites on the mainland, Novozymes is committed to localization of both management and product for China. Novozymes began training and promoting Chinese managers from the beginning, and was one of the first companies to integrate foreigners from headquarters into departments under Chinese managers, rather than insisting that expatriates had to lead the operations; their top executive for China is Chinese. Intel is another example of a company known for its development programs that fully utilize the gamut of tools. What stands out most in its operations in China is the commitment of resources, shown in mentoring programs of high-potentials often by executives in another country, of world class executive education programs for managers here, and for rotating Chinese staff into positions in the USA, usually for 6-24 months to increase both functional and corporate process knowledge and to build personal networks. "I know they want to consider me for my boss' job when I return," said one senior middle manager at Intel before he left for a US assignment.

Succession planning is essential to the effectiveness of development programs. If staff capabilities are grown but they cannot take on new responsibilities, the result is frustration rather than thanks. And timely rotation and promotion is the best way to retain employees.

3.3 *Resources committed*

Most human resources and training managers have been taught to carefully examine the finances committed to paying for education, including the cost of business schools or trainers and of the participants' travel expenses. Some also consider the cost of lost work time; unfortunately this is rarely balanced against the plus of better work afterwards. However very few companies budget for the cost of not educating and improving their staff capabilities. In 2000, McKinsey & Co. surveyed 410 corporate officers at 35 large American corporations, asking "How much more does a high performer generate annually than an average performer?" The results for operations, general management and sales roles showed differences of 40%, 49% and 67% respectively (McKinsey 2000 War for Talent survey). Asked whether their company developed talent quickly and effectively, only 3% of the respondents strongly agreed. This means that, despite the opportunity to improve performance in high double-digit numbers, few organizations prioritize people development

This does not apply in China to the same extent. Since entering China, foreign firms have emphasized education of staff and managers, and are rewarded by the Chinese employee's eagerness to learn. In fact, training opportunities - or the lack thereof - directly impact a corporation's ability to hire and retain good local talent. Nonetheless training and development budgets are limited. Experience on the ground indicates that most firms invest between 2-5% of an employee's annual salary per year in training, with junior staff at the lower and executives at the higher end of the scale.

3.4 *Trend 1: high-potential programs*

High potential programs were the flavor of the decade in the nineties, as MNCs expanded operations and desperately needed to fill the pipeline with Chinese managers. Many corporations decided training was easier than re-training, and so focused on relatively inexperienced young employees who spoke good English and showed ability and good attitude. Some examples of these programs are Motorola's CAMP program, ABB's Management Localization Program, and Nortel's HiMAX.

Motorola, as one of the early movers in the PRC, has often served as a model for other foreign firms here. Their China Accelerated Management Program (CAMP) was designed to develop Chinese middle and then senior managers in five phases over a period of twelve months:

Example. Motorola's CAMP

Program Steps	Subject Focus
High potential nomination and screening	
3 weeks training on site	Culture and Ethics, Business Improvement, Quality, Productivity and Project Management
4 months on the job action learning project	Benchmarking, Leadership, Influence
6 weeks job rotation	
4 months self-directed learning	Finance
1 week simulations	Team Building, Business Strategy

Motorola used the CAMP approach not only to develop and retain managers, but also as a team building and public relations exercise. By building cross-divisional cohorts, the firm encouraged networking across business groups and building the personal ties that keep managers in companies as well as making them effective. In addition, the program was highly visible and so demonstrated the corporation's commitment to China while building goodwill with the government.

3.5 *Trend 2: MNCs prefer non-degree, Chinese prefer degree programs*

Since the late 1990's part-time MBA and EMBA programs have become widely available in China's cities, with wide choice of both local and joint sino-international programs. Many corporations supported their key personnel in attending such programs, with participants commonly spending weekends studying, often flying across the country to attend classes. Since 2001, there is a trend away from paying for degree programs because many of the participants seek new positions after graduation.

As a result, multinational corporations in China increasingly focus on customized management development programs to develop staff without providing a widely appreciated degree. These programs range from essentially internal mini-MBA courses to functional programs tailored specifically to the needs and processes of the corporation. The specific courses can be extremely effective when tied closely to succession planning, however many Chinese managers would prefer the portable degree.

3.6 Trend 3: separate "learning functions"

In the last ten years, Motorola University and the Nokia Learning Center in Beijing and the joint training center held by Henkel and BASF in Shanghai were early movers in separating the training and development function. From early on, Motorola University provided a range of training and degree programs for their own employees and those from related companies. Programs are provided through the corporate university but usually presented by outside providers including universities, business schools and training companies. The courses are also used to promote corporate relations with government, suppliers and customers. A similar model has been followed by other corporate universities in China, which are increasingly seen as profit centers, in competition with training companies and universities.

Companies in China participate in these trends to varied extents. As many foreign invested businesses mature in China, and as Chinese companies face international competition in their own market and enter the markets of other countries, we see new trends emerging that bode well for the manager of tomorrow.

4. Management Development Tomorrow

As most of the leading global corporations gear up for further expansion of Chinese and Asian operations, six trends seem to be crystallizing that include more of the focused development tools shown on the right hand side of Illustration 5. This overview sketches what is visible today, on the ground in 2004.

Developing talent over time requires a flexible but structured process strong enough to defeat the natural barriers that accompany it. When localizing management in China, for instance, the thought of being replaced is often uncomfortable for expatriate incumbents, who must be rewarded for successfully bringing up successors. Yet high potential managers need support from mentors and peers to mature into new responsibilities rather than just being intellectually pushed. We observe an increasing willingness by multinationals to accept that talent development is not magic, but takes professional processes including internal projects, external coaching, and attention to both the professional and the emotional skills growth necessary to form a real leader (Lynton 2002[2]).

Significantly, all the changes discussed below reflect one main trend: after years of management exploration and fast-pace economic growth, companies in China are attaining a level of maturity at which they are willing to modify their objectives from what used to be a consumer mode to a controlled process of management development. High potential Chinese managers will still rise more rapidly than their Western counterparts, but they will be given the necessary time and practice to reach an international level of competency.

4.1 *Future trend 1: increased focus on mentoring and succession planning*

Despite giving unreasonably high salary and benefits increases in the past few years in an effort to keep key managers, companies continue to find it very difficult to retain their employees. This has resulted in a slow but tangible switch in mindset. Companies are no longer trying to retain their stars at any price; rather they seek to better understand key performers' motivations, and use coaching and management development to satisfy those drives while concentrating the performers on key areas. This means that the company puts resources on strategic projects for a reasonable timeline, while accepting the risk that they may lose their high potentials within 2 to 3 years. By keeping the process as transparent as possible, the corporations make their key staff aware that developing their successor is a high priority right from the start. Training their own successor, with clear and measurable objectives and the resources to do it, is a much more realistic vision of retention and it mitigates the worry of having invested significant amounts of money on an individual only to lose everything when he or she leaves the company.

4.2 Future trend 2: fast tracking is disappearing

After years of accelerating young Chinese managers' "maturity process" through intensive training and fast promotion tracks, companies in China have realized that the secret to developing high profile local managers in the long run is to give them enough space to grow into broader roles. The main symptom of a drastic shortage of management talent in the past 10 years in China, the "job hopper phenomenon" does not only apply outside the company as most recruiting firms emphasize, it also happens within companies where young profiles, cherished as the company's treasures, develop an oversized ambition and ego and become motivated by the desire to accumulate impressive track records in a limited amount of time.

Carried away by regular praise and rewards, not only do they burn themselves in the fire of quick success and recognition, but they also maintain the illusion for companies that managerial talent can grow almost overnight. This is one of the reasons (added to a frenetic raise in young managers' compensation packages), for companies to move back to the good old models of one to two years learning curves before promoting a manager to the next level with the objective to help him reach a performance climax on the third year so that he also has time to groom a decent pool of potential replacement for the current position.

4.3 Future trend 3: from segmented to cross-functional responsibilities and roles

The new challenge for multinational companies grooming new generation Chinese managers is preparing them to move away from micro-management to a broader vision of the organization and a wider grasp of how different functions of the company interact with and impact each other. Chinese cultural patterns encourage in-group behavior and paternalistic leadership styles (see illustrations 2 and 3). The risk for the company from this is segmented actions rather than a one-voice strategy, autonomous entities functioning with their own rules and objectives rather than a whole organization moving in the same direction.

Training the managers to look outside of their clan and evaluate team performance in relation to the other functions of the company has become a milestone in the development of a new generation of Chinese leaders; their natural sense of belonging has to be "extended" to the whole organization rather than applying to their own "reduced corporate family". This is a major change in management development in China, a change that cannot be achieved through classroom training but through field practice and strategic support to grow a new managerial conscience.

4.4 Future trend 4: from conceptual knowledge to action knowledge

Whereas classroom training remains the most economical and fastest way for companies to train their Chinese managers, Management Forums are becoming more common as a way to support high potential managers in maturing into broader roles and responsibilities. For the past three years, multinationals in China like Cisco, Oracle and most of the High Tech companies have been organizing Leaders Forums and Leaders Labs where high potential managers can reflect, comment and act on the company's vision, values and strategy.

At first rare and reserved for a privileged audience of managers working in innovative companies, this practice is now spreading to a larger number of organizations and becoming an important part of a new corporate training culture where top managers from the group leave their "high spheres" and meet with their potential successors. This is a strong message that success comes from a strong operational grasp of a company's reality as well as from a helicopter view to anticipate the future and prepare the answers to constantly renewed challenges.

The practice of a Leaders Forum thus touches on a sensitive dilemma companies face when growing a high-flyers pool for their China operation: training Chinese managers to address short term as well as mid to long term objectives. Naturally gifted in dealing with high pressure, emergency situations and changes overnight, Chinese managers have developed an outstanding ability to react to a fast-moving environment. However, when they are pulled away from their daily management "burning fires", they have a hard time projecting daily issues and priorities into a wider picture where their actions reflect an overall strategy rather than daily trouble-shooting. The core result of a Leaders Forum is the commitment to link operational with strategic managers through common projects and networks.

4.5 *Future trend 5: projects /coaching*

Softer and personalized development approaches such as competency development through specific projects or coaching are already in wide use. Increasingly, companies are using group coaching for middle managers across functions and departments to create peer dynamics. In a case study, Bressot (2003) describes developing managers through concrete experience of what their next job will entail. This was achieved by a combination of executive education programs, shadowing the executive they would replace, and mentoring. The shadowing gave the young managers the experience – what Bressot calls the "déjà vu" – of the responsibilities the new leaders would have a year later. In order to create the "deja-vu" experience, the transition team designed concrete projects drawn from the company's current strategic plan that allowed the candidates to develop the identified competencies in context. Each candidate was assigned two to three individual projects with planned resources, a timetable and measurable targets. The project developed key leadership competencies and provided a context for developing efficient managerial practices.

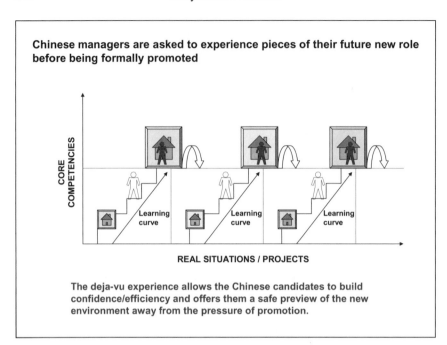

Illustration 6. The Deja-vu Experience

The core of this trend is the emphasis on real-life projects and coaching as part of management development. Most tailored executive education programs must now include company projects to give participants hands-on use of their new theoretical skills.

4.6 *Future trend 6: specific use of international experience*

In the 1990's in China, the ultimate reward by a foreign company's top management was to send its most promising managers abroad to be trained in the head office. The objective at that time was to literally transform the best local assets of the company into international management champions who, having returned to China could re-inject key management models from head office onto the China operation almost immediately. For the newly returned managers, applying fresh concepts into what used to be their familiar world proved to be extremely difficult.

The typical pattern was that, despite a one or two-year immersion abroad, the main learning was still based on observation rather than practice. Lengthy culture shock and integration slowed the individual's ability to integrate into the new situation and to acquire new management practices. Once back in China, the pressure of unrealistic expectations led to a double-face welcome within the company: returnees were seen as heroes and future management gurus by the top management and some Chinese staff, and as new "foreign" bosses for others who suddenly saw the returned managers as future competitors for their own jobs. Returning therefore necessitated a long period of re-integration and re-assimilation into a world unfamiliar after several years away.

Today the same MNCs continue to send their high potentials abroad but they have become more realistic in their expectations. The HR Director of a Shanghai-based international pharmaceutical group described this: "Rather than unrealistically expecting to see a whole new manager return from intensive training, we now assume that exposure to different management standards and regular participation in projects in an international context will spur the managers' flexibility and open their minds, demonstrated in soft competencies on their return. This way we avoid attitude problems, from oversized egos to signs of nervous breakdown because of praise or pressure. Our managers take the international experience as part of their personal development rather than as a key milestone in their promotion track."

5.   The New Role of Management Development

Corporations in China need to develop and retain managers in order to maintain their competitive edge. Overall, there is a move away from pushing managers to ascend silos as fast as the economy grew in any way possible, towards a controlled process of development focused on growing managers with a broad and integrated view of the organization. Human Resources executives and line-managers alike have begun to focus on discovering the potential talent they already have in the organization, and to apply a variety of tools for growing these candidates.

The last fifteen years have seen shifts in this development process. Painting with a broad brush, one can see several shifts. Training methodology has moved from primarily frontal instruction to primarily participative learning and projects with accompanying coaching. Pushing candidates up the career ladder as fast as possible is giving way to thoughtful succession planning and mentoring, and reliance on training courses has been replaced with a range of degree and non-degree, open and customized programs from outside providers as well as in-house universities and Management Forum type programs. Overseas training and postings are now also being used in more focused fashion, replacing the previous pressure to produce a fully changed Chinese person with a Western mindset, with the rather more reasonable expectation that candidates will grow and become more flexible with international exposure.

What remains constant is the appreciation that most Chinese candidates have excellent hard skills but need to develop the soft skills of management. There is a new realization, however, that rather than starting with unlearning old habits, in fact effective management development in China depends on integrating useful habits and skills that Chinese managers have already learned through their culture, and to leverage soft factors such as clan, networks, and leadership styles.

What we are thus seeing in management development in China is a move away from the old star system to an integrated talent model as companies switch from an automatic focus on "rare profiles on the market" to a system in which managers have the responsibility to build tomorrow's leaders from their entry in the company. The duty to prepare their successors is not new for top managers and the reliance on the group for support means that younger managers look to the leaders for mentoring and guidance. However, Human Resources used to decide on promotion and succession tracks with the support of line managers. Today's management development priority has operated a complete u-turn. The company now wants to convince high potential managers that, by preparing their own succession with the support of HR, they boost the company's performance as well as their own. Becoming a mentor or a coach does not just mean giving free time to the company's younger talent because it is the right thing to do. It means acquiring the soft competencies that the market lacks tremendously as well as preparing one's own transition to another position within or outside the company.

A major change is the new emphasis on integrating coaching and mentoring within the organization into management development plans. In a few years, Chinese managers will no longer need to be automatic stars themselves as this trend will allow some of them to discover a new source of motivation: self-fulfillment through developing others. The status of having built enough expertise to be able to share knowledge with the future generation of managers is beginning to grow. At a time when high compensation packages no longer rank first on a manager's priorities list, developing others becomes an ideal opportunity for reflecting on what they have learned before they move further up in the organization.

In summary, the changes in management development in China today are based on integrating inherent strengths in the Chinese cultural patterns of group reliance and leadership while focusing emphasis on:

- Allowing the time to develop mature managers with an integrated view of the company rather than pushing "fast trackers" up functional silos.
- Emphasizing action learning, especially the use of hands-on projects.
- Implementing coaching and mentoring alongside formal training as steps in the succession planning process.
- Defining precise international experiences for personal development and exposure to other ways of working and thinking.

This chapter has described the framework within which specific learning events are designed and implemented to support the development of a new generation of Chinese managers. In the age of globalization, that new generation will affect us all.

References

Bressot, Fabienne (2003). Awakening the Manager Within. China Staff. IX (9), 1-6
Business Digest (2004). Les Lecons a Tirer de l'Entrepreneur Chinois ("Lessons Learned from the Chinese Entrepreneur"), n°144 September issue.

Economist Intelligence Unit White Paper (2004). Coming of Age. Multinational Companies in China.

Faure, Sophie (2003). Manager a l'ecole de Confucius ("Managing the Confucian Way"), Editions d'organisation.

Furst, Michael. (2004) Personal Correspondence.

Hoon-Halbauer, Sing Keow. 1994. Management of Sino-Foreign Joint Ventures. Lund University Press: Lund.

Li J.T., Tsui Anne S., Weldon Elisabeth (2000). Management and organizations in the Chinese Context, Macmillan Press.

Lynton, Nandani (2002[1]) HR in China: People Power. AmChat, the Business Journal of the Shanghai American Chamber of Commerce. March 2002.

Lynton, Nandani (2002[2]) "Change Management" in HR Strategies China. CCH Asia Pte Limited, Singapore.

Pye, Lucian W. (1992). Chinese Negotiating Style. Commercial Approaches and Cultural Principles.Quorum Books: N.Y.

Seligman, Scott. (1999). Chinese Business Etiquette, A guide to protocol, manners and culture in the People's Republic of China, Warner Books.

Tang, Zailand and Bernhard Reisch. 1995. Erfolg im China-Geschaeft. Von Personalauswahl bis Kundenmanagement. Campus Verlag: Frankfurt/N.Y.

Warner, Malcolm (1992). How Chinese Managers Learn, Management and Industrial Training in China, Macmillan Academic and Professional.

Warner, Malcolm (1995). The Management of Human Resources in Chinese Industry, Saint Martin's Press.

Warner, Malcolm (2004). Human Resources in China Revisited, Routledge.

Whiteley, Alma, (2001). Management Education in the Chinese Setting, The international Business Press and the Journal of Teaching in International Business, Volume 12, Number 2.

Whiteley, Alma, Cheung Sara, Zhang Shi Quan (2000). Human Resources Strategies in China, World Scientific Publishing.

Yang, Mayfair Mei-hui. 1994. Gifts Favors & Banquets. The Art of Social Relationships in China. Cornell University Press: Ithaca, N.Y.

Chapter 13

Managing Learning and Learning to Manage: Pedagogies for HR and OD Graduate Education in China

Diana J. Wong-MingJi
Eastern Michigan University

Mary E. Vielhaber
Eastern Michigan University

Fraya Wagner-Marsh
Eastern Michigan University

1. Introduction

China's economic reform from a centrally planned economy to a market system and its entry into the World Trade Organization triggered a high demand for managers with global standard business capabilities. Since 1979, China's economic growth rate has been over 8% annually, which is one of the highest in the world (X Si & Bruton, 1999). At the end of 1998, China had 1.36 million private enterprises that employed 17.84 million people (People's Daily, 1999). By 2003, private enterprises contribute over 40% of China's GDP (Wu, 2003). The rapid growth also involved some painful high costs with bankruptcies and layoffs of poor performing organizations. From 1996 to 2000, the economic restructuring resulted in a dramatic decrease of workers in urban SOEs from 112.44 million to 81.02 million, a drop of 31.42 million (Wang, 2003). The number of urban SOEs dropped from 30.16 million to 14.99 million, a decrease of 15.17 million in the same time period (Wang, 2003). From 1995 to 2002, 7,798 state owned enterprises (SOEs) went bankrupt with another 2,000 that may go bankrupt from 2003 to 2008 (China Daily, 2003). In sum, new private Chinese enterprises and influx of foreign firms are not able to absorb the number of unemployed.

At the beginning of the transformation process, over 400,000 SOEs required substantial development to become globally competitive enterprises (Fan, 1998) At the end of 2002, the State continued to control 159,000 industrial and commercial enterprises (China Daily, 2003). "Despite an oversupply of ordinary workers, China is seriously short of high-quality technical, operational and management personnel who are qualified to assist the readjustment of the industrial structure (Wang, 2003: 24)." The process to improve competitive capabilities requires millions of managers who can improve the competitive capabilities of these newly transformed enterprises. The complex array of decision making and management of organizational change processes required professional managerial competencies. Managers need to make good decisions about what to produce, how much, what quality standards, what production methods, etc. The complex array of decisions to make progress with organizational change processes depend on professional managerial competencies. The demand for such competencies came not only from the Chinese SOEs but also from the entry of transnational companies into China. Learning from foreign joint venture partners is one means of transferring managerial knowledge and skills with trial and error in a learning by doing process.

Graduate business programs provide another critical venue for generating the requisite professional management knowledge and skills. The programs are expanding beyond general Master of Business Administration (MBA) programs to more specialized ones. This chapter provides an overview of the first specialized graduate degree in human resource management and examines how three innovative pedagogical practices in the program relate to current and future transformational needs of organizations in China. Continuous improvements with pedagogical innovations are important for graduate professional education to be relevant in China's context of rapid turbulent changes. Due to the cross-cultural nature of the Master of Science in Human Resources and Organization Development (MSHROD) program in China, we acknowledge that the notion of being innovative is relative to the perspective of the stakeholder.

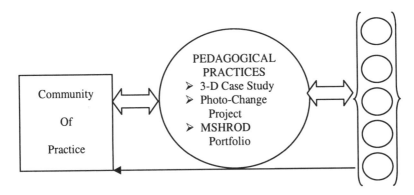

Figure 1. A Pedagogical Framework for Managing Learning and Learning to Manage

We consider the process of pedagogical innovation as a dynamic and continuous iterative process between a community of practice, faculty, and students (see Figure 1.). The designing, developing, and implementing of pedagogy involves multiple iterations between a faculty and the community of practices and a faculty and the learners. The faculty member designs and develops a set of pedagogical practices by drawing from a community of practice and body of knowledge. The development and implementation is a process of re-creating and reconstituting knowledge between the faculty and the learners. For this process to be effective, faculty members need to adapt their set of pedagogical practices to the Chinese context

Transferring management knowledge from western countries to China takes place in tandem with both the rapid pace of economic development and intellectual exchanges between educational institutions. The key for effective transfer of managerial knowledge and skills fundamentally depends upon appropriate pedagogical practices that support relevant learning for future added value. In 1980, the case-study teaching method and simulated decision making pedagogies were introduced in China when Mr. Deng Xiaoping initiated the adoption of the first joint China-US MBA program at the China Industrial Management Training Center in Dalian University of Technology (Wu, 2003).

Continuous improvement of innovative pedagogical relevance needs to go further with applications of managerial concepts, integration across course materials, and reflective critical thinking. In order to address these issues, the following discussion is divided into three major sections. First, a brief background of business education in China provides a context for the need to continue developing pedagogical practices, especially in specialized degree programs. Second, we present three innovative pedagogical practices for the first graduate HR program and explain how they are relevant to organizational change in China. Last, the discussion identifies cross-cultural lessons in how we manage learning with the Chinese students and how the Chinese students learn to manage human resources and organization development in China's great transformation.

2.   Business Education – The Chinese Context

China experimented with graduate business education in the 1980s. MBA programs were formally introduced in 1990 with 86 students enrolled in nine authorized universities (People's Daily, 2000). At the same time, China established the first modern enterprise system to relinquish state control over some industrial and commercial production units. From the 1990s to mid-2000's, China's business education evolved in three successive overlapping waves. In the first wave of the early 1990s, business education focused more on macro-economics and management engineering with business students receiving degrees in either economics or engineering. In the second wave of the mid-1990s and early-2000s, China created a comprehensive business education system with undergraduate, postgraduate, MBA, and PhD degree programs. In 1991, the first MBA program received official recognition by the Ministry of Education and the first EMBA program started in 2002 with 30 approved programs. Business education shifted away from economics and engineering to business administration, accounting, tourism, technology economics, and management. With the US leading the way, many higher educational institutions from other western countries such as the UK, Canada, and Australia also launched MBA programs in China. Three types of MBA program exist: 1) Local programs are run solely by PRC institutions; 2) Joint programs are run by a PRC and a foreign institution; and 3) Imported programs have a passive Chinese institution and run by a foreign institution. Recently, the third wave of graduate business education expanded beyond general MBAs with more specialization such as aviation management, finance, high-tech administration, technology management, hospital management, urban management, and marketing management (Hulme, 2004). The joint MSHROD degree program between Tianjian University of Commerce and Eastern Michigan University (EMU) is one of the examples of specialization with a focus on the function of human resources. It initially started with discussions of an MBA program but the focus shifted given EMU's unique capabilities in the area. Many researchers and practitioners documented China's significant human resource challenges and serious market demand for HR expertise (Park, 2004; Lewis, 2003; Pacific Bridges, 2001; Bruton, Ahlstrom, & Chan, 2000; Sun, 2000). Tsang (1999: 92) provided a succinct quote from a Singaporean director of a company in China, "Personnel is always the biggest issue: How to train people, how to motivate people, how to get them, particularly, to become managers. That's the biggest headache." The MSHROD curriculum addresses these issues with a strong reputable established program that spans over a 20 year history. The program enables future managers with a deeper level of expertise to manage a wide range of personnel issues in organizational change processes.

Information concerning the demand and supply for specialized graduate degrees is mainly anecdotal. However, indicators about the state of MBA programs in China provide a basis for extrapolation. In 2001, the MOE approved 62 institutions with about 10,000 MBA students enrolled in 2003 (Hulme, 2004). The first decade of MBA programs produced about 5,000 MBA graduates (People's Daily, 2000) compared to about 100,000 MBA graduates per year in the US (Newsline, 1998). But the demand far outstrips the supply. The Shanghai Education Commission estimates that by 2006 China will need 37,500 MBA graduates per year. The AACSB (Newsline, 1998) reported that 1.4 million MBA graduates are needed over the next decade. Jack Gosnell of the US Embassy in Beijing commented that, "[i]t would require 200 to 300 years to meet China's current need for management personnel (Scalberg, 2001: 7)." Thus, the demand and supply for specialized managerial expertise probably parallels the situation for generalists but on a smaller magnitude. An important key for the future lies in building management teams that effectively integrate MBA generalists with specialized experts. Herein is a critical role and responsibility for an MSHROD graduate.

3. Managing Learning – Pedagogical Practices

Faculty members need to bridge incredible chasms of historical and cultural contexts to make managerial knowledge relevant for Chinese students. Without a shared system of meaning, the communication of knowledge is seriously compromised (Trompenaars, 1995). The codified management knowledge that is translated and transferred in the classroom is not readily used or applied. In other words, the student may parrot the words and concepts in class but make limited meaningful connections or understanding when confronted by situations in the workplace. The students do not have a shared code or mental model with their western counterparts to understand, value, and accept the knowledge (Schwenk, 1986). Hence, the fundamental challenge for faculty teaching business in China centers on constructing common grounds to connect the tacit knowledge system of the Chinese students with the radically different tacit knowledge of those articulating management knowledge from the west (Newell, 1999).

Before addressing specific pedagogical issues, we need to briefly outline the purpose and structure of the joint MSHROD program. The five major goals of the MSHROD program seeks to prepare future managers to manage organizational change process, relate appropriate human resource and systems to organizational needs, apply appropriate HR and OD techniques to increase organizational effectiveness, contribute to improving HR and OD, and provide access to the expertise of both faculty and students. TUC is responsible for teaching the business foundation pre-requisites and five courses of twelve three-credit courses in the curriculum. EMU faculty travel to Tianjin to teach seven courses in compressed formats. During the US academic semester, each faculty makes two trips per course to teach for five consecutive days on each trip. Courses scheduled for spring and summer run for ten consecutive days. The students take two courses at the same time and the program is completed within a period of 18 months and the students receive an EMU degree.

Faculty draw from an existing community of practice, a body of knowledge, and vicarious lessons from others who worked in China to design and adapt the MSHROD course materials (see Figure 1). However, the process of recreating and reconstituting knowledge depends upon not only the appropriateness of pedagogical practices but also on the interactive dynamics with students in the moment. Clarke III & Flaherty (2002) compared a variety of educational tools used in a MBA marketing course and found that nine (academic readings, computer simulation, field research, guest speakers, homework problems, Internet communications, lecture, practitioner readings, and videos) had different impacts on Chinese student compared to US and UK students and five (case analysis, library research, marketing plan, lecture outlines, and videoconferencing) had similar impacts. They recommended that faculty consider including lectures, lecture outlines, homework problems, and academic readings for Chinese students. Also, Chinese students regard case studies to be especially important for a good MBA course, especially ones with a local focus, use of real names, and decisional rather than illustrative (Thompson, 2000).

Given differences between Chinese and US students in learning styles, relationships with teachers, experience with lectures, language barriers, family influence, and societal attitude toward failure (Waller, 1993; Zhang, 1999), the EMU faculty revised their courses to address the alternative format for the courses and the Chinese cultural context. A preliminary trip to launch the program and face-to-face discussions with the TUC administrators, faculty, and students provided some initial contextual insight and experience for the EMU faculty's preparations. The faculty members tend to already use a wide range of pedagogical practices in the MSHROD program, especially highly experiential and interactive exercises for knowledge application and skill development. While many exercises are standard practices in the US context, the Chinese students experience the activities as refreshing and innovative from their traditional education experience which featured mainly lectures and exams.

An important underlying approach for faculty was to model and construct learning opportunities for students to transform information into applicable knowledge for the workplace. Specifically, this meant that information needed to go beyond being clearly translated from English to Mandarin. (The program is officially conducted in English but some translation happens for difficult concepts.) Students needed tangible experiences to support their construction of mental models with tacit knowledge. Important pedagogical practices demonstrated knowledge in action.

The pedagogical practices we highlight emphasize the mutual development of tacit and explicit knowledge that Newell (1999) advocates for in a community model of management knowledge. The three pedagogical practices are a 3-D case study, photo-change project, and the MSHROD e-portfolio. Each one is briefly outlined below to illustrate how western management information is transformed in a process of recreation and reconstitution to become meaningful knowledge in the Chinese context.

3.1 3-D Case Study – ASIMCO and Mr. Jack Perkowski, CEO

Keeping in mind the important purpose to bridge the gap between US academic graduate and the Chinese workplace, an important goal was how to support our Chinese graduate students in applying their learning to both their current and future work lives. Thus, selection of human resource development case studies followed recommendations by Thompson (2000), which included local Chinese context, real identities, and decisional situation. One case, "ASIMCO: Developing Human Capital in China" (Wong & Weist, 2002) provided the exemplar that we were looking for to introduce HRD best practices in China. The case told the story of an American investment banker, Jack Perkowski, who created an automotive components company in China ten years ago and built the company into the largest, independent, diversified manufacturer in China. The case focused on the ASIMCO leadership development program designed to grow managers for key leadership roles.

We contacted ASIMCO to invite one of their Chinese executives to tell their story as a guest speaker in our class. Not only did ASIMCO accept our invitation, but they surprised us by telling us the CEO, Jack Perkowski would be our guest speaker. Because of Mr. Perkowski's professional commitments, we scheduled his presentation for the morning of the first day of class. Mr. Perkowski captivated the students with his story of the creation and remarkable success of ASIMCO.

Students learned first hand the value of a well-designed and implemented human resource development strategy. Mr. Perkowski described the ASIMCO year long program where high potential managers attended seminars, engaged in action research projects and worked with executive mentors. Students read the case before class began and came prepared to ask questions.

During the session, the students also learned the importance of teamwork, a key to our own learning model that we used in developing our graduate courses. Since individual achievements are typically emphasized in Chinese education, we knew that many students would not immediately embrace team projects, a standard pedagogical tool in American business schools. When Mr. Perkowski strongly emphasized the importance of teams at ASIMCO, he converted several skeptical students into team advocates.

Mr. Perkowski was accompanied by his top Chinese executive and several newly hired young Chinese managers and salesmen. All of the guests talked informally with small groups of students following the presentation. Many business cards were passed out, a first step in building the all important business connections in China. Given the visit from Mr. Perkowski and his team, students experienced a tangible reality dimension of the case. The issues came alive for them beyond the abstractions of the written word on paper.

Throughout the HRD course, the class referred back to the ASIMCO experience when discussing HRD challenges, program design, training techniques and evaluation. With a common example, the Chinese students discussed how the concepts and techniques they were learning could be applied in their own organizations. Hence, the case provided context for the reconstitution of knowledge and more specifically, the construction of tacit knowledge.

At the completion of the course, teams of students were required to write their own HRD case study based on a Chinese or multinational company where one of them worked. The ASIMCO case again served as an example of the way to tell a company's story. The students were instructed to describe the current approaches to HRD as well as their recommendations for improving those practices. By applying what they learned from readings and class discussions, the teams not only demonstrated their knowledge of HRD, but they also created practical action plans that they could apply to both their current and future work lives.

3.2 OD Photo-Change Project

The economic and societal changes in China provide a rich vibrant context for students to study organization development and change (OD&C). However, change introduces substantial ambiguity and chaos. The challenge was to create tangible applications of OD &C to the Chinese workplace with ways of seeing beyond the abstraction of words. The underlying pedagogical purpose of the photo-change project was to bridge the western based organization development and change concepts with the Chinese students' cultural perspectives. We drew from the documentary traditions in visual anthropology and visual sociology to develop a new pedagogical practice by using photography.

The photo-change project required students to take pictures that represented organizational change happening in Chinese organizations. They were not permitted to download pictures from the internet. The photos could be from different places and did not need to be connected into a story, which imposes a different level of work on the learner. Learning objectives for the project were to apply OD&C concepts to the many changes taking place in and surrounding the lives of the students; to reflect on organizational change processes; to draw connections between different stakeholders in the change processes; to evaluate organizational change processes; and to draw implications about the trajectory of organizational changes. The students selected ten photographs to fulfill the requirements of the project. For each photo, students titled the picture, provided a description of the subject matter, applied OD&C concepts, and discussed relevant dimensions of the organizational change process. Most students completed the project with digital cameras and used on-line learning technology to disseminate information after the face-to-face class sessions were over.

The photo-change project facilitated learning for the Chinese students, which engaged them in a transformation process to recreate abstract information into knowledge. The words were recreated into visual images and then reconstituted into explicit knowledge that became contextually meaningful at a deeper level. The photographs provided a channel to embed OD&C ideas into the Chinese context through the eyes of the learner. Also, photographs allow for the freezing of moments in history. Requiring students to write, discuss and share the photographs provided opportunities for reflective and critical thinking.

The use of photographs is a pedagogical innovation for both students and the faculty to an OD&C graduate course. Visual images helped to address language issues by providing students with a focal point for constructing ideas and words. Some of the images were quite powerful. For example, one student shared photographs of leadership change and downsizing in her firm with pictures of moving boxes all over her office. Her unit was downsized from 7 to 1 with her remaining as the sole person in her unit. Her discussions were very intense with applications of theoretical concepts to make sense of the rapid changes in her immediate work environment. She discussed how the OD&C concepts enabled her to analyze the organizational situation and navigate through the chaos with much more confidence. Examples of salient OD&C concepts included restructuring, leadership change, organizational culture, and performance improvements. Several students expressed similar sentiments with somewhat less emotional intensity because their situations were not as intense.

In sum, the visual images and written discussions support an iterative process of managing learning and learning to manage between faculty and students. To manage learning, the faculty can make progress toward addressing language issues, cultural differences, conceptual abstraction, and conceptual embeddedness in the Chinese context. For students learning to manage, the abstract concepts became much more tangible as they struggle with the application process in organizational environments. Most students gained access to organizational change situations. But their learning challenge centered on how to frame the situation and bracket the information into a coherent picture story. Students found the writing process easy once the pictures were selected. The photo-change assignment was the term project for one course which contributes toward the customized learning pedagogy in the MSHROD e-portfolio.

3.3 MSHROD e-Portfolio

A critical pedagogical approach in the MSHROD program is to support students' on-going professional development. MSHROD students must prepare and submit a portfolio that demonstrates the achievement of learning goals in the program. The portfolio may include any material that students believe demonstrates that they have met the program learning goals as well as evidence of their writing skills, analytical and problem solving skills, and interpersonal skills. Students write a reflective statement that describes why they have chosen each item, what they believe it demonstrates about their achievement relative to the program's learning goals and whether there are any modifications they would make in the future doing this type of work. Also, they provide a written statement of their management philosophy that demonstrates an understanding of the knowledge base and ethical values underlying HRM/OD management practices including diversity. A typical example of a MSHROD student's portfolio includes statement of management philosophy, videotape of delivery of training program, practicum project summary with client evaluation and journal, case analysis or term project from an elective course, work place, or community organization, and a reflective essay addressing the above components. The MSHROD portfolio development process involves multiple iterations of work with different faculty. The MSHROD portfolio is not graded but is a graduation requirement for the program.

The purpose of the MSHROD portfolio is 1) to provide the faculty with an integrated mechanism for examining student learning and mastery so that this information may be used to assess the strengths and weaknesses in the MSHROD program; 2) to illustrate the cumulative development of skills and analytic abilities so that the student has a structured opportunity to examine his/her own skill levels and learning; 3) and in conjunction with program faculty, to discuss accomplishments and needs for continued professional development.

For the MSHROD program in China, we made a number of important adaptations. First, the students use an electronic portfolio format to post their work products on a website to facilitate access for both students and faculty. Instead of one faculty member evaluating the e-portfolios, all faculty members who taught in China have responsibility for evaluating several e-portfolios and providing feedback to students. Second, we revised the fifth learning goal to be more realistic for the Chinese students: "To prepare professionals who can apply human resource management strategies effectively as strategic business partners in global organizations." Third, the number of work "products" for the portfolio was reduced from four to three in order to address the potential limited use of case analysis and applied products in the classes taught by the Chinese professors. Last, diversity in the management philosophy statement focused on "cultural diversity" for greater appropriateness in the Chinese environment.

A significant challenge for faculty in managing the learning process with the MSHROD e-portfolio concentrated on being able to communicate clearly the idea of a "portfolio". It was a completely foreign idea to the Chinese students. During the orientation, explanation of the portfolio concept took over an hour. An interim discussion half way into the program provides additional reinforcement as well as reminders from different faculty members. Particular projects can be identified as potential work "products" for the inclusion in the MSHROD e-portfolio. Samples of MSHROD portfolios from EMU counterparts in the US also provide the Chinese students with another avenue to figure out how to develop their individual portfolios. An important key with the MSHROD portfolio is to provide faculty with important information to engage in continuous improvement of the program for future cohorts.

The MSHROD e-portfolio introduces an important and innovative pedagogy to the Chinese graduate students. The MSHROD e-portfolio can be considered the program's rite of passage which involves three phases – separation (divestiture), transition (liminality), and incorporation (investiture) (van Gennep, 1960; Trice & Beyer, 1993). The reflective learning process in the written statement for the portfolio requires students to consider how their achievement of program goals differentiates them, hence separating them from their state of learning upon entry into program. The MSHROD e-portfolio development process situates the Chinese learner into a liminal space, a common anthropological term denoting a threshold in terms of time and space. Within the liminal space, students are required to suspend the norms of learning that focus on information acquisition to step back in order to look at their achievement holistically. The students need to review, reflect, and integrate to retrospectively make sense of their accomplishments in the program. The last phase of investiture unfolds when students enter into an HR/OD position. Thus, the MSHROD e-portfolio enables students' learning to manage by intentionally structuring the liminal space in their rite of passage through the program.

Learning to Manage – Lessons in the Chinese Context

Given the turbulent environment of the economic transformation of China's economy and society, pedagogical practices in business management education must strive for cultural relevance with best practices, especially in human resource management and organization development. The challenge in this charge is not only achieving cultural relevance but also keeping up with the revolutionary changes. US based management ideas for HR and OD can make a recognizable added value contribution toward raising the skill level of management personnel. This discussion focuses on how the above three pedagogical practices – 3-D case study, photo-change project, and the MSHROD portfolio – relates to changes in the Chinese context.

First, acquiring an HR knowledge base and developing related HR skills enable managers to advance the level of human capital in an organization. HR management knowledge includes a foundational understanding of recruiting, selecting, hiring, training, and exiting processes. The 3-D case study of ASIMCO with guest speaker visit by Jack Perkowski, CEO and his executive team provided real life application of the HR management process. The students related conceptual readings to the case, in discussions with Mr. Perkowski, and gaining insights from the new executive recruits who were being socialized into ASIMCO. The ASIMCO managers provided perspectives from both sides of the table – the employer and the new employees – about the human resource management processes and organizational change. The embedded story in the ASIMCO case also integrated how human resources affected the bottom line financial performance of the organization and the critical need for skilled personnel. By applying theoretical concepts with the ASIMCO case and in a variety of experiential exercises, students develop HR managerial skills that are transferable into their future workplaces for human performance improvements. This addresses a fundamental need in the current state of economic changes.

Second, both the 3-D ASIMCO case study and the photo-change project required students to constantly create tangible connections between abstract theoretical concepts with existing organizational practices. Students had to engage in intellectual struggles to analyze, evaluate, compare and contrast, and create options to address organizational change situations. By examining different organizational change processes, students gained a broader perspective with multiple ways of seeing that allowed them to create multiple interventions. These intellectual processes support a range of information processing and cognitive developments for making complex managerial decisions related to product development, quality standards, production methods, target markets, business processes, organizational design, and strategic direction. While the content material is not specific to all functional business areas, the MSHROD students have in depth expertise with HRM as well as the opportunity to develop systematic thinking skills that are relevant to a wide range of decision making areas of an organization. Furthermore, systematic managerial cognitive processing skills are also applicable across organizations and industries.

Third, the MSHROD e-portfolio enables students to engage in two powerful learning processes. One, students are situated in a liminal state to retrospectively make sense of their own personal transformation learning processes within the macro spectrum of China's economic revolution. Second, students employ a holistic perspective to evaluate and synthesize the breadth of knowledge and skills they acquired in the MSHROD program. The MSHROD e-portfolio also provides a forum for students to articulate and crystallize their managerial competencies to strategize for career development beyond the program. At the same time, MSHROD faculty are afforded an opportunity to learn from student feedback what needs to be reconfigured in the curriculum to address the dynamic needs in the Chinese economy with future students.

Last, the MSHROD program addresses a critical need for global standards in business managerial skills in the Chinese economy. By focusing on human resource issues and organization development, future Chinese managers gain the necessary knowledge base to improve their managerial competency with the human resource assets in their organizations. Increasing the managerial skill level supports necessary organizational changes for Chinese firms to compete in the global arena more successfully. The Chinese students gain valuable managerial competencies in learning to manage and as faculty members, we learn to increase and stretch how we manage learning processes. The following section briefly identifies cross-cultural lessons from the faculty perspective to contribute toward future business management education in China.

4. Conclusion

The magnitude of structural changes in China's economy and labor force affect tens and hundreds of millions of people (Wang, 2003). Demand for professional managers and for graduate business management students come from both multinationals entering China and SOEs. The gap between supply for managerial skills and demand continues to widen (Shi, 2000). This means that business graduates will face good job prospects in terms of number of offers and salaries. The salary of mid-level managers in foreign investment firms in China rose by more than 60% from $7,305US in 1995 to $12,154 in 1997 (Anonymous, 1997). In comparison, teaching faculty in Chinese universities earn about $3,600. This presents interesting implications for business students and faculty. The growing pressures to entice faculty away into industry is just one challenge to develop business education in China. More importantly, to meet the changing demands of the Chinese economy, graduate business education need to address both the quantity and quality for relevance.

References

Anonymous. (1997). National examination of MBA in 1997. *Beijing Review,* 3-9.

Bruton, G., Ahlstrom, D., & Chan, E. (2000). Foreign firms in China: facing human resources challenges in a transitional economy. *S.A.M Advanced Management Journal, 65*(4), 4-11.

China Daily. (2003). Money-losing SOEs to face bankruptcy. *China Daily.*

Clark III, I., & Flaherty, T. (2002). Teaching internationally: matching part-time MBA instructional tools to host country student preferences. *Journal of Marketing Education, 24*(3), 233-242.

Fan, Y. (1998). The transfer of western management to China. *Management Learning, 29*(2), 201-221.

Lewis, P. (2003). New China-old ways? A case study of the prospects for implementing human resource management practices in a Chinese state-owned enterprise. *Employee Relations, 25*(1), 42-60.

Newell, S. (1999). The transfer of management knowledge to China: Building learning communities rather than translating Western textbooks? *Education & Training, 41*(6/7), 286-293.

Newsline. (1998). China steps up pursuit of western management education (Fall 1998 ed.) Message posted to AACSB Newsline: http://ww.aacsb.edu/publications/printnewsline/NL1998/fachinawme_1.asp

Pacific Bridges, Inc. (2001). Recruiting and human resources in China: Summer 1998. *SHRM's International Focus.* Abstract retrieved from http://www.pacificbridge.com

Park, S. (2004). Dean's Corner Column. *eNewsline-AACSB, 3*(8). Retrieved from http://222.aacsb.edu/publications/enewsline/Vol-3/Issue8Deans-Corner.asp

People's Daily. (1999). *People's Daily.*

People's Daily. (2000). 5000 MBA graduates trained in China. *People's Daily.*

Scalberg, E. J. (2001). Lesson from China. *Selections,* 6-13.

Schwenk, R. C. (1986). The cognitive perspective on strategic decision-making. *Journal of Management Studies, 25*(1), 41-55.

Shi, Y. (2000). A status report on MBA education in China. *International Journal of Educational Reform, 9*(4), 328-334.

Si, X., & Bruton, G. (1999). Knowledge transfer in international joint ventures in transitional economies: The China experience. *Academy of Management Executives, 13*(1), 83-90.

Sun, J. (2000). Organization development and change in Chinese state-owned enterprises: A human resource perspective. *Leadership & Organization Development Journal, 21*(8), 379-395.

Tompenaars, F. (1995). *Riding the waves of culture: Understanding cultural diversity in business.* London: Nicholas Brealey.

Trice, H., & Beyer, J. (1993). *The Cultures of Work Organizations.* Englewood Cliffs, NJ: Prentice Hall.

Tsang, E. (1999). Internationalization as a learning process: Singapore MNCs in China. *The Academy of Management Executives, 13*(1), 91-99.

Van Gennep, A. (1960). *Rites of Passage.* London: Routledge & Paul Kegan.

Waller, D. (1993). Teaching marketing to Asian students: Are they missing the message? *Journal of Marketing Education, 15,* 47-55.

Wang, Y. (2003). Structural change of China's labor force and the unemployment issue. *China & World Economy,* 18-25.

Wong, G., & Wiest, N. C. (2002). *ASIMCO: Developing human capital in China* (HKU236). University of Hong Kong for Asian Business Cases.

Wu, J. (2003). Business education in China: Internationalization and Consolidation.. *Newscenter.*

Zhang, L. (1999). A comparison of US and Chinese university students' cognitive development: The cross-cultural applicability of Perry's theory. *Journal of Psychology, 133*(4), 425-439.

Chapter 14

Building a Qualified Team of Management Consultants: The Professional Training and Certification of Management Consultants in China

Wenxian Zhang
Rollins College

Yenming Zhang
Beijing Taiji Times Management Consultancy

1. Introduction

By the early twentieth century, a number of consulting firms specializing in comprehensive diagnosis of business organizations began to emerge in the industrial nations. For example, James O. McKinsey, widely regarded as one of the founders of the consulting profession, established his consulting firm in 1923 (Rasiel and Friga, 2001). Over the years, the full benefits of hiring consultants were gradually recognized by business organizations.

As summarized by Nelson (2000), a qualified management consultant usually can offer extensive knowledge and access to resources not available internally. Skilled consultants can also contribute broad experience in the field. In addition, consultants possess the time to research and analyze the problem. Consultants are themselves professionals. They are generally independent of their clients and are able to make objective decisions the client might not be able to make. Furthermore, consultants have the ability to implement the recommendations they provide to their clients. For all these reasons, the practice of management consultation has spread to every aspect of business operations, and the profession has been swiftly developed into a multi-billion dollar industry during the twentieth century.

China, with its rapidly growing economy, is regarded as the last and ultimate testing ground for modern management consulting practices. This article will review the development of management consultation in the People's Republic of China, and explore the opportunities and potential difficulties of conducting management consulting service in the emerging Chinese market. Presently, there is a great need for qualified management consultants to meet the growing demands of economic development. In this paper, the current practices in the professional development of Certified Management Consultants (CMC) around the world will be studied, and efforts by the National Human Resource Exchange Center (NHREC, 全国人才流动中心) and the Chinese Management Academy (CMA, 中国管理科学学会) on the professional training and certification of Chinese domestic management consultants will be examined in detail.

2. Development and the Market of Management Consulting Services in China

During the early years of the People's Republic of China, consultants had played a key role in the rebuilding of the nation's economy. In the 1950s a fleet of foreign experts, most of them from the former Soviet Union and a few from other East Bloc countries, were invited to China for their practical advices on how to construct a new industrial base after decades of wars and chaos. With backgrounds mostly in sciences and engineering, those experts tended to focus on technical side of business undertaking, and more importantly, they operated within the framework of a centrally planned economy. Their practice was vastly different from the Western-style management consultation services known today, and their impact was somewhat limited.

After China split up with the Soviet Union, those foreign consultants were quickly pulled out, and the country thus entered into an era of self-isolation, followed by the turmoil of the Cultural Revolution (1966-1976). The tide finally turned in the late 1970s when the reform-minded Deng Xiaoping took over the helm of the nation. Under his leadership, private ownership was re-created and recognized, special economic zones were established along the Southeastern shoreline, and reforms on the state-owned enterprises (SOEs) were launched. Those vigorous measures successfully attracted billions of dollars in foreign investment, and revitalized the nation's stalled economy. Along with investment funds came the new concept and practice of business management, thus creating a new marketplace for management consultation services in China.

Starting from the early 1980s, modern management methods and techniques from the West and Japan began to arrive in the Peoples Republic of China through the teachings by foreign professors and management consultants. Most Chinese managers at that time came from local engineering backgrounds, and they were likely to emphasize specific skills rather than broad concepts (Burstein, 1983). In general, the traditional roles of Chinese managers tended to clash with the new challenges of China's ambitious economic modernization, which created a gap between traditional training and sought-after skills (Borgonjon, 1992). In China's centrally planned economy, managers for the most part took a reactive approach, waiting for customers to come to them. However, in a competitive market-driven economy managers must adopt a proactive approach to willingly identify and appeal to customers.

Since the 1980s, Deng Xiaoping's powerful drive to deepen economic reforms has forced Chinese managers to embrace the concepts such as marketing and consumer behavior, which for decades were omitted from Chinese management seminars. To fill the gap, some foreign business experts were invited into the country, and short-term training strategies were quickly developed (Hickey, 2004; Wonacott, 1997). The foreign input has resulted in some seminars that attracted over 200 participants, including top government people. Those short programs have given a limited number of Chinese managers the experience they desperately needed (Burstein, 1983).

Meanwhile, some Western consulting groups eagerly attempted to enter China with an aim of attracting international clients who were keen to do business in the newly opened Chinese market. For example, Anderson Consulting worked on a project in China in the early 1980s even though it did not establish its mainland office in Shanghai until 1993 (Wilson, 1995). Engle (1986) also summarized some of the early experiences of management consultation services in China. This group of management firms realized a potential for profit in this emerging market, and were confident that they were able to provide the feasibility studies required of multinational corporations and joint venture partners in China.

As to the domestic clients, initially management consultants had to give free advice and information as they taught, since Chinese companies were not yet used to buying consulting services (Burstein, 1983). Nevertheless, management consultation services gradually caught on, and fees for strategic advice have become an accepted business cost for many Chinese firms. It merits pointing out that from early on not all management consultants are foreign, as Chinese domestic consulting sector has also experienced dramatic growth over the years. Yet in general, management consulting services are still underdeveloped and misused in China, according to a recent study (*Business China*, 2001).

As shortages of Chinese personnel experienced in advanced Western management practices will likely continue for some time, foreign companies having strategic commitments to China will find it is increasingly important to build a qualified local management force (Borgonjon, 1992). Schlevogt (2000) predicts that a new wave of economic growth in China will also create a great need for management advice in the coming years, and such opportunities will include: privatization – ownership diversification of state-owned enterprises and their sales to the public; liberalization – opening of sectors to foreigners; deregulation – breaking up monopolies; mergers and acquisitions – absorbing overcapacity; development of hinterland – special incentives for foreign investment in the West; and a general move toward knowledge and service industries.

The case of BearingPoint, a global business consultancy services company, is an excellent example to illustrate such argument. In just over two years, the company has substantially grown its business in China, from being non-existent in China in 2000 to a firm employing 500 people by 2003 (*Asia Today International*, 2003). Apparently, China has become the firm's most promising market, and the growth is coming from state-owned enterprises seeking to re-engineer themselves to remain relevant in today's dynamic China. BearingPoint clients include the Bank of China (中国银行) and China Telecom (中国电信). Those large state-owned companies are eager to seek out international management consultants to help them achieve world best practice in sectors ranging from accounting to strategic planning.

Another example is the China National-Native Produce & Animal By-Products Import & Export Corp. (中国土畜产品进出口总公司), China's oldest state-owned trading company, which is undergoing a mid-life makeover forced on it by economic reform. Like other state trading-companies, its client base declined over recent years as the government opened the import-export business to foreign-invested companies and allowed some manufacturers to trade directly. Faced with such challenges, the company has turned to the German management consultancy Roland Berger and Partners for advice. Based on the recommendations of a team of five-consultants, the firm has since developed a long-term strategy, and is making efforts to downsize its workforce by reorganizing its overstaffed headquarters and numerous subsidiaries (Saywell, 1999).

China's recent entry into the World Trade Organizations creates another powerful incentive for management consultation services. Unlike the early practice of helping multinational firms enter the Chinese market in the 1980s, most of the consulting firms today are dealing primarily with Chinese companies trying to restructure or cope with the competitive pressures of deregulation and China's WTO membership.

Many Chinese industries, such as telecommunications, airlines and power, are being thoroughly restructured by the government, and the country's "Big Four" state-owned banks are paying consultants to tell them how to build consumer orientated businesses. In addition, the increasingly vibrant private sector is starting to become a big customer base for management consultations in China. Even parts of the government have bought the consulting concept: McKinsey did a high profile report for the Shanghai municipal government on how to redesign the famed Nanjing Road into a world-class shopping district, and A.T. Kearney has advised Beijing's government on fostering its flourishing software industry (Dolven, 2002). In Shenyang, the municipal government co-funded a World Bank project, which invited the management consult firm EDS Business Planning to assist in the rejuvenation of the Shenyang Machine Tools Co. EDS' contract is to provide corporate strategy in five key areas: strategic planning, human resources, product development, financial management, and manufacturing and sales (*Business China*, 1997).

In brief, all those organizations with different forms of ownership in China - state, collective, private, and foreign - share one characteristic as noted by Schlevogt (2000): they all desperately need advice and help! While most multinational companies (MNCs) treat China as a production center and export platform in their global strategy, many have also begun to enter the domestic market. Whereas a few years ago their major concerns were market-entry strategies, now they often have to solve problems in the area of joint-venture restructuring and human resource management. Competitive strategy at the corporate and business unit level, as well as penetration of the domestic market, have become additional pressing issues. All these lead to the notion of huge Chinese management consulting market that is waiting to be explored.

Despite vast market potentials, there are also substantial obstacles for management consulting companies to conduct their businesses in the People's Republic of China. Schlevogt, in a two-part article in *Consulting to Management* (2000), summarized a dozen or so of those obstacles, such as too much emphasis on hardware, neglect of software; insufficient knowledge of consulting; managerial short-termism; underdeveloped legal framework; sprawling bureaucracy with ethical problems; scarcity of qualified human resources; cultural barriers; Chinese "special situation;" internal mismatch; lack of appropriate strategies; lack of appropriate organization; unqualified consultants and leaders; and lack of knowledge and information base. These problems can be further classified into three categories: large society issues, organizational cultures, and knowledge and training of management consultants. Clearly there is a great need for a large number of qualified management consultants to meet the demands of rapid economic development in China.

The next section of this paper will review the current practices in the training and professional development of management consultants around the world, and its implications for Chinese market.

3. Professional Development of Management Consultants in the World

A management consultant, as defined by the Institute of Management Consultants USA (1996), is an independent professional who, for a fee, helps the management of client organizations define and achieve their goals through better utilization of resources. The consultant may do this by helping to define and identify current or future problems or opportunities. Management consultants are change-agents who not only propose change but help implement it as well. As an independent professional, a management consultant's sole concern is the welfare of the client's organization. Clearly to be competent, a management consultant needs to have among other things an excellent educational background, strict professional ethics, and years of applicable experience.

Since consulting on how to do a job is different from actually doing that job, it is generally agreed that consulting should have its own special training requirements that are additional to what a new consultant may have learned at university, at business school, and in former employments (Kubr, 2002, p. 799). Over the history of management consulting profession, learning on the job has been recognized as a proven method of learning. By actually practicing consulting, more than likely an individual will have some meaningful learning opportunities of dealing with real-life situations and problems of his or her clients. However, there is a growing belief within the management consulting circle that learning on the job alone is not sufficient and should be supplemented by other learning experiences, such as formal training courses, workshops and professional certification. Advocating in this regard are some leading professional associations of consultants around the world, such as: the International Council of Management Consulting Institutes (ICMCI) and the Institute of Management Consultants USA (IMC USA).

The Institute of Management Consultants USA was established in January 1968 to set standards of professional conduct and competence and to accredit individual member consultants meeting those standards (Shays, 1985). Its mission is to "promote excellence and ethics in management consulting through certification, education, and professional resources." Over the years its most active function has been on accrediting consultants as certified management consultants (CMC). More than half of the 2,600 members of the IMCUSA now hold the CMC title (Savin, 2000). This accreditation by one's peers is regarded as a mark of success, although it has no legal status in the United States except for signifying accredited membership in the organization. IMC USA has developed a Code of Ethics, the standards of competence, and is committed to the development of the profession and adding to the field of knowledge in management consultation services.

The *Consulting to Management* (*Journal of Management Consulting*) is published by the organization. Currently, the United States is clearly the most advanced country in terms of the use and development of management consulting services. The *U.S. Statistical Abstracts* (2003) show the revenue for management consulting services reaching over 9.67 billion dollars in 2001; and it is reported that half of the world management consulting population resides in the U.S. (Nelson, 2000). Besides IMC USA, several other large groups in the country are also actively devoted to training and certifying management consultants, including: the National Bureau of Certified Consultants (NBCC), the Institute for Investment Management Consultants ((IIMC), and the Investment Management Association (Bergsman, 1995; Chapelle, 1999; NBCC, 2004).

In the international arena, other developed nations such as Great Britain and Canada also have well-designed systems in place for the training and development of management consulting profession. A key player with global reach is the newly arrived International Council of Management Consulting Institutes (ICMCI). Initially with only seven institutional members, ICMCI was founded to build better working relationships between member institutes, to provide a common communication platform, to institute a code of ethics, and to establish a minimum of standard for quality in management consulting services.

The birth of ICMCI was attributed to John Roethle, chairman of IMC USA in 1987, when he organized a congress of management consultants from ten countries to address burning issues faced by the profession (ICMCI, 2002). The mission of ICMCI is to elevate the standards of management consultants worldwide, and to provide the international community with the confidence that these standards, combined with the certification process of its member institutes, will ensure that certified management consultants serve their clients with world-class competency and professionalism.

In 2001, ICMCI was recognized as a Non-Governmental Organization (NGO) and granted Special Consultative Status by the United Nation's Economic and Social Council (ECOSOC). Today with more than 20,000 members from 40 nations, ICMCI stands as the global association of national management consulting institutes from all over the world. These national institutes administer, in accordance with established standards, the international CMC certification earned by individual management consultants. By setting the global benchmark for the CMC designation, ICMCI has developed an International Code of Professional Conduct, the Competency Framework and the Common Body of Knowledge to assess the qualification of management consultants (ICMCI, 2002).

What is a CMC? According to ICMCI, a Certified Management Consultant is an individual who has met strict certification requirements of the Institute of Management Consultants in his or her country. If that Institute is a member of the International Council of Management Consulting Institutes, the initials mean the consultant has met established standards of competence, ethics and independence, and is eligible for reciprocity between ICMCI member institutes. These standards include: three years in management consulting; recognized degree or professional qualification or additional five years in management consulting in lieu of a degree; 1,200 hours per annum in active management consulting during the three qualifying years over the preceding five years, and currently active in management consulting; owner or employee of a firm in independent practice, or internal consultant in organization meeting institute's independence criteria (ICMCI, 2002). To qualify for a CMC designation, written examination or structured interview designed to test the understanding of professional codes of conduct and common body of knowledge is mandatory, in addition to five client references and two sponsors who are full members or fellows of the institute. IMC USA has a similar structure and higher standards for its CMC title.

When certified, a CMC will make a pledge in writing to abide by the institute's code of professional conduct. Adherence to this code signifies voluntary assumption of self-discipline above and beyond the requirements of law. Every institute member of ICMCI has such a code that meets the minimum standards of ICMCI. Institutes enforce their code by receiving and investigating complaints of violations and by taking disciplinary action, including revocation of certification, against any member who is found breaching the code.

It should be pointed out that current certification efforts have been vigorously opposed by some people within the profession (Weiss, 2003; Evans and Saunders, 1978). They believe that certification cannot guarantee anything more than the application of general and rather elementary criteria of admission to the profession. It cannot show whether a consultant is actually suitable for a given job. After all, consulting to business is itself a business and a consultant who passes the market test by finding enough clients does not need a paper certifying his or her competence. Nevertheless, despite its controversy, certification is believed by many to be a step towards a wide recognition of management consulting as a true profession. To be a profession, according to Vieira (2004), every avocation needs to meet five criteria: 1) a body of knowledge that is continuously upgraded; 2) a system of certification or accreditation; 3) ongoing training and updating; 4) a commitment to service before self; and 5) a code of ethics.

As a general rule, business, government and the public at large prefer to have a guarantee that management consultants associated with important decisions in the private and public sectors are proven professionals. Therefore, certification should enhance the international position of management consulting, and help it to compete with other professions where certification is a long-established practice. As Kubr (2002) summarizes, it should put more order into the consulting business and help to separate the wheat from the chaff.

The world "certified" represents more than just training, it also stands for experience, ethics and a commitment to professionalism (Savin, 2000). Although the CMC designation is yet sufficiently known or respected, the ICMCI and its member institutes are making efforts to meet the needs of the majority of management consultants (70%), who do not work for the few elite consulting firms, by exposing them to a body of knowledge, supplying ongoing training and development, and helping to implement a code of conduct (Vieira, 2004).

Hence, despite its limits, it is fair to say that the ICMCI's programs have made a positive contribution to the promotion of competence and ethical standards in management consulting from a global perspective, and to the collaboration of consultants around the world sharing common interests. Those efforts have also profoundly influenced the current initiatives on professional training of management consultants in the People's Republic of China, which currently holds a provincial membership in ICMCI.

4. Development of Management Consulting Profession in China

From the late 1970s to the early 1990s, the Chinese domestic market of management consultation services was only in a rudimentary stage of development. Early Chinese consulting firms were emerging as "idea companies" (点子公司). The lack of professional operation of these companies and distance between their "ideal ideas" and practical realities faced by their clients resulted in a downturn of credibility. However by 1992, Deng Xiaoping's visit to Southern China especially to Shenzhen had swiftly shifted the country's economic engine into high gear. Some government agencies began to realize the indispensableness of management consulting to the national as well local economy, and made tremendous efforts to promote the development and use of Chinese consultation services.

Early emphasis was in the areas of investment, technology and financial services. According to a report by the Science and Technology Society of Jiangsu Province (江苏省科协), the return ratio for research and development was one to seven in the region; however for successful consulting service it could reach as high as one to twenty-two. In 1994, the cities of Beijing, Tianjin, Shanghai and the Jiangsu Province were designated by the Chinese State Council (国务院) as experimental regions for promoting the development of scientific consultation China, as those areas all possessed a mature business market, well educated population, high growth rates and able research capabilities.

As China's various more advanced regions were developing into market-driven economy, many private or foreign companies of information consultation and market research started to emerge. Firms like Gallup Consulting (盖洛普咨询), Horizon Research (零点调查), Haochen Commerce (浩辰商务) and Huicong Information (慧聪信息) began to provide valuable consulting services to Chinese businesses. Meantime, the world elites of consulting industry such as McKinsey and Boston Consulting Group, believing China's emerging market was the last and ultimate testing ground for management consulting, also rushed in with their well-equipped troops of consultants.

By the mid-1990s, with strong support from the central and local governments, Chinese management consulting sectors have enjoyed a period of remarkable growth. In 1996, the gross income for information consultation and service industry related to computers was 6.2 billion RMB in Beijing; the following year with a growth rate of 14.5% it reached to 7.1 billion; and by 1998 with 42.8% surge it was already a 10-billion RMB business. Excluding computer-related industries, the gross revenue for the consulting services in Beijing in 1998 was 4.73 billion RMB, which counted for 1.1% of GDP for the Beijing region in that year. Data from the Beijing Municipal Statistics Bureau (北京市统计局) indicated that a total of 53,000 people were employed by 2,200 consulting firms in the region (北京市统计局国民经济和社会发展统计公报, 2003). Many of the companies have been developed into very successful business corporations, including: Hanpu Management (汉普管理), Yuanzhuo Management (远卓管理), Great Wall Strategies (长城战略) and so on. Evidently, management consulting has become an integral part of the nation's economic system, and such a rapid growth has created an enormous pressure for the sector to develop efficiently a large number of well-qualified management consultants to meet the market demand.

The following statistics present a quick glance at the scope of consulting industry in China. According to the records of business registration in 1999, there are over 130,000 companies engaging in businesses related to consulting, employing nearly a million people. However its total revenue only counted about 0.2% of the GDP in China (Xinhuanet, 1999). A recent survey by the Horizon Research indicated that management consulting sector consisted up to 15.4% of total consulting industry in the country. The level of satisfaction for management consulting services in China was about 55% (Horizon Research, 2004).

Generally speaking, companies engaging in the Chinese management consulting market can be classified into two categories: large international consulting companies and small-scale domestic operations. The large international firms are known for their rich global resources, well-established systems and procedures, and lofty consulting fees. They tend to focus on strategic planning and panoramic issues. On the other hand, domestic firms have fewer employees, and are usually more involved in short-term projects and problems with day-to-day operations. They compete with large international companies with low expenses and their deep understanding of specific problems and issues unique to Chinese businesses.

The domestic sector can be further divided into two schools of practice: academic consulting and empirical consulting. The model for academic consulting is typically a management professor with several graduate students. They usually can produce studies that are pleasant to read, with advanced theoretic research and systematic plans and strategies. However they tend to be short on real-world experiences, and their recommendations are sometimes difficult to implement. Empirical consulting, on the other hand, is likely to develop reports with pragmatic plans of action and clear implementation strategies. Although they are rich in real-life experiences of business operations in China, they are short of knowledge of most recent management research and advancement, and their proposed solutions usually lack forward looking perspectives and innovations. These shortcomings undoubtedly hinder the further growth of the Chinese domestic management consulting sector and its ability to compete with large international firms.

Nowadays it is very common to see multiple consulting companies competing for a single client. In 2002, eighteen firms fought to win a contract from the China Southern Airlines (Dolven, 2002). Tough competition drives down profit margin, and with low operating income, it is very difficult for domestic consulting companies to grow in size. Therefore, it has become a daunting challenge for Chinese firms to attract and keep highly qualified team of management consultants in the long run. A gloomy statistical result shows that 70% of Chinese consulting companies are operating at a loss, and a majority of those firms go out of business only after nine months (中国管理咨询网, 2004). When their services are in demand, new consultants are hired in a hurry; when projects are done, layoff is likely to follow. Because of this lack of consecutiveness, their businesses are by and large stuck with low-level, low-quality, small-scale, and cyclical operations.

From the perspectives of business organizations that engage consulting services, many Chinese companies usually do not have a clear and comprehensive understanding of what a management consultant and a consulting firm can contribute to their operations. Since there are no governing authorities assessing the qualification of management consultants and quality of consulting services in the country, Chinese enterprises generally have low confidence in engaging such services. They tend to ignore or overlook the use of consulting services; when forced to deal with serious emerging issues, they usually have unrealistic expectations on management consulting, hoping it will magically solve all their problems. Even when proposals are made and outline of strategies developed, sometimes it is difficult to implement the proposed plans by consultants. Under the heavy influence of Eastern philosophy, the management of many Chinese companies is complicated with various human factors, unlike their Western counterparts where everything is straight business, governed by the rule of law. The breach of apparent link between proposal and implementation, lack of forceful enforcement and other issues all hinder the further advance of management consulting services in China.

Problems with the Chinese domestic consulting sector are closely correlated with people employed in the industry. A recent online survey shows the annual income for a Chinese consultant ranks number five in the nation, ahead of finance, investment, and insurance professions (iUserSurvey, 2004). Because of its huge potential, many people rush in the business without appropriate training and preparation. The composition of current Chinese management consultants lacks diversity; some firms are straight MBA graduates. People with backgrounds in technology, information studies and engineering are scarce in the occupation. This is in sharp contrast with large international firms that have a much-diversified human resource structure, where both management personnel and people with special scientific expertise assist and compliment each other. On the whole, the major problems with the Chinese management consulting profession are a narrow and obsolete knowledge base, lack of strategic outlook and systematic approach to problems, lack of the overall notion of market competition, limited meaningful managerial experience, lack of awareness of concepts of modern management consulting practices, low sense of professional responsibilities and inferior ethics. Training and development of a sufficient number of qualified consultants has become an urgent, bottleneck issue to the further growth of Chinese management consulting industry.

5. Professional Training of Management Consultants in China

As discussed above, since there are no central authorities assessing the qualification of management consultants, no standard accreditation or registration system in place, and no appropriate laws and regulations governing the use of consulting services, the Chinese management consulting market is in somewhat of a chaotic status. Realizing the imperativeness of the matter, some local Chinese government agencies and professional associations have recently begun to make efforts to address such an issue. Among them, the early initiatives by the Chinese Enterprise Confederation (中国企业联合会) are most noticeable. Over the years the organization has formulated the "Recommendations on the Development of Chinese Management Consulting Profession" (关于发展我国管理咨询事业的意见), a "Tentative Plan on the Accreditation of Management Consulting Organizations" (关于管理咨询机构认证试行办法), and a "Tentative Plan on the Certification of Management Consultants" (管理咨询顾问试行办法). Some of the plans are included as a part of economic regulations of the National Business and Trade Commission (国家经贸委). However, for various reasons those documents are never officially released.

    Some of the local efforts in this regard include: in Beijing in 1996, the Beijing Association of Scientific Consultation (北京科技咨询业协会) developed a "Tentative Plan on the Accreditation and Management of Certified Consultants" (注册咨询师认证及管理暂行办法) and detailed implementation procedures. The plan was approved by the Scientific Commission of the Beijing municipal government (北京市科委), and went on as a small-scale experiment; in Shanghai, regarded as a key part of human resource engineering into the 21st century, the city's Human Resource Bureau (上海市人事局), the Municipal Educational Commission (上海市教育委员会) and Adult Education Commission (上海市成人教育委员会) have authorized the Shanghai Enterprise Federation (上海市企业联合会) to organize a program on the "Certification of Mid to Senior Level Management Consultants" (中高级管理咨询师资格证书); in Shenzhen, a training program for "Internationally Certified Management Consultants" (国际注册管理咨询师认证教程) has been initiated by the Shenzhen Enterprise Federation (深圳市企业联合会) and the Shenzhen Training Center for Managerial Personnel (深圳市企业管理干部培训中心); and in Chongqing, a new set of "Assessment Standards of Management Consultants" (管理咨询师职业鉴定试行标准) has just been issued by the Bureau of Labor and Social Security (重庆市劳动和社会保障局). As a result of the local scope and experimental nature of these plans, the development of the management consulting profession in China, although positive, is somewhat limited. In light of the current situation, the Ministry of Human Resources (人事部) has stepped in to take a leadership role in the training and professional development of management consultants in the country.

    A key entity, the Office of the Training and Certification of Management Consultants (OTCMC, 管理咨询师培训与认证管理办公室), is to be established from the ambitious plan, and the National Human Resource Exchange Center (NHREC, 全国人才流动中心) will be responsible for the funding and implementation of the program. With an overall goal of promoting professional development of management consultants in China, the plans are designed to provide training, assessment and certification to the profession, to seek collaboration with international organizations on common interests, and to establish a national framework of management consulting services in China, with an information network and professional training institutes across the country.

The objectives of the plan are to establish thirty Regional Training Centers (RTC, 授权培训中心) that are authorized by the program office, and when in place, these RTCs will seek to train a total of 3,000 management consultants within a given year for the OTCMC to certify. Currently, the proposed plans have been submitted to and approved by the Chinese governing authorities, and NHREC has entered in the official contract to commence the program. The implementation will begin in 2005, with each center sending two to three trainers to the national office in Beijing to be trained and briefed with most advanced theories and practices in management consultation services.

The NHREC's master plan for the development of management consultants has four core components – the national office, regional training centers, training curriculum and certification process – each will be examined underneath.

5.1 *Office of the Training and Certification of Management Consultants (OTCMC)*

Designed as the national authority for certification of management consultants in China, the Office of the Training and Certification of Management Consultants has three key elements: the Curriculum Committee, the Assessment Committee, and the Certification Center.

The Curriculum Committee is in charge of the design of the curriculum, selection of textbooks, and overall implementation strategy for three different levels of training courses. It has seven to nine members, consisting of the leading Chinese and international professors and influential professionals in management science and consulting business.

The Assessment Committee is responsible for the development of standards of qualification for CMC in China, the design of assessment, the quality control and supervision of the review and certification process. With one chair and one secretary, it contains seven members of senior experts on enterprise management, consulting research and practices around the world.

The Certification Center includes nine to eleven members, among them a director, an assistant director, a senior research follow, and a secretary. Its main goal is to review the qualifications of applicants, and issue different levels of certificates to qualified candidates. The center is also in charge of establishing a partnership with the ICMCI, and responsible for organizing annual conferences and international seminars on management consulting services in China and around the world.

5.1.1 Regional training centers

The establishment of authorized regional training centers is the key to the success of the NHREC program. The center's selection is based on self-nomination combined with special invitations to certain reputable organizations. Basic requirements for such endorsement include: established institution with sufficient funding and facilities to meet the training needs in the region; leading personnel with rich experience in management education; minimum of three eligible instructors to be trained by the national office; and signing of official contract with the national office. The comprehensive qualification of applying agencies is to be carefully assessed by the OTCMC. After a center passes its initial appraisal, it will go into a probation period of six months before receiving its full accreditation, and there will also be a yearly review based on its annual operations to ensure the quality of the program. When approved, a center will enter in an official partnership agreement with the OTCMC, and be issued license for training and certification of management consultants in its region.

The main goals of a regional center are to provide qualified instruction to management consultant candidates using established curriculum and teaching methods; advance market development in the area, promote awareness of the training program and the CMC designation; coordinate the application, interview and examination of CMC candidates in the region; provide management training programs to businesses and government agencies; offer management consulting to companies or recommend qualified CMCs for such services; seek opportunities to collaborate with allied organizations, and establish comprehensive regional network of educational resources.

Conversely, the responsibilities of the national office are to provide the recognized brand name and structured training programs; organize intensive training and reinforcement to regional instructors, provide needed textbooks and educational support to each center; establish the main benchmark for the assessment of CMC in China; review and approve applications for certification, store information into the National Database of Enterprise Management Personnel (全国企业经营管理人才库), and make recommendations to client organizations; solicit support from government agencies; provide promotion and market development on the national level; and organize national and international conferences on management consulting in China.

5.1.2 *The training curriculum*

The Chinese consultant training program will focus on the essential professional knowledge and skills needed for successful management consulting practice in China. Based on a candidate's qualifications, the proposed training will be offered at basic, intermediate and advanced levels and classes will be conducted during weekends. The length of each program will be approximately two to three months. Objectives of such training are to enhance a potential consultant's understanding and capabilities in strategic planning, leadership and innovations, market development, enterprise and project management, information processing and business communication, continuous learning and teamwork among others.

Table 1 illustrates some of the core courses and contact hours designed for those three different levels of training programs.

Emphasis of training will be on the introduction and use of the new concepts and advanced theories in management research, demonstration of applicable models in contemporary practices, and practical skills critical for management consulting services in emerging market. Candidates who successfully finish particular courses of training will receive credentials issued by the NHREC, and will be eligible for applying for different levels of certificates of management consultant designation in the country.

Table 1. Course Requirements

Categories	Basic	Intermediary	Advance
Core Courses	Organizational Behavior (30)	Management and Organizational Behavior (30)	Organizational Development Strategies (30)
	Fundamentals of Management Science (30)	Enterprise Cultures (30)	Organizational and Capital Management (30)
	Principles of Economics (20)	Management of International Organizations (20)	Management of Knowledge Industry (20)
	Foundation of Financial Management (20)	Accounting and Financial Management (20)	Analysis and Assessment of Enterprise Commerce (30)
	Effective Business Communication (30)	Leadership Skills (30)	International Commerce and Collaboration (20)
Electives	Psychology of Management Consulting (12)	Pursuit of Excellence in Business Operations (12)	Path of Success of World-class Enterprises (18)
	Individuals and Teamwork (12)	Essentials of Human Resource Management (12)	Human Resource Strategies (18)
		Arts of War in Business Operations (6)	*Arts of War* in Business Operations (12)
Total Class hours	154 hours (21 days)	160 hours (23 days)	178 hours (26 days)

5.1.3 *Certification of management consultants in China*

Based on the qualification of individual candidate, the CMC designation is to be issued at three different levels: Certified Management Consultant Trainee (CMCT, 见习管理咨询师), Certified Management Consultants, and Sr. Certified Management Consultants (SCMC, 高级管理咨询师). A CMCT is likely to be a new grassroots employee with basic knowledge and limited experience in management consulting. The requirements include: bachelor degree from nationally accredited institution, five years work experience, with two years in management consulting; or master degree from nationally accredited institution, three years work experience, with two years in management consulting; experience in enterprise management, strong interest in and commitment to management consulting.

The basic qualifications for the CMC designation are: bachelor degree from nationally accredited institution, six years of work experience, with three years in management consulting or master or above degree from nationally accredited institution, four years work experience, with two years in management consulting; or CMCT holder for two years, with a minimum of two formal consulting experiences each year; or sufficient knowledge of the industry, with scholarly research and publication in management and consulting practice.

A SCMC is an individual with extensive knowledge and rich practical experience in the management consulting profession, likely to be a CEO, VP or director in a consulting firm or a senior-level manager of an established business organization. Qualification for such title includes: bachelor degree from nationally accredited institution, ten years work experience, with five years in management consulting or master or above degree from nationally accredited institution, seven years work experience, with three years in management consulting; or CMC holder for two years, with a minimum of three formal consulting experiences each year; and a well respected reputation in the management consulting profession.

Candidates who complete different levels of training and meet the above qualifications will need to file individual applications for certification, along with personal IDs, diplomas, training credentials, recommendations from sponsoring institutions and references from consulting clients to the Certification Center for review and approval.

A key component of the assessment process is the face-to-face interview with each candidate. Scheduled on the first Sunday during the months of March, June and September, this 45-minute interview will be conducted by a minimum of two representatives from the national center, with a focus on a candidate's personal preparation and his or her capability of dealing with issues in management consulting. The first five to ten minutes are to review and verify an applicant's background information such as educational qualifications, working experience and so on, the remaining session is to assess the candidate's understanding of knowledge and competency requirements by posting various questions in management consulting.

At the conclusion of the interview, the representatives will conduct a comprehensive appraisal according to the established standards and procedures, reach a consensus, and forward the closing recommendation to the center for final approval. This recommendation will then be evaluated by a national review committee to ensure the integrity of the process. Lastly, within ten business days, candidates should be notified with the results of their applications, certificates will be issued to qualified individuals, and information entered into the national management personnel database.

6. Conclusion

As China becomes increasingly integrated with the global economy, its market for management consulting services has experienced a period of dramatic growth. Various Chinese government agencies and non-profit organizations, realizing the importance of management consultancy to the national and local economy, have been actively promoting the use and development of management consulting services in the country. Meanwhile, with the notion that China will become the last and the largest emerging market in modern history, many elite international consulting firms have also eagerly jumped on the Oriental express. China's recent entry into the WTO, the massive reengineering of SOEs, deregulation, privatization, mergers and acquisitions, and a general move toward knowledge industries have all contributed to the creation of a huge potential market for management consulting services in China. Professor Dongtao Huang of Guanghua School of Management, Peking University estimates that the market for management consulting services in China was about $100 million in 2000; more strikingly, it will grow ten times a year for the next few years, and reach over $10 billion by 2010 (Chinese Enterprise Confederation, 1999). If his prediction turns out to be true, it is highly unlikely the number of people in the profession will grow ten fold a year as well.

Despite its enormous promise, substantial obstacles also exist to the growth of management consulting services in China. Nationwide, the legal framework is still underdeveloped, bureaucracy and corruption widespread. Chinese business culture and organizational structure could also become barriers to the further development of consulting services in the country. Furthermore, various problems are associated with the Chinese domestic consulting profession itself, including: narrow and obsolete knowledge base, lack of strategic outlook and systematic approach to problems, lack of the overall notion of market competition, limited meaningful managerial experience, lack of awareness of concepts of modern management consulting practices, low sense of professional responsibilities and inferior ethics. Industry wide, there are no central authorities to assess the qualification of management consultants, no standard accreditation or registration systems in place, and no appropriate laws and regulations governing the use of consulting services. All these factors have severely hindered the growth of the Chinese management consulting profession and its competence in the marketplace.

Clearly there is a great need for a large number of qualified management consultants to meet the demands of rapid economic development in China. Facing this challenge, the National Human Resource Exchange Center has formulated an ambitious plan to promote the training and certification of management consultants in China. Its main goals are to introduce the advanced theories and methods of management practices into China, to establish standards and regulations for management consultants, to provide competency training and qualification certification to practicing consultants, and to promote communication and professional cooperation across the country and the exchange with world industries. The training and certification program has been endorsed by the Chinese Management Academy.

Based on the working documents released so far, this plan seems to be well researched and deliberated; and with the support of governmental agencies, it has a huge potential to change the face of the Chinese management consulting profession in the coming years.

Compared with other similar programs and practices, a professional code of conduct needs to be developed, and an independent discipline organization established. The key to the success of this plan may well rest on NHREC's ability to coordinate the current development efforts in various parts of the country, design and effectively promote a systematic training curriculum, establish authoritative training centers in strategic locations, and ensure an objective and thorough process of certification for management consultants in China in a timely fashion.

The Chinese training and certification program of management consultants is clearly under the influence of Western practices such as IMC USA and ICMCI, yet it has its own distinctiveness. Combining the prestige of the leading management research institution in the nation with the power of a central government agency, it has a convincing authority that is lacking in other programs. Comparing the development of management consulting practices in the United States and other Western countries where growth has been largely shaped by market force over a century, the Chinese management consulting profession proliferates in a relatively a short period of time, benefiting from the achievements in research and practice around the world. More importantly, various governmental agencies have played much more active roles in the establishment of policies and standards, and the promotion of professional development in management consulting services in the country. Since the Chinese training and certification program will be fully implemented in the near future, its broad and long-term impact on the market is yet to be seen.

Although the Chinese management consulting service is derived from Western management theories and practices, its development is also under the heavy influence of Eastern philosophies, e.g., Confucianism, Taoism and Buddhism that guide people's organizational and social behavior. The core of these philosophies is the "value systems." Take Confucianism, for example. On one hand, an essential value is benevolence (仁), meaning to treat others with kindness. This functions as a guiding principle in people's social life. In organizational or political life, on the other hand, the Confucian value is functioning "conformity" (致), meaning subordinates must conform to the will of the leader. Such deep-rooted value has been affecting the lives of Chinese for over two thousand years that people take it for granted. In social life, people treat others kindly, while in organizational life individuals are more protective. Subordinates are supposed to be submissive, and those who challenge authorities will have a hard time inside any given organization.

This is in sharp contrast to a Western society where equity is at least a value, and people are less status conscious. In the West, people and organizations capitalize on new theories and research findings, and depend more on operational rules and regulations; while in the East, people tend to depend more on *guanxi*, meaning personal relations with others, which plays a crucial role in one's political power base in an organization. These fundamental differences account for why Western management consultancy finds it difficult to "land" in China at the early stage of sector growth. But as pointed out earlier in the paper, dramatic changes are happening while the market matures, and organizations and businesses will be more open to consulting services from both within China and around the world.

References

Asia Today International. 2003. Post-TWO China embraces consulting firms. 21:4 (Aug./Sep.): 23.

Beijing Municipal Statistics Bureau (北京市统计局). 2003. *北京市统计局2003年国民经济和社会发展统计公报.*

Bergsman, Steve. 1995. Consultant training: IMCA certification program popular among consultants and sponsors. *Pension Management*, 31:5 (May): 5.

Borgonjon, Jan and Wilfried Vanhonacker. 1992. Modernizing China's managers. *China Business Review*, 19 (Sep./Oct.): 12-15.

Burstein, Daniel. 1983. China gropes for perfect blend of management techniques. *International Management*, 38 (4): pp. 57-60.

Business China. 1997. Guru time. 23 (14): pp. 8-9.

Business China. 2001. A piece of advice. 27 (2): p. 12.

Chapelle, Tony. 1999. Street talk: consultants' group changes name and membership requirements. *On Wall Street* (Aug. 1): p. 1.

Chinese Enterprise Confederation (中国企业联合会). 1999. *中国企业发展报告.*

Chinese Management Consulting Network (中国管理咨询网). 2004. http://www.chnmc.com/articleshow00.asp?articleid=1313 [cited 28 August 2004].

Dolven, Ben. 2002. The great consulting pile-up. *Far Eastern Economic Review*, 165:19 (May 16): pp. 26-29.

Engle, Paul M. 1986. Consulting in a Chinese factory. *China Business Review*, 13:5 (Sep./Oct.): pp. 46-47.

Evans, Robert C., and David J. Saunders. 1978. What is a nice businessman like you doing in a profession like this? *Optimum*, 9 (3): p. 62.

Nelson, Kevin. 2000. Consultants. In Marilyn M. Helms, editor, *Encyclopedia of Management*. 4th edition. Detroit: Gale Group, pp. 137-138.

Hickey, Will. An evaluation of foreign HR consulting company effectiveness in China. *Performance Improvement Quarterly*, 17 (1): pp. 81-101.

Horizon Research (零点调查). 2004. http://www.horizonkey.com/index.asp [cited 16 July 2004].

The Institute of Management Consultants USA. 1996. Selecting and utilizing a management consultant. http://www.cmcglobal.org/FAQs.cfm [cited 14 July 2004].

International Council of Management Consulting Institutes. A measure of excellence. http://www.icmci.org [cited 15 July 2004].

ICMCI. 2002. http://www.icmci.org/AboutUs/index.htm [cited 15 July 2004].

iUserSurvey. 2004. http://www.iusersurvey.com/new_case.asp [cited 18 July 2004].

Kubr, Milan. 2002. *Management Consulting: a Guide to the Profession*. 4th edition. Geneva: International Labour Office, pp. 799-822.

NBCC. 2004. Certified Professional Consultants to Management, National Bureau of Certified Consultants. http://www.national-bureau.com/ [cited 15 July 2004].

Rasiel, Ethan M. and Paul N. Frida. 2001. *The McKinsey Mind: Understanding and Implementing the Problem-Solving Tools and Management Techniques of the World's Top Strategic Consulting Firm*. New York: McGraw-Hill, XIII.

Savin, Jerald. 2000. A Matter of certification. *New York Times*, (Oct. 29): 3. p. 16.

Saywell, Trish. 1999. Taking advice: China's oldest state trading firm calls in consultants. *Far Eastern Economic Review*, 162 (14): p. 60.

Schlevogt, Kai-Alexander. 2000. The nascent Chinese consulting market: opportunities and obstacles (Part 1). *Consulting to Management*, 11:2 (September): pp. 28-34.

Schlevogt, Kai-Alexander. 2000. The nascent Chinese consulting market: opportunities and obstacles (Part 2). *Consulting to Management*, 11:3 (December): pp. 15-22.

Shays, E. Michael. 1985. Institute of Management Consultants, Inc. - a profile of the organization. *Journal of Management Consulting*, 2 (2): pp. 36-44.

Science and Technology Society of Jiangsu Province (江苏省科协). http://www.jsast.com/kx/ [cited 16 July 2004].

U.S. Census Bureau. 2003. Professional, scientific, and technical services – estimated revenue for employer and nonemployer firms: 1998-2001 (Table 1272). *Statistical Abstracts of the United States of America*. Washington, DC: Government Printing Office, p. 793.

Vieira, Walter E. 2004. Reflections. *Consulting to Management*, 15:1 (March): pp. 27-31.

Weiss, Alan. 2003. Avoiding the tribalization of consulting. *Consulting to Management*, 14:1 (March): pp. 13-15.

Wilson, Brian. 1995. Anderson Consulting provides expertise to Westerners: interview with B. Wilson. *Management Review*, 84 (August): p. 15.

Wonacott, Peter. 1997. Foreign firms spend heavily in race to train staff in China: teaching local managers leadership, team building, they aim to replace expensive expatriates. *Asian Wall Street Journal Weekly*, 19 (October 13): p. 2.

Xinhuanet. 1999. 中国经济. http://news.xinhuanet.com/ziliao/2003-01/25/content_707610.htm [cited 18 July 2004].

Chapter 15

The Case of Educating Chinese Travel Industry Executives for the Globalized Market

J. Mark S. Munoz
Millikin University

1. Introduction

Globalization has intensified business interactions worldwide accelerating capital flows, while increasing economic and political interdependencies (Greenberg and Baron, 1997:37). This landscape was shaped by (1) lower transportation and communication costs, (2) trade liberalization, and (3) export expansions and cross-border foreign direct investments. The trend has spearheaded economic growth and competitive activities.

Chinese scholar Cai Tuo (1998) defined globalization as an "objective historic process and tendency of contemporary human development beyond nation-state boundaries, unfolding as global communication, global networks, and global interactions." Dumlao (2003) reported that most Asians held positive attitudes towards globalization but there exists inherent concerns on its impact on national independence and culture.

Globalization has implications on business operations. Technological innovation and market integration increases the speed and volume of cross-border information and knowledge flows. These changes forces organizational adjustments and innovation. Corporate universities are in vogue, and brick and mortar and virtual learning approaches are being combined. In China, IBM and the Ministry of Education collaborated to use grid technology to facilitate education. (IBM, 2003).

In the travel industry, cross-border knowledge flows are critical. Gained efficiencies in technology, communication, and education is norm. Cross-cultural social interactions enhance personal development and network expansions constitute an international learner's experiences (Clyne & Rizvi, 1998; Pittaway, Ferguson, & Breen, 1998).

The convergence of education and technology is taking place in China. Xinhuanet (2001) reported that 30 Chinese travel agency managers attended a three-month course run from Australia over the Internet. Intel (2004) launched IntelTeach across China in 2000 and trained over 120,000 educators in information technology and innovative pedagogies. Ji (2004) noted that the 2003-2007 Action Plan for Invigorating Education aims to :) establish a system that is life-long with Chinese attributes, 2) create top rate and innovative workers, 3) promote integration of education, technological innovation, and economic construction

China's travel industry needs to respond to evolving opportunities and growth. In 1999, the country received 72.8 million foreign tourists leading to US$14.1 billion in revenue (China National Tourism Administration, 2004). Indicators of the large industry are: 10,481 tourist hotels, 8,993 travel companies, 5.6 million tourism employees, and US$ 4.2 billion in tourism investment.

Euromonitor (2004) characterizes China's travel industry as : 1) abundant in tourism resources and diversifying, 2) fast developing infrastructure, 3) possessing flexible tourism policies, 4) expanding with 97 million tourists in 2003, 5) internationalizing with standardizations in hospitality service, 6) growing transport sector, and 7) liberalizing, as foreign tourism entities enter the market.

China's tourism education resources are foundations for growth. Currently, there are 1,195 tourism colleges with 327,938 students. Locations like Beijing, Jiangsu, and Anhui have over 100 training centers offering higher education and secondary vocational tourism programs (China National Tourist Office, 2004).

The World Tourism Organization (2004) predicted that East-Asia and the Pacific will be among the top three tourist recipients by 2020 with an estimated 397 million visitors. Tourism expansion coupled with globalization dynamics pose challenges and opportunities for Chinese travel executives and require strategic approaches.

This article explores the views of international travel executives on issues relating to globalization, presents research on international education and cross border knowledge, and recommends strategies for educational enhancement in the Chinese travel industry.

2. Research Study on Globalization

This article is based on a multi-country survey that sought to determine the impact of globalization on contemporary business. The study gathered the views of senior level travel executives worldwide and explored concepts advanced by Thomas L. Friedman that: (1) there are changes in communication patterns due to globalization ; and that (2) technology transforms business modalities. Additionally, that there are psychological and educational implications arising from globalization.

The perceived business changes observed by travel executives worldwide has an impact on Chinese organizations, since it shapes the way information and knowledge is acquired and spread internationally.

Travel executives were selected in this study for reasons of linguistic congruency, or English proficiency. Additionally, international perspective, multi-cultural exposure, cross-industry involvement, and technological aptitude were considered.

2.1 Characteristics of the sample population

The travel executives surveyed were individuals engaged in ventures such as travel agencies, travel research and consulting, travel technologies, hotels and resorts, hospitality management, travel media, airlines and aviation, car rental, tour operators, tourism boards, convention and exhibition bureaus, travel distribution systems, travel and tourism education, travel media, destination management, and destination investment companies.

The executives were members of the Pacific Asia Travel Association (PATA). Based on sector involvement, 35% were in Travel Services, 34% in Tourism, 7% in Airlines, and 24% in Hospitality. The respondents were from 35 countries, including China.

Respondent composition was 73% male, and 27% female.

All of the respondents were college graduates. The profile of the respondents based on their level of education was as follows: 50% with

Bachelor's degree, 47% with Master's, and 3% with PhD's. The average industry experience of all the respondents was 20 years.

2.2 Research methodology and findings

Survey forms were sent out to 1,000 members of PATA, and 118 valid surveys completed.

The author collected data regarding the respondents' perceptions on the potential impact of globalization on business communication, technology frameworks, psychological implications, and international education deliveries.

Each of the statements in the survey corresponded to a five-point Likert-type scale. The respondents were advised to select answers from a scale provided. The quantitative and qualitative scales were 5 for Strongly Agree (SA), 4 for Agree (A), 3 for Undecided (U), 2 for Disagree (D), and 1 for Strongly Disagree (SD).

Since the purpose of the study was to determine the central tendency of the responses to each statement, the weighted mean for each statement was calculated. In order to arrive at a definite interpretation of the respondents' central tendency, the researcher assigned the following hypothetical mean range:

Range	Scale	
4.21-5.00	Strongly Agree	(SA)
3.41-4.20	Agree	(A)
2.61-3.40	Undecided	(U)
1.81-2.60	Disagree	(D)
1.00-1.80	Strongly Disagree	(SD)

The data were recorded on tables, showing the frequencies and percentages of responses in a survey factor. The weighted mean, along with the qualitative equivalent, were recorded, presented, analyzed and interpreted.

2.2.1 Industry perceptions on cross-border communication

The executives agreed that "our present world has resulted to changes in the way we communicate with others." Breakthroughs in communication technologies facilitate personal and business communication across borders. This scenario allows an endless stream of global communication described by Friedman (2000) as the "democratization of information."

The respondents agreed that "globalization has resulted in our ability to reach out to people in other countries in a faster, deeper, cheaper manner." Cross-country travel is no longer a hindrance to the spread of information and knowledge. The declining cost of international communication, technological conveniences, and market expansion have aggregately accelerated information and knowledge flows.

In China, individuals and organizations become increasingly exposed to international markets. Yu (2004) describes the Internet in China as the largest medium for the exchange of information, and facilitates the access of information from all parts of the world, across all fields of society, and all aspects of human life.

2.2.2 Industry perceptions on technology

The travel executives agreed that "companies that do not modernize or have top-notch technologies would likely fail." Their agreement is predicated on the idea that the pursuit of business growth is closely aligned with the efficient and timely use of technology.

The respondents agreed that "globalization requires companies to restructure to take advantage of new technologies." This finding implied that the respondents were aware of the need to adopt a new structure in conjunction with new technology or an internationalization effort.

The respondents agreed that "the greater a country's bandwidth, the greater the likelihood of its prosperity." Communication technology predicates a country's global preparedness. Digital infrastructure enhances E-commerce activities, cross-border informational flows, and international communication.

Agreement was signified by the respondents to the statement that "countries exporting IT and services would likely become more prosperous than those that export basic raw materials." With high expectations placed on IT, the respondents believed that its by-products and services offer a lucrative path to the future.

Based on a measurement of a country's preparedness for a digital economy, Bishop (1999) listed China in the lower tier countries possessing poor online infrastructure. However, since 1999, China's infrastructure and business environment has blossomed as indicated by the CIA World Factbook (2004): GDP of $6.449 trillion (2003 estimate), GDP growth rate of 9.1%, 214.42 million telephone lines, 206.62 million mobile phones, and 156,531 internet hosts.

Though challenges continue to exist in the country's socio-political landscape, the infrastructure and internal market is adequate for the travel and tourism sector to build successful and globally oriented enterprises.

2.2.3 *Industry perceptions on the psychological impact of globalization*

Strong agreement was shown by the travel executives to the statement that "globalization has set in at our world today, and most of what we do have international repercussions." This finding has three implications: 1) globalization affects an individual's perception of suitability to globalization, 2) globalization affects the way in which people utilize technology, and 3) individuals who tend to resist technological changes, will eventually realize that modifications in lifestyles and work processes are necessary.

The respondents agreed that "the globalized system has changed the way I perceive the world to be." The executives are aware that countries are not isolated and are growingly interconnected.

The respondents agreed that they "felt pressured and threatened as our world further globalizes." Globalization brings pressures to excel, compete with others, and meet demanding standards. Gudykunst and Hammer (1988) indicated that individuals exposed to cross-cultural environments and are unfamiliar with cultural codes may experience high level of stress in social encounters, and suffer from anxiety and self-doubt.

Indecision was shown by the executives pertaining to the statements that "there is a risk that those who are left behind in a globalizing world will create chaos and a backlash." Despite the anxiety and pressures for change, the executives were unsure that a potential backlash on globalization would take place.

Globalization in China affects individuals since convenient access of international information impacts its culture. Jinwen (1998) views globalization as a phenomenon resulting from political and cultural homogenization brought about by an integrated global economy. Yu (2004) points out that a global culture and global socialization exists in China and has shaped "global persons" surrounded by global cultural information.

The forces of globalization affect individuals in a physical, mental, and social level. In China, the emergence of universal value systems transcending national borders, social systems, and political ideologies have been observed (Junjiou, 1998). The path towards the assimilation of foreign value systems is not easy. Ling (1998) noted that globalization raises a number of problems relating to conflicts between traditional culture and modernization, conformity with the world economy versus the pursuit of national interests, as well as issues pertaining to legal pluralism and sovereignty.

These global issues confront individuals and organizations and require strategic responses. Chinese executives need to be proactive in order to adapt. Rongjiou (1998) noted the emergence of globally directed skills among individuals and a growing interest in international trade and management practices.

2.2.4 *Industry perceptions on international education*

The respondents strongly agreed that "the academe has a major role to play in educating and preparing the youth for globalization. They acknowledged the role of academic institutions in revolutionizing technology, imparting new and radical business concepts, and refining the students' skills and competencies to suit global demands.

The executives strongly agreed that "studying in another country would heighten an individual's chance of succeeding in a globalized world." The respondents affirmed the importance of experiential learning in foreign venues, especially in locations with technological and scientific advancement. Studying in another country provides the learner with opportunities to expand networks, and appreciate divergent cultures, business and political systems, and technologies.

The executives agreed that "online education is an effective methodology in providing educational access across borders." They affirmed that unbounded knowledge is gained through on-line education. Clark, Johnson *et al.* (1995) noted that academics have gained inroads in innovating and developing on-line support materials that augment student learning and enable students to work collaboratively.

However, the respondents were uncertain that "they would spend over $500 for a relevant short term course offered by an academic institution in another country via the Internet." Their uncertainty is attributable to concerns regarding technological incompatibility, divergence in instructional platforms, price values, and trust issues.

Ji (2004) noted educational reforms taking place in China. The developmental approaches highlight the role of the academe in preparing students for globalization. Yu (2004) observed that "the Chinese government has taken very active approaches to participate in the progress of globalization by implementing policies that open its economy to the world." According to China's Ministry of Education (2004) the total educational expenditure in 2002 reached RMB 548.003 billion (approximately US$66 billion).

Data from China's Ministry of Education (2004) indicate that: 1) there are 1.17 million educational institutions, 2) rapid growth of higher education enrollment with 3.82 million enrollees in 2003, an increase of 19%, 3) Significant growth of post-graduate enrollees numbering 269,000 in increase of 34%, 4) China sent 450,000 students to 103 countries in the past 20 years, and 5) IT and distance education is being implemented by government and academic institutions. As of 2002, there were 1,373,000 IT enrollees in 140 programs.

The educational system in China is not without challenges. The Economist (2003) characterized China's educational system as 1) one that has failed to produce enough innovative thinkers, 2) anchored on learning by rote, 3) heavy on fact-gathering but low on creativity, 4) generally disliked by students, and 5) presently undergoing reforms as the government and academic institutions endeavor to make education more pleasant, useful, challenging, and geared towards independent-thinking.

Meanwhile, new modes pertaining to the delivery of education are being applied. Bi (2004) observed the growing interest on the use of online technology such as Blackboard for course offerings in Chinese universities. Bi (2004) cited the value of these technologies for post-graduate degree-seekers, private corporations, and government offices. Recent statistics indicate that China has 31 universities providing on-line educational packages with approximately 50,000 students receiving distance education (People Daily, 2001). Educational websites have expanded as international players set up their own Internet platforms. (Liu, 2004)

The dynamics of China's learning environment is evolving and can lead to paradigm shifts in knowledge dissemination across academic institutions, government entities, and private corporations.

3. Chinese Organizations and the International Learning Environment

As China's educational landscape is transforming, academic institutions, government entities, and private corporations need to heighten the compatibility of existing systems with the global environment. This section sheds light on the characteristics of the Chinese learning environment and discusses its implications to international knowledge transfers.

In the process of globalization, Chinese firms face technological changes and new manpower demands. Newell (1999) noted the limited supply of experienced Chinese managers and the rapid growth in business and management education in China. Enrollment in post-graduate education, specifically the MBA programs have increased sharply.

There exist impediments towards learning. Chan (1999) observed the strong influence of cultural values and beliefs on Chinese thinking. These values, combined with years of rote and repetitive learning shaped educational attitudes towards learning. Chan (1999) indicated that Chinese learners : 1) lack abstract thinking, 2) are constrained by attitudes towards face, 3) rely heavily on concrete examples, 4) possess limited creativity, and 5) feel the need to compromise in group settings. The Economist (2003) attributed China's traditional educational methods to a political culture and era that required citizens to submit blindly to authority.

Negative attitudes towards learning curtail the speed of information and knowledge flows required in a global environment. Clarke (1999) point out that the conservative social values in China were promoted by the educational system and if not addressed becomes a deterrent to economic progress.

There is need for reform and quality enhancement. Hallinger (1998) reported the changing context of education in Southeast Asia and that global educational ideals, multiculturalism, and technological innovation in knowledge deliveries should be strengthened. Cheng and Wong (1996) noted though, that some educational features in East Asian schools coincide with effective characteristics in Western academic institutions – community support, teacher professionalism, attention to quality, and high expectation.

Assessments and comparative approaches are necessary. Dimmock and Walker (1998) emphasized the need for cross-cultural comparative analysis in educational administration and management across borders.

Chinese organizations should undertake readjustments to capture cross-border knowledge flows. Li (1999) observed the diversity of management styles among foreign companies, and pointed the need for the reconciliation of internal differences between value systems and management styles.

Cross-cultural sensitivity needs emphasis. Mangan (1997) highlighted the importance of cultural sensitivity in offshore learning experiences. Intensive offshore teaching can contribute to an organization's internationalization process (Watkins, 1993; Mangan, 1997).International actors should employ cross-cultural awareness skills and knowledge that allow service readjustments, satisfaction of international expectations, and effective communication across cultures. (Mallison, 1997:35). International learners and process-doers unfamiliar with divergent cultural codes experience high level of stress in social encounters, suffer from interpersonal anxiety and self-doubt, and may withdraw from the interaction process. (Gudykunst & Hammer, 1988; Zaharna, 1989, Fan & Mak, 1998).

Organizational learning adjustments are important. Gorman (1999) cited the need for awareness of an international learner's cultural disadvantages, such as adaptations pertaining to information gathering and presentation, dealing with status, gender and family roles, financial security issues, and diversity. Mendenhall, Punnett and Ricks (1995) cited the relevance of studying other cultures and considering interrelationships between labor, globalization, and ethics in the global environment., while Robey and Sales (1994:462) highlighted learning global ethical conduct.

Language needs to be considered in cross-border knowledge transfers. "It is impossible to consider any form of education - or even human existence - without first considering the impact of language on our lives" (Cole and Scribner, 1974). Ji (2004) indicated that China's education reform includes the promotion of Chinese language teaching, learning in other countries, and the exploration of international market for education services.

In an interview by the People Daily, Ma Qizhi, governor of the Ningxia Hui Autonomous Region pointed out that "High-quality human resources are a key factor for economic and social development in this period of accelerated global economic integration and rapid development of information technology,"

As Chinese organizations are exposed to countless opportunities and challenges relating to the cross-pollination of information, effective strategies need to be planned to tap into the huge reservoir of global knowledge.

4. Strategic Educational Approaches for China's Travel Executives in a Globalized Market

The results of globalization study show that the global business environment impacts communication abilities, organizational and process technologies, employee mindsets and attitudes, international education approaches, and cross-border knowledge flows.

J. M. S. Munoz

As far as travel executives in China are concerned, the global environment has redefined business dynamics and requires strategic adaptation. Technology and communication empowerment facilitates informational flows across countries. As the World Tourism Organization (2004) predicted future tourism expansion in East Asia, travel executives in China should plan for business enhancements to capture emerging opportunities.

In the quest for growth, organizations should transfer information strategically. Research suggest the importance of : 1) assessment of technological compatibilities, as well as the learner's psychological preparedness and learning predisposition with globalization, 2) strategic partnering and value-added arrangements with corporate or field-related institutions, 3) establishment of foreign institutional alliances that facilitate cross-cultural learning, 4) incorporation of online learning methodologies, and 5) sensitivity to the variations on the value and price of knowledge across borders.

When adapting to global changes, Cateora and Graham (1999:117) recommend ten (10) criteria that international organizations need to meet : (1) open tolerance, (2) flexibility, (3) humility, (4) justice/fairness, (5) ability to adjust to varying tempos, (6) curiosity/interest, (7) knowledge of the country, (8) liking for others, (9) ability to command respect, and (10) skills that fit the environment. It is useful for Chinese organizations to evaluate, plan, and strategize in accordance with these criteria.

With regard to informational flows, Chinese travel organizations should prepare for greater internationalization. Authors Mak et al. (Mak, Westwood, Ishiyama, & Barker, 1999) recommend overcoming barriers relating to ineffective coaching and limited feedback, feelings of inadequacy, interpersonal anxiety to other races, and threats to the international learner's original identity.

Additionally, Chinese travel organizations should use technology systematically. Rochester (1994) points out the case where 3M developed a European order entry system using the Nolan Norton formula. The introduced technology worked out well for the following reasons : (1) linked IT to the firm's global strategy; (2) initiated a global IT architecture process creating a dynamic system model; (3) recognized opportunities offered by global portfolios; (4) differentiated global and local infrastructure needs; and (5) developed a global IT resource allocation and deployment strategy. Buss (1982) recommends the consideration of infrastructure divergence.

With globalization's impact on knowledge flows in Chinese organizations, the selected readjustment approaches is critical. These adjustments can be in the form of enhanced infrastructure, improvement of systems and organizational frameworks, and careful planning of effective modalities that heighten the efficiency of information flows globally. Outlined are viable approaches.

Formulation of a Global Vision. Travel organizations in China should understand the dynamics of the global environment, and develop organizational visions within a global context. Hallinger (1999) highlighted the need to institute changes in education in Asia. The development of a vision provides a foundation for the pursuit of an integrated strategy and allows the identification of effective methodologies in knowledge acquisition and dissemination. Hallinger (1998) cited the critical role of system leaders in furthering educational changes in developing nations.

Organizational Assessment. There should be an assessment and understanding of organizational needs in conjunction with the training and educational requirements of the global environment. In addition, the globalization study indicated that individuals have innate fears of globalization. These fears should be understood, measured, and planned for. With the proper assessment of strengths and weaknesses, effective action may be implemented.

Develop Organizational Commitment. Employees in China's travel industry can be active global learners only if they are committed to the cause. It is important for top management to articulate organizational advantages clearly and draw a strong commitment from employees. Clarke (1999) articulated that conservative value systems impede change and progress.

Introduce Creative Learning Methodologies. Chan (1999) noted that Chinese learning behavior has developed through rote and repetitive learning. Employees in the travel industry are products of this educational culture. In organizational learning, The Economist (2003) identified the need to stimulate creativity and steer away from the mere accumulation of facts. Livelier and creative learning approaches can stimulate learning in the workplace. The use of online methodologies and communication technologies helps accelerate the pace and broadens the scope of cross-border information transfers.

Address Needs Pertaining to Multiculturalism. Li (1999) observed a variety of managerial styles in use in China. Employees in these organizations have limited exposure to foreign value systems. Training and educational support in this arena stimulates cross-cultural appreciation and successful international interactions.

Enhance Language Skills. Language skills impede effective cross-border communication. Development of language skills in employees facilitates the absorption of international information, allows the sharing of knowledge, and enhances the firm's ability for network expansion and relationship building.

Encourage Employees to Pursue Post-Graduate Education. The globalization study highlighted the role of the academe in preparing individuals for globalization Newell (1999) cited managerial supply challenges and interest in MBA education. Chinese travel organizations can gain competitive advantages by encouraging and supporting employees who wish to pursue further studies.

Introduce Learning Approaches Within a Group Environment. Chan (1999) noted the importance of groups in the Chinese learning environment. Modes of learning can be initiated by a group and implemented within a team setting.

Motivate and Reward Independent and Innovative Employee Behavior. Chan (1999) observed the lack of abstract and independent thinking among Chinese learners. In Chinese travel organizations this learning impediment may be addressed through positive reinforcement such as cash prizes and awards for innovative projects.

Provide Attention to Training Quality and Performance. Cheng (1996) observed that Chinese schools give emphasis to quality and have high expectations of learners. This educational approach can be used by travel organizations. Cheng (1996) recommends the consideration of effort-ability as well as the holistic-analytic tendencies of learners.

Engage in International Benchmarking As Chinese travel companies globalize, national standards and norms should not only be met, but exceeded. Benchmarking should be made with global leaders. Euromonitor (2004) noted efforts towards internationalizing standards in China's hospitality industry. Dimmock and Walker (1998) cited the need for comparative emphasis of educational administration and management internationally.

Capitalize on Competitive Advantages. The Chinese travel industry is connected to a global network. In order to be competitive, a clear understanding of competitive strengths is critical. The firm should capitalize on its identified strengths whether it is technology, communication, information process flow, or a highly skilled and globalization-ready workforce.

Weave Through the Challenges. Rarely is an organization completely endowed with all favorable factors for global success. Bishop (1999) cited inadequacies in China's preparedness for the digital age. Travel organizations in China must learn to deal with endemic challenges relating to organizational capacity, skills and competencies, divergence in technological infrastructure, economic disparities, and institutional bureaucracies. Proactive action is needed despite domestic constraints.

Engage in Synergistic Organizational Alliances. The globalization study indicated the ease of communication flows across borders. Opportunities towards development of strategic partnering are enhanced. Chinese travel organizations can form linkages with academic and government institutions to further its educational agenda.

Take Small Yet Immediate Global Approaches. The globalization study suggested that changes are taking place in the contemporary business landscape. Chinese travel organizations need to take small but immediate measures towards technological upgrades, international participation, and effective knowledge management.

Pursue Development in a Strategic Manner. Chinese travel organizations should utilize strategic global approaches. Adopted strategies should simultaneously address domestic and international issues. A small and remote hotel may be constrained by inadequate technological infrastructure, manpower skills, and institutional support. The hotel's strategic plan may include: 1) heightening employee knowledge of international hotel practices over the Internet, 2) participating in online hospitality and language training programs, 3) launching a website to draw global patronage, 4) affiliating with international organizations, and 5) joining international marketing campaigns.

Technological advancement accelerates information flows in and out of China. A dynamic web service anywhere in the world makes information about a travel product or service accessible to all stakeholders. Pollock and Benjamin (2001) identify the benefits of web services as: (1) enabling full interoperability between platforms; (2) accessibility; (3) global support; and (4) enabling automation. Starkov and Price (2001) advocate the adoption of more aggressive eBusiness strategies that lower operating cost and enhance marketing efficiencies. Technology is the means for China's travel organizations to increase organizational performance and enhance international informational flows.

As in China, global knowledge transfer and international education has expanded elsewhere in the world. Companies worldwide are building competitive advantages by accelerating knowledge flows and raising the bar for productivity and profitability. Organizations are using innovation to tap into the global information bandwagon.

The access to cross-border information, cutting-edge technologies, and unique educational approaches is growingly convenient for travel organizations in China. Travel executives in many parts of the world have succeeded in responding to globalization by building efficiencies in business management, strategy formulation, technology, communication, and international knowledge flows.

References

Bi, X. (2004). E-learning vs. course management system. Center for Innovations in Technology for Learning (CITL) Ohio University news feature at the China Education and Research Network. (accessed August 2004), [available at http://www.edu.cn/20040519/3105937.shtml]

Bishop, B. (1999). *Global Marketing for the Digital Age*. NTC : Illinois.

Buss, M. (1982). Managing international information systems. *Harvard Business Review*, 60 (5), 153-162.

Chan, Sally (1999). "The Chinese learner – a question of style." *Education + Training.* Asia Pacific Management Forum, 41 (6/7), 294-305.

Cheng, K. & Wong, K. (1996). "School effectiveness in East Asia : Concepts, Origins, and Implications." *Journal of Educational Administration* ; 34 (5), 32-49.

China National Tourism Administration. (2004). China tourism introduction." (accessed August 2004), [available at http://www.cnta.com/lyen/index.asp]

China National Tourist Office. (2004). Statistics on China's tourism, 2000. (accessed August 2004), [available at http://www.tourismchina-ca.com/statistics015.htm]

CIA – The World Fact Book. (2004). China, (accessed August 2004), [available at http://www.cia.gov/cia/publications/factbook/geos/ch.html]

Clark, E. E. & Johnson, S. (1995). The role of information technology in university teaching, *Journal of Law and Information Science*, 6 (2), 131-163.

Clarke, T. (1999). "Economic growth, institutional development and personal freedom : the educational needs of China." *Education + Training*, Asia Pacific Management Forum ; 41 (6/7), 336-343.

Clyne, F., & Rizvi, F. (1998). Outcome of student exchange. In D. Davis & A. Olsen Eds.), *Outcomes of international education* (pp. 35-49). IDP Education : Sydney, Australia.

Cole, M., and Scribner, S. (1974). *Culture and Thought.* John Wiley : New York.

Dimmock, C. & Walker, A. (1998). Towards comparative educational administration : building the case for a cross-cultural school-based approach.. *Journal of Educational Administration*, 36 (4), 379-401.

Dumlao, D.C. (2003, December 28). Filipinos favor opening up of RP to global competition. *Inquirer News Service.*

Economist. (2003, January 23), Roll over, Confucius. Economist Online Edition (accessed August 2004), [available at http://www.economist.com/world/asia/displayStory.cfm?story_id=1548706]

Euromonitor International. (2004). Travel and tourism in China. (accessed August 2004), [available at : http://www.the-infoshop.com/study/eo18170_travel_tourism_china.html]

Fan, C., & Mak, A. (1998). Measuring social self-efficacy in a culturally diverse student population. *Social Behavior and Personality*, 26, 131-144

Friedman, T. L. (2000) *The Lexus and the Olive Tree*, Anchor Books: New York.

Gorman, D. (1999, December). Cultural disadvantage of nursing students. *International Education –ej* (On-line Serial), 3(4). (accessed August 2004), [available at http://www.canberra.edu.au/education/crie/1998-1999/ieej12/ie12-Don.html]

Greenberg, J. and Baron, R.A. (1997) *Behavior in Organizations: Understanding and Managing the Human Side of Work,* Prentice-Hall International: Upper Saddle River, New Jersey.

Gudykunst, W. B., & Hammer, M. R. G. (1988). Strangers and hosts: An uncertainty reduction based theory of intercultural adaptation. In Y. Y. Kim, & W. B.

316   J. M. S. Munoz

Gudykunst (Eds.), *Cross-cultural adaptation: Current approaches* (pp. 105-139). Sage : Newbury Park: CA.

Hallinger, P. (1998). "Educational change in Southeast Asia : The challenge of creating learning systems" *Journal of Educational Administration*, 36 (5), 492-509.

IBM. (2003). IBM and China's ministry of education launch 'China grid' (accessed August 2004), [available at : http://www-1.ibm.com/grid/grid_press/pr_1013.shtml]

Intel. (2004). Global tour of Intel in education : China at Teachfuture.com (accessed August 2004), [available at http://www.intel.com/education/projects/global_tour/H_05_china/]

Ji, Z. (2004). The implementation of the 2003-2007 action plan for invigorating education. China Education and Research Network, (accessed August 2004), [available at http://www.edu.cn/20040324/3102182.shtml]

Jinwen, Z. (1998). Some issues on globalization in Hu Yuanzhi ed. *Globalization and China*, Beijing : Central Compilation and Translation Press, p. 102-119.

Junjiou, T. (1998). Thinking and arguing on globalization," in Yu Keping, ed. *Globalization and Antimonies*, Beijing : Central Compilation and Translation Press, p. 127-132

Li, S.K. (1999). Management development in international companies in China. *Education + Training* ; 41 (6/7) , 331-336.

Ling, L. (1998). Chinese legal development under the background of globalization," *Studies and Inquiries* (1), 93-94.

Liu, J. (2004). Advanced distance learning. China Education Daily, (accessed August 2004), [available at : http://www.edu.cn/20010830/200786.shtml]

Mak, A. S., Westwood, M. J., Ishiyama, F. I., & Barker, M. C. (1999). Optimising conditions for learning sociocultural competencies for success. *International Journal of Intercultural Relations*, 23, 77-90.

Mallison, H. (1997), 'Sensitivity to Japanese cultural baggage: a key attribute for front office staff,' *Australian Journal of Hospitality Management,* Spring, 35-38.

Mangan, K. S. (1997). Business schools promote international focus, but critics see more hype than substance, *The Chronicle of Higher Education*, September 12, 1997, A14.

Mendenhall, M., Punnet, B. & Ricks, D. (1995). *Global Management*. Blackwell : Cambridge, Mass.

Ministry of Education. (2004). Survey of the educational reform and development in China." (accessed August 2004), [available at http://www.edu.cn/20040107/3096934.shtml]

Newell, S. (1999). The transfer of management knowledge to China : building learning communities rather than translating Western textbooks. *Education + Training*, Asia Pacific Management Forum ; 41 (6/7), 286-294.

People Daily. (2001). First ever distance education platform sold in China. China Education and Research Network. (accessed August 2004), [available at : http://www.edu.cn/20011015/3004975.shtml]

Pittaway, E., Ferguson, B., & Breen, C. (1998). Worth more than gold: the unexpected benefits associated with internationalisation of tertiary education. In D. Davis & A. Olsen (Eds.), *Outcomes of international education* (pp. 61-71). IDP Education : Sydney, Australia.

Pollock, A. and Benjamin, L. Shifting sands : the tourism ecosystem in transformation" a white paper at the DESTICORP website, (accessed August 2004), [available at http://www.desticorp.com/whitepapers/TourismEcosystemwhitepaperWTM.pdf.

Qizhi, M. (2001, November).West autonomous region offers distance learning. As quoted in an interview in the People Daily, (accessed August 2004), [available at http://www.edu.cn/20011102/3007988.shtml]

Robey, D. & Sales, C.A. (1994). *Designing Organizations*. The McGraw-Hill Companies : Boston.

Rochester, J.B. (1991). Building a global IT infrastructure. *I/S Analyzer*, 29 (6), 1-14.

Rongjiou, X. (1998). The impact and challenge of economic globalization, *World Economy* (4), 46.

Starkov, M. and Price, J (2001).eBusiness levels the playing field. (accessed August 2004), [available at : http://www.eyefortravel.com/papers/hotel2.doc]

Study Abroad. (2004). Graduate program search. (accessed August 2004), [available at http://www.studyabroad.com/gscobrand/outside.html]

Tuo, C. (1998). Globalization and contemporary international relation. *Marxism and Reality*, (3), 20.

Watkins, B. T. (1993). Internationalizing graduate education, *Chronicle of Higher Education*, November 17, A48.

World Tourism Organization. (2004). Long-term prospects : tourism 2020 vision. (accessed August 2004), [available at : http://www.world-tourism.org/market_research/facts/menu.html]

Xinhuanet. (2001, September). "Australia trains Chinese tourism specialists via internet", China Education and Research Network, (accessed August 2004), [available at : http://www.edu.cn/20010907/3000670.shtml]

Yu, K. (2004). "From the discourse of "Sino-West" to "Globalization" : Chinese perspectives on globalization a paper prepared for the China Center for Comparative Politics, March 2004. (accessed August 2004), [available at http://globalization.about.com/gi/dynamic/offsite.htm?zi=1/XJ&sdn=globalizat ion&zu=http%3A%2F%2Fwww.humanities.mcmaster.ca%2F%7Eglobal%2Fw ps%2FKeping.pdf]

Zaharna, R. S. (1989). Self-shock: the double-binding challenge of identity. *International Journal of Intercultural Relations*, 13, 501-525.

Chapter 16

A Cross-Cultural, Cross-Discipline Business Education Program in Mainland China: Training a Managerial Workforce for China's Economic Transition

Howard Kleinmann
Queens College, City University of New York

Le Lu
University of Shanghai for Science and Technology

1. Introduction

The paramount task of business education in China today is to produce a trained managerial workforce for the large number of foreign companies operating on the mainland and Chinese firms seeking to expand their markets worldwide. What is required of the workforce is cultural flexibility, communicative competence in both general and business English, and familiarity with business standards and practices. To achieve this purpose, the local educational system must deal with a spectrum of difficulties, including textbook availability, business education concepts and Chinese tradition. This paper describes how an experimental business educational program, co-sponsored by two universities, one Chinese and one American, addresses these difficulties. The paper further discusses how an integration of business knowledge, language and culture within the curriculum distinguishes the program but also creates other pedagogical and program administration problems.

2. Business Education in China - Challenges

An increasing number of foreign enterprises have flocked to China as a result of the opening of its markets. These enterprises require qualified employees to be hired from the local population. At the same time, more and more Chinese enterprises are internationalizing their operations, formulating strategic development plans to expand overseas. While this has created a variety of opportunities in a burgeoning job market, it has placed new demands on China's higher education system, particularly in the area of business education.

Because China only began its transformation to a market economy in the 1990's, modern business education there is still very much in its infancy. It has not been able to keep pace with the demands of a growing market in an arena of global competition. Although it has enormous potential, as evidenced by the growing number of business schools and students, this quantitative growth has rarely been accompanied by a corresponding qualitative growth. Indeed, business education in China today is facing problems to which there are no immediate solutions.

One of the obstacles to educational reform is China's educational tradition. Residual educational concepts rooted in the Chinese cultural tradition and planned economy still make themselves felt in today's educational system in China, at times interfering with the critical goals of developing productive workers, successful entrepreneurs, and informed consumers (Madison Metropolitan School District Career/ Technical Education Department: Business Education Description, 2001). Education in China has traditionally been embedded in Confucian culture. In this tradition, the purpose of education is moral, stressing the betterment of society through improved citizenship (Porter, 1990). Under the traditional planned economy, students were supported financially by the government and were assigned a job after graduation. Because they were 'cadres of the country', they were expected to implement the policies of the government. Both the educator and the educated understood and agreed that the former provided what he thought was beneficial to the latter. What the learner thought he needed to learn did not matter (Alon and Lu, 2004). Since the market was totally controlled by the government, the objectives of the government-oriented education were moral and normative.

Although business educators may welcome the concept of market orientation in higher education, for many reasons it is difficult for them to actualize it. First, until a new model is successfully formulated, it is impossible to abandon the old system. Because transitional steps are difficult to implement, the approach is basically to continue within the old framework. Second, the personnel charged with the delivery of business education services are often undertrained. It is not unusual, for example, for professors from a different discipline, such as engineering or linguistics, to become professors of business education merely by taking a few business-related courses. Furthermore, it is common for recent MA graduates, who are inexperienced and underqualified, to teach business courses immediately after graduation. The shortage of qualified business educators is essentially a result of an imbalance in supply and demand: There simply are not enough qualified business educators. Third, the teaching methodology used in the classroom is often unsatisfactory. Teachers without substantial classroom or business experience often merely repeat information from textbooks to students. There is little meaningful interaction between professors and students about concepts. Instruction is mechanical, with little opportunity for discussion, debate, and consideration of other ideas. Underqualified faculty using outmoded teaching techniques are a poor mix for effective pedagogy. With the student body growing faster than the faculty, this situation is unlikely to change significantly in the near future.

Business education in China has many other problems, aside from teacher qualifications and teaching methods. For example, there is a serious shortage of textbooks. In recent years, some universities with MBA programs have begun to purchase some textbooks used in Western countries, but this practice is by no means widespread. The high cost precludes most programs from doing this. Indeed, in many programs, a box of chalk and one copy of a textbook might be all the resources a business teacher has at his disposal. Moreover, because students are accustomed to learning characterized by rote memorization, they do not do well on tests that require critical thinking and analysis. Essential components of state-of-the-art business education programs, such as case studies, group projects, simulations, and internships are only beginning find their way into the pedagogy in China. As a result, what is taught often has little practical significance in real business settings.

Unquestionably, the most pressing need is the training of a workforce equipped with knowledge and skills that conform to internationally acknowledged standards. With more and more Chinese businesses wishing to expand globally, the demand for employees who have the skills to conduct business in an international context is increasing rapidly. At present, the demand greatly exceeds the supply of qualified business professionals.

Furthermore, the job market in China is growing increasingly competitive. Whether applying for job vacancies in state-owned enterprises or foreign ventures, applicants have to go through numerous job interviews before they are hired. While foreign ventures are more appealing than state enterprises, due to the higher salaries and training opportunities, it is more difficult to secure a job there. It is estimated that in state owned enterprises, 80% of job applicants can secure a position, while only 10% of job applicants will be fortunate enough to be hired by a foreign venture (China Job Hunting Website, 2003). The disparity is attributable mainly to the applicants' English language proficiency. Foreign-funded ventures want employees who are proficient in English, especially spoken English. Even state-owned businesses are increasingly demanding English-proficient applicants due to their internationalization. Applicants who are not competent in English are at a distinct disadvantage even if they have other specialized business knowledge (Guangzhou Daily, 2002).

In addition, foreign and Chinese partners in joint ventures are frequently faced with cultural conflicts that can result in misunderstandings. This is predictable whenever two cultures come into contact. It is exacerbated by the fact that the Chinese are often dependent on the foreigner's capital investment. This dependence can remove the feeling of equality in the cultural interaction. Because of the power imbalance inherent in the business relationship, feelings of resentment can surface when cultures clash. Differences are more difficult to resolve in such a context, especially when one group is reluctant to air issues and when the other does not see the need to. If there is a lack of communication between the parties, this problem may be unsolvable (World Business Review, 2004). That is why foreign employers prefer to employ workers with bicultural competence. It increases the likelihood of adaptability and reduces the likelihood of cultural clash.

In sum, because of the rapid transformation of the economic system in China, the business education system is faced with the daunting task of responding to and keeping pace with this change. Especially critical is the pressure that is brought to bear on workforce needs, where increasingly sophisticated qualifications, specialized knowledge of business products, a wide array of business skills, foreign language proficiency and cultural adaptability are required. The government and educators are concerned over China's heretofore unsuccessful struggle to meet this demand. The following program, which integrates business, cultural, and pedagogical components, may be a model for addressing this problem, at least in the sort term, until China has developed the educational infrastructure for addressing the problem without outside assistance.

3. A Model Joint Program

In 1996 the University of Shanghai for Science and Technology (USST) and Queens College (QC) of the City University of New York (CUNY) entered into an agreement to co-sponsor an undergraduate program in international trade, finance, and investment. The program, located on the campus of USST and housed in the College of Foreign Languages, was designed to serve undergraduate Chinese students majoring in English who wished to specialize in English for Finance and English for International Trade.

The relationship that USST sought with QC was not accidental. In the mid-1980's, QC had been involved in English language teacher training programs at several colleges in China under the now defunct Ministry of Machine Building. One of the colleges was USST, which at the time was known as the Shanghai Institute of Mechanical Engineering. The relationship between the institutions was cultivated over a ten-year period through joint programs, exchanges, and ongoing communication between administrators. As a result, when USST was interested in partnering with an American university in a business education program, it approached QC because of the strong ties that had been established in English teacher education. From the Chinese standpoint, a trusting relationship had been developed with QC in a number of programmatic areas over a substantial period of time, and it was logical to try to deepen the relationship by extending the partnership to another area rather than approach a new institution. This approach reveals much about the high value that the Chinese place on the cultivation of relationships (Wang et al., 2000), which are seen as long-term rather than short-term objectives, and should be instructive to other institutions seeking to establish collaborative programs with Chinese institutions.

Just as the USST business education partnership with QC was not accidental, organizing the program within the College of Foreign Languages at USST was purposeful from an administrative and programmatic standpoint. The College of Foreign Languages specializes in English and German for Specific Purposes instruction, particularly science and technology. English and German language majors are exposed to a rich curriculum in language, literature, and linguistics. In the past, when most students were to be assigned jobs at state-run technology enterprises after graduating, the curriculum included a small amount of vocational preparation. But the emphasis was predominantly on language. This turned out to be essential in establishing a foundation for the joint program. Because of the highly developed English language skills that students brought to it, the program could effectively use American college professors to teach state-of-the-art business courses in English. The students' ability to comprehend and use academic English satisfactorily was a given. As a result, QC professors could concentrate on teaching content, knowing that students were proficient enough in English to follow lectures, participate in class, and do assignments.

4. Program Features

The program's integration of language, culture, and discipline-specific business content is accomplished through the curriculum, which is composed of a statement of goals, objectives, and learner needs, with instructional material designed to meet them. In the joint USST-QC program the primary goal is to produce a trained workforce for the business community in China that can function skillfully in a multicultural business environment. A main objective is the development of English language ability for a specialized purpose, namely, business. This objective is not limited to developing knowledge of a particular part of the English language. As in all English for Specific Purposes (ESP) instruction, it also addresses the skills required to use the language in particular contexts (Orr, 2002). Other objectives include ESP listening comprehension, speaking, reading, writing, translating and interpreting skills, cultural competence, and specialized business knowledge. This constellation of skills is designed to enable the student to function in a multilingual and multicultural business environment. In short, it aims to develop communicative competence in business settings (Boyd, 2002).

Apart from its market orientation, the program is cross-disciplinary and cross-culturally oriented. The program's two tracks, international trade and international finance and investment, determine its cross-disciplinary feature. Thus, it is a business-oriented language program, incorporating business education with language training. The language emphasis enables the learner to acquire language and cultural competence to adapt to a foreign language environment while the emphasis on business content develops in the learner the skills necessary to function in an international business setting.

The curriculum takes into consideration the working environment the students are likely to find themselves in after they graduate by emphasizing cultural competence, as well as language competence and business knowledge. St. John (1996) and Boyd (2002) have distinguished between business English for learners who are already in the workplace and those who are preparing to enter it. The students in the USST-QC program fall into the latter category; they recognize the relevance of ESP to their careers although they do not yet know the exact relationship.

The program is defined as cross-culturally oriented in three ways. First, the program prepares the students to work in the English-speaking culture embedded in the wider Chinese culture. Second, some subjects taught in the program relate to content specific to Chinese culture and some to English-speaking culture. Third, the program is itself in a bicultural environment in the sense that the students receive classroom education from both American professors and Chinese professors; some of the courses are taught in English and some in Chinese.

It is important to keep in mind that the goal of the language-culture integration in the curriculum is not cultural assimilation. Rather, it is to develop bicultural individuals who have a sensitivity to and appreciation of cultural diversity (Lu and Hua, 2003) and who can navigate both cultures comfortably. To this end, the curriculum contains two categories of culture-related courses. The first involves courses about cultures per se, both target and home culture. Courses in this category include such offerings as A Survey of Han Culture, Introduction to Western Cultures and Intercultural Communication. The second category includes courses containing peripheral cultural information, such as Modern Chinese, A General Survey of America and Great Britain, American and British Literature, and Appreciation of Movies of the West. Both types of offerings are important in developing bicultural competence in the students.

The curriculum of the program is divided into three main modules: compulsory courses, optional courses, and a practicum. Compulsory courses are further divided into three sub-modules: courses for general education, courses for language majors, and specialty courses, which mainly include specialized business courses. The curriculum includes two types of business courses: business-oriented language learning courses and specialized business courses. Business oriented language courses are taught by Chinese faculty members. These courses include Correspondence in Foreign Trade, Business English Reading, and Translation in Economics and Trade. They are usually embedded in writing, reading and translation training. This language-business integration prepares the students in vocabulary and business discourse necessary for the specialized business courses.

Ten specialized business courses are taught by QC professors. QC is part of the seventeen community and senior colleges comprising the City University of New York, and professors are recruited from these institutions to teach in the program. The ten courses that they teach comprise 22% of the compulsory courses and 14% of all the courses in terms of credits. The courses include three core courses, Micro/macro-economics, Management, and Business Statistics, and seven elective courses based on the core: Entrepreneurship, Marketing, Financial Markets and Institutions, Negotiation, International Business,

Investments, and Corporate Finance. Students begin to take these courses at the end of their third semester when they have satisfied the prerequisite language training. The materials used in the specialized business courses are either recommended or compiled by the American professors, and every link in the pedagogical chain, from syllabus to teaching methodology to testing, is under the purview of the invited professors.

By program design, QC professors are typically sent to USST in pairs to teach two courses each. Aside from the advantage of covering four courses in the curriculum in one "semester," this arrangement also has the advantage of creating a mini-community of QC staff, who can interact with each other socially and professionally. This is important because the QC professors are not proficient in Chinese and, as other foreign teachers in China have experienced, cannot really penetrate the foreign culture (Porter, 1990). Notwithstanding the hospitality extended by the Chinese hosts, feelings of loneliness and isolation can set in. Pairing the QC professorial staff allows them to navigate the foreign culture together and communicate about their experiences, both within and outside the program, freely.

A key feature of the program allowing QC to recruit highly qualified professors successfully is the scheduling of the specialized business courses. QC professors typically have teaching commitments at their home institution in the Fall and Spring semesters, which run approximately September 1 through December 20, and February 1 through May 20 respectively. While it might be possible occasionally to find qualified professors who are on sabbatical or are retired to go to China during these periods, it would not have been possible to sustain an ongoing flow of faculty to teach at USST over the seven years that the program has been running. Faculty members receive their full-time salaries based on their teaching assignments at CUNY during the Fall and Spring semesters. They are not given release time for teaching at USST. To solve this problem a creative approach to scheduling was devised which entailed scheduling QC professors to teach in the period between the end of the Fall semester and the beginning of the Spring semester (approximately December 21 through January 25) and in the Summer (approximately June 1 through July 15). This arrangement allowed the professors to participate in the program and fulfill their teaching commitments at CUNY.

5. Benefits and Problems

Partnering with an American university has definite pedagogical advantages. American professors bring with them different approaches, methods, and techniques, which are reflected in the ways they organize classroom activities. In contrast to the traditional educational model still used in China today that emphasizes theory over practice, memorization of facts, verbatim repetition, and teacher-centered classroom activity, the USST-QC program exposes the students to a totally different pedagogical style, where teacher-student interaction, case study, critical thinking, group discussion and team presentation are emphasized. Classroom activities are managed to encourage active student participation and creativity. Student evaluations have confirmed that over time, students see the advantages of this approach, not only preferring the methodology to what they had been accustomed to in their educational careers, but recognizing the opportunities that it offers for deepening their understanding of the subject matter. Furthermore, the advantages are not limited to technique because by being exposed to expertise in and materials on economic theories, management concepts, and operational processes in the West, the students are able to obtain familiarity with business standards and practices in international settings rather than processes that are limited to Chinese markets.

Moreover, the mixed faculties, Chinese and American, constitute a bicultural environment in which the students develop their cultural sensitivity and flexibility. Graduates of the program have commented on their ability to communicate and function with ease and confidence in English in international business settings as one of the most valuable outcomes of their experience.

The success of the program has led to its growing popularity, as evidenced by the increasing number of applicants every year. Moreover, the program has attracted students with national entrance examination scores well above the average for colleges of the university. Most telling perhaps is that a majority of the graduates from the program are admitted to universities all over the world to pursue graduate studies or find jobs in foreign companies and large state financial institutions.

While the USST-QC program has been successful in many ways, it has not been without problems. Program features that have positive characteristics sometimes have a downside as well. Scheduling is a perfect example of this. The program offers courses taught by QC professors in the winter intersession between the Fall and Spring semesters and in the Summer because these are the times that the faculty members are available to teach in China. However, because the semesters of Chinese universities do not coincide with the American system, schedule adjustments need to be made. In addition, because of the limited stay of the QC professors, teaching hours have to be packed into the schedule, which is crowded with other courses the students have to take. Students would prefer the instruction of the specialized business courses to be spread out over an entire semester for both convenience and learning reasons. The short four to six week period of instruction makes it difficult to digest and internalize the material being taught.

There are also issues related to faculty structure. As the program is built within an academic unit that is primarily composed of language teachers (the College of Foreign Languages), there is not a permanent staff of business teachers who can mentor the students or deal with pedagogical issues related to business courses. Most of the students, when choosing a topic for a graduation thesis, prefer to write on business or business-culture issues over purely language or language-culture themes. Although the program has a consulting body consisting of Chinese business teachers, they are not the faculty of the college and thus their direct contribution to the students and the program is limited. In addition, their language proficiency is not adequate to supervise theses written in English.

Integrating the various curricular modules is not free of problems either. The program integrates language, culture and business modules in one curriculum, which requires a well-balanced distribution of credit hours. The students are required to take two national tests at the end of the second year and at the end of fourth year as a measurement of their language proficiency as language majors. Failure to pass these exams means not graduating and obtaining the degree. Therefore, it is essential that the program offer a sufficient number of language courses and learning hours to ensure the development of advanced language-culture competence. On the other hand, the attractiveness of the program lies largely in its business orientation. When the ten business courses comprising a total of 30 credits and 400 hours are added to the curriculum, the total credit hours exceed the required limitation. In the general education module, six politics-related courses totaling approximately 258 credits hours are required, which leaves little room for balancing the language, culture and business modules. Some of the culture courses and language courses have to be moved to elective parts of the curriculum or canceled entirely.

Instructional materials are an ongoing difficulty. A main purpose of the joint USST-QC program is to make use of Western educational resources, including textbooks. However, two factors restrict the use of published textbooks. One is the high cost of the textbooks published and purchased in the United States. The students are unable to bear the heavy expense, and unauthorized copying of published material violates intellectual property laws. In those relatively few instances where textbooks are available at an affordable cost to Chinese students, they are not the newest editions, and they are often too advanced for undergraduate students. For the majority of business courses that do not have textbooks, the students have to rely exclusively on the professors' lectures. For Chinese students, who are accustomed to textbook learning, this requires a difficult and uncomfortable adjustment in learning style.

As in any joint program, administrative issues arise and require attention. This is all the more true when the two cooperating institutions are separated by distance, language, culture, and administrative style and practice. Much depends on the communication skills and good will of the chief administrators. To illustrate, in the USST-QC agreement one item stipulates that two students from each graduating cohort will be granted a one-year tuition scholarship to study for an M.A. at QC. Unfortunately, because scholarship recipients to date have not been successful in obtaining a visa from the U.S. Consulate in Shanghai, despite vigorous efforts by QC to support their applications, no one has been able to take advantage of this award. From the QC view, it is has done everything it can by offering the scholarship and supporting the visa applications; from the USST standpoint, the scholarship, in effect, does not exist if students cannot obtain a visa. Both sides are correct, and the program could be jeopardized if the problem went unaddressed. As a compromise, the parties agreed that in the event a scholarship recipient is not be able to obtain a visa, QC will offer a nominal cash award in lieu of the scholarship. This is an example of open communication, compromise and good will overcoming a problem that could undermine a program if left unaddressed.

Finally, notwithstanding its many advantages, the USST-QC program can only have limited impact. It cannot alter the fact that there are an insufficient number of higher educational institutions in China to accommodate the number of students who seek admission. In China, there are approximately 1,000 higher education institutions with a total of 7,120,000 registered students. In comparison, the U.S. has 4,000 higher education institutions with a total of 14,500,000 registered students (China Education News, 2002). In addition, against the background of globalization, world economies must be interdependent and mutually penetrating. A global vision and international orientation are required. However, China's higher education is in many ways still influenced more by notions of the planned economy than by the modern international educational standards of the free market system. There is still a huge gap between what China's higher education system can presently do for the market and what the market requires of it. Joint international educational programs like the QC-USST partnership can only help narrow this gap in small increments.

The connection between China's admission to the WTO and education internationalization has been discussed and researched by both the government and academia (China Education and Research Network, 2001; China Education and Research Network, 2002). The topic is no longer just a matter of theoretical discourse but one of practical application. At present, there are already a few foreign educational institutions with branches in China. There are also some foreign degree-granting programs, and there are some joint programs that send students to the foreign partner's institutions for one or two years, with students receiving degrees from both institutions. Finally, there are joint programs like the USST-QC initiative, where professors are sent by partner foreign institutions to teach various specialized courses at Chinese universities. The State Education Committee is now evaluating all these joint programs in China in an attempt to regulate their management. This is clearly an indication that the Chinese government is advocating international educational cooperation and will use the existing programs as the springboard for continued and even more developed international cooperation.

6. Conclusion

China's unprecedented rate of economic growth since opening up its system to the world economy requires the higher education system to provide qualified workers not only for domestic enterprises and organizations but also for foreign ventures. The traditional education system is challenged and disadvantaged by the new demand of the market for a workforce that requires international competitiveness. In the face of a shortage of educational resources, Chinese higher education has turned to the corresponding sector in the economically advanced West, looking for resources that may assist the system in its transition from a domestic focus to an international one, from central planning to market orientation. Business education takes the primary place in the efforts of the higher education system to solicit international assistance because of the urgent market need and a serious lack of business education resources.

In this transition, a variety of international cooperative projects in China's higher education sector have come into existence. Of all the forms of international cooperation in business education, the USST-QC suggests an approach that can be a model for those programs that combine business education with language–culture training. Viewed from the general social and economic background of China, the USST-QC program is a pioneering international cooperative endeavor designed to meet the challenge brought about by China's economic globalization and admission into the WTO. It is invaluable for the reform of China's higher education in two important aspects: the utilization of Western educational resources and as a prelude to the internationalization of higher business education in China. Notwithstanding some difficulties, it certainly represents a first step in successfully integrating language, culture, and business components. With her advancing internationalization and membership in the WTO, China will experience further international cooperation in the field of higher education, which will bring in more resources from the outside, enabling a freer and more varied exchange of educational services to take place. Business education in China will surely be the beneficiary of this cooperation, and many of the problems experienced by international programs today will be solved. The question no longer is "if" but rather "when," and as long as the political situation in China remains stable, the timing is likely to be sooner rather than later.

References

A Comparison of Interviews in State Owned Enterprises and Foreign Ventures.(no author indicated) 2003-07-04. from China Job Hunting Website. Retrieved November 4, 2004, from http://www.hao86.com/test-skill/570.htm.

Alon, I. and Lu, L. (2004). The State of Marketing and Business Education in China. *Marketing Education Review*, 14 (1), (pp. 1-10). (Lead Article)

Bai, Y. China's Higher Education after its Accession to WTO. (n. d.), from China Education and Research Network. Retrieved November 8, 2004, from http://www.edu.cn/20011226/3015310.shtml.

Boyd, F. (2002). An ESP program for students of business. In T. Orr (Ed.), English for specific purposes (pp. 41-56). Alexandria, Virginia: *Teachers of English to Speakers of Other Languages.*

Chen, J. (Education Section of American Embassy in China). China's Accession to WTO --- Proactive Role Required of Education. (n.d.), from China Education and Research Network. Retrieved November 8, 2004, from http://www.edu.cn/20020118/3017968.shtml.

Experience. (n. d.) Criterion by Foreign Ventures at Recruitment Market: English Weighs More Than (no author indicated.) from Guangzhou Daily. Retrieved November 5, 2004, from http://www.chinatalent.com.cn/news/080602.html.

Daimler Crysler: HR should look up. (no author indicated) 2004-06-29, from *World Business Review* ICXO.COM. Retrieved November 5, 2004, from http://cho.icxo.com/htmlnews/2004/06/29/253804.htm.

Hu, W. and Grove, C. (1999). Encountering the Chinese (2nd ed.). Yarmouth, Maine: Intercultural Press.

334   H. Kleinmann & L. Lu

Madison Metropolitan School District Career/Technical Education Department: Business Education Description. (no author indicated) Last updated January 10, 2001, from http://www.madison.k12.wi.us/tnl/voced/business-intent.htm.

Lu, L and Hua, Y. (2003) Guiding Principles for Developing Cultural Flexibility in Bi-cultural Business Environment. *Foreign Language Education*, 3, pp. 224-229. ISBN 7-5609-2915-X/H 465

Orr, T. (2002). The Nature of English for Specific Purposes. In T. Orr (Ed.), English for specific purposes (pp. 1-3). Alexandria, Virginia: *Teachers of English to Speakers of Other Languages.*

Porter, E. A. (1990). Foreign teachers in China. New York: Greenwood Press.

St. John, M. (1996). Business is booming: Business English in the 1990s. *English for Specific Purposes*, 15, 3-18.

Wang, M. M, Brislin, R. W., Wang, W., Williams, D., and Chao, J. H. (2000). Turning Bricks into Jade. Yarmouth, Maine: Intercultural Press.

Chapter 17

Conclusions and Reflections

John McIntyre
Georgia Institute of Technology

The post-1987 Chinese economic reforms (often referred to as *gaige kaifang*—"reform and opening up") set in motion a complex and rapid period of transition from a planned economy to a market-based society. It has meant a radical evolution in the values and beliefs as well as educational systems which have guided society. These economic reforms have come to emphasize the idea that to "get rich is glorious," thereby jettisoning the 1950's Iron Rice Bowl policy predicated on the notion that workers had the right to life-time employment and state-supported social programs. As China transitions to a market economy, fully engaged in the process of globalization, economic actors are finding that they face daunting challenges as they reform not only society but the economic operators' values, business practices, and laws. Moving an economic system from a socialist command economy to a market economy poses a unique set of challenges for the education and development of economic and business professionals.

The existence of a ready pool of trained managerial talent is one of the acknowledged foundations to propel an economic system towards a mixed economy model. Moreover, the requisite and gradual privatization of many classes of assets presupposes the existence of legal and financial talents of well-schooled managers, as state ownership increasingly vests in private individuals and international strategic alliances. Privatization may involve laying off a large number of employees, dealing with poorly trained managers, and also removing the job security of workers under the previous system: management skills are therefore essential in handling the human resource functions. Another salient feature of market transitioning is the deployment of open-market policies. They present numerous opportunities as companies gain access to new markets and at first cheap and then later skilled labor.

Hence, professional education becomes a keystone of this transitioning process since strategic planning, finance, accounting, marketing, and human resources management have been heretofore neglected, if not ignored. Drastic measures are often required to turn around inefficient state companies into privatized firms able to perform essential business functions in a globally integrated and hypercompetitive economy. Professional education then increasingly provides the institutional framework within which more impersonal exchanges are made possible rather than traditional networks of familial or other personalized ties. Multinational companies do face obstacles as they hire employees in former socialist societies. The training needs speak for themselves but also paramount is the building of trust that socialist economies may have failed to foster among economic actors and reversing risk-averse patterns, as noted by Bruton, Ahlstrom, and Chan (2000).

China is simultaneously climbing, at an accelerating pace, the industrialization escalator—a process initiated in the post-World War II era--and becoming an industrial society characterized by the dominance of manufacturing actors. Its production is increasingly integrated in the global supply chains of an interdependent world economy. The notion of China as the "factory of the world," often cited in the West, reflects deep structural shifts, under way for the past generation or longer.

With over one thousand universities and a population of one billion three hundred million, China compares poorly to the United States' four thousand universities for some two hundred and eighty million. Overall, China's higher educational needs for a reforming and globalizing economy of its size are not being met. Within the existing higher education system, management and business education have little tradition and its roots are not well laid. Since the 1980s, paralleling the instoration of economic reforms, modern management education in China has followed an importation model. This phenomenon can easily be understood as part and parcel of the *"kaifang"* notion, viewed in China as access to the foreign products, technology, and know-how. Westerners have interpreted this process as fraught with opportunities for greater trade and investment to generate demand. But the process has deeper implications, often connoting not only a door opening but also a blossoming, as in the image of a flower opening up.

Foreign business schools have established Chinese operations or returning Chinese academics with business school training have joined existing Chinese universities not fully addressing Chinese managerial training needs.   These needs are further underlined in   Human Values and Beliefs: A Cross-Cultural Sourcebook, in which Inglehart, Basanez, and Moreno show that countries undergoing industrialization have high rankings on the materialistic index.   China, in fact, scores the highest on such a ranking, indicating that individuals with professional and entrepreneurial aspirations in China are achievement-oriented and favor material gains. These are essential components, *inter alia*, as hinted by Professor Liu Ji, President of the China Europe International Business School (CEIBS) of Shanghai in this book's foreword.

Such a trend line is fully consistent with some of the traditional Buddhist values perennially found in Chinese society: a work ethic that encourages workers to engage in their best efforts and fosters qualities such as taking initiative, persistence, and hard work (Nanayakkara, 1992.)   More fundamentally, China has been strongly influenced by Confucianism.   This philosophy—condemned during the Cultural Revolution—continues to influence values, attitudes, and behavior, particularly in the workplace.   The leader at every level has to perform not only an administrative function but also plays a moral role.   When people are successful in their businesses, they like to refer to themselves as "Confucian businessmen" (*ru shang*) (Lu Le).

Some ninety Chinese universities have indeed been given the status of "experimental MBA institutions" by the State Council. Standing out among these are Renmin,   Qinghua,   Xi'an Jiaotong, Nankai, and Fudan Universities. Many of these do not in fact offer their own Chinese-language MBA degree programs. Beyond these State Council-approved and Chinese university-based programs, there is an additional 150 or so MBA programs offered either in the form of foreign MBA degrees awarded through a Chinese partner university, through free-standing MBA programs offered directly   by foreign universities which the Chinese government closely monitors,   and through programs licensed by Chinese universities largely with local faculty trained in China. As China designs its own business education system, consistent with China's opening up to the world economy, it will have to grapple with the design of management curricula and training methods which encourage its future business leaders to become more   innovative and creative.   Chinese students often go through grueling hardships to succeed through schooling experiences based on rote learning. Different training methods are evolving and Chinese business education programs may lead the way for the rest of the professional educational   system (The Economist, 2003). The challenges of designing a large-scale business and management educational system in China, responsive to the opening up of the Chinese economy, its forced march towards industrialization, and its achieving a world-class—some say, foremost— role as an economic actor on the world stage have not been fully grasped in the West (World Bank, 2002). In business education, China can choose from the best existing approaches and methods and draw from its own rich educational tradition in creating state-of-the-art entrepreneurial and knowledge-intensive mechanisms to train global leaders steeped in a unique cultural tradition and cognizant of best global practices (Clark, 1998).

This collection of carefully selected and reviewed contributions was assembled and organized in four major thrusts—economic transition and development, pedagogical issues for Chinese business education, professional business training in China and the development of international alliances— which offer a repertory of "best practices" in business education, pathways to adaptation and reforms, collaborative opportunities and provide explanatory frameworks to understand and prescribe in the China context.

It is the first book to combine authorship and expertise drawn both from East and West in addressing the contribution of the two educational and professional training traditions and how cross-learning may occur. Previous efforts are scant and often more social science-based (Whitelee). It is distinct also because of its emphasis on the pedagogy of management (organization development, management, ethics, consulting, and marketing) and the transfer cross-cultural knowledge. The text is focused largely on mainland China. It is hoped that this book-length contribution to an emerging stream of management literature paves the way for a better and more focused understanding of how dominant management educational designs—characterized by a stress on analysis, efficiency, optimization, marketing, and based on rationality and the scientific method—can be adapted and adjusted to the ascendancy of China and its managerial cadres as a world economic power. In this regard, the potential reverse flow of contributions inherent in Chinese work values and styles should not be underplayed and points the way towards new research paths. Managerial convergence cannot solely mean the predominance of a Western style of professional education, problem solving, and decision making.

References

Bruton, Garry D., David A. Ahlstrom, and Eunice S. Chan. 2000., "Foreign Firms in China: Facing Human Resources Challenges in a Transitional Economy," *SAM Advanced Management Journal,* Autumn: 4-36.

Clark, B. 1998. *Creating Entrepreneurial Universities: Organizational Pathways of Transformation,* International Association of Universities, Oxford, U.K.: Pergamon Press.

Inglehart, Ronald, Miguel Basanez, and Alejandro Moreno. 1998. *Human Values and Beliefs: A Cross-Cultural Sourcebook,* Ann Arbor, Michigan: University of Michigan Press.

Le, Lu. 2003. Influences of Confucianism on the Market Economy of China. In Ilan Alon, Ed., *Chinese Culture, Organizational Behavior, and International Business Management,* Westport, CT, Praeger Publishers.

Mintzberg, Henry. (2004). *Managers, Not MBAs.* San Fransisco, CA: Berrett-Koehler Publishers, Inc.

Nanayakkara, Sanath. 1992. *Ethics of Material Progress: The Buddhist Attitude,* The World Fellowship of Buddhist Activities Committee, Colombo: Sri Lanka.

"Roll Over, Confucius," *The Economist.* January 25, 2003:. 40-41.

Whitelee, Alma M., Ed. 2001. *Management Education in the Chinese Setting,* Binghamton, NY: International Business Press.

World Bank. 2002. *Constructing Knowledge Societies: New Challenges for Tertiary Education,* Washington, D.C.: Word Bank.

Index